The Great Awakening

What the Spirit Guides Say

James McQuitty

The Great Awakening

What the Spirit Guides Say

James McQuitty

A James McQuitty Book

First Published 21st March 2023

Many other books in both paperback and kindle formats by James
Are available worldwide through Amazon

Other titles include:

Escape From Hell

Golden Enlightenment – Twenty Year Anniversary Edition

The Reason Why You Were Born

Find the Author at Facebook:

https://www.facebook.com/jamesmcquittysharing

Cover Artwork by Elaine Thorpe

https://www.elainethorpe.com/

The complete artwork:

Testimony One

'In these increasingly dystopian times one may be forgiven for wondering where salvation might be sought. Yet where better to look than from some of those enlightened souls in the afterlife whose guidance and wise counsel has brought comfort to countless individuals over the years? To this end the author has brilliantly drawn together the wisdom of several powerful spirit teachers, who although speaking independently of each other share the same vital information through a common thread that both warns of current and forthcoming events whilst also pointing towards the solution. Indeed, one cannot help but wonder, that had these wonderful spirit sages been brought together simultaneously and asked to address the issues now facing humanity, the resulting narrative would have precisely reflected the collective wisdom found within these pages. I congratulate James McQuitty on his diligence, determination and skill in sourcing, collating and bringing together this vital information so needed by humanity – he is truly a voice for spirit and a power for good.'

Robert Goodwin
Medium & Author
https://www.whitefeatherspirit.com/

Testimony Two

'This book is full of truth and I am delighted to have some of my channelled messages included. It's interesting to read the various perspectives coming through each medium, with the golden thread of truth stitching everything together.

'There are many great messages published, and after reviewing these I have been surprised at their lucidity and level of truth. Sometimes I forget how earnest the angels are in their efforts to communicate with us.

'I wish James great success in this publication and his intentions to help wake up humanity. It's a formidable job but as we are blessed and guided, we will enter through many doorways of opportunity to share and uplift others. Much love and appreciation to you my brother.'

Al Fike

Trance Medium

https://divinelovesanctuary.com/

Truth Coming Out of Her Well

By Jean-Léon Gérôme, 1896

The Naked Truth & Well Dressed Lie
The painting tells the story of when
The Truth and the Lie met on a summery day...

'The Lie said to the Truth: "It's a marvellous day today"! The Truth looked up to the skies and sighed, for the day was really beautiful.

'They spent a lot of time together, ultimately arriving beside a well.

'The Lie said to the Truth: "The water is very nice, let's take a bath together!" The Truth, once again suspicious, tested the water and discovered that it indeed was very nice.

'They undressed and started bathing. Suddenly, the Lie came out of the water, put on the clothes of the Truth and ran away. The furious Truth came out of the well and ran everywhere to find the Lie and to get her clothes back.

'The World, seeing the Truth naked, turned its gaze away, with contempt and rage. The poor Truth returned to the well and disappeared forever, hiding therein, its shame.

'Since then, the Lie travels around the world, dressed as the Truth, satisfying the needs of society, because, the World, in any case, harbours no wish at all to meet the naked Truth.'

With Love and Gratitude to:

Carolyn, for being there; and to the Spirit guides and Mediums who have contributed to this book. And to every truth teller mentioned within, and worldwide, for the truths, revelations, and wisdom that collectively has been and continues to be shared.

Also to Gwen Glover, who drew my attention to the lovely, *"Truth coming out of her well"*.

Please note:

Throughout this book, all text of spirit communications and quotes from other sources are in *italics* – and often abridged extracts.

Bold Text Lettering displays the passages that 'stood out' to me in some way as of particular interest, inspiration, relevance, or importance.

Additional note:

In my opinion, if one wishes, "The Dark Agenda" and "Truth Tellers on Earth" chapters within can be read before "What the Spirit Guides Say" without spoiling the overall reading experience.

Poem: The Great Reset

'Fiery furnace of my soul, crush my fears and make me whole.
Show me how to shine my light, through the blackness of the night.
Lead me to right actions, away from all distractions.
Clear my way so I clearly see that there is nothing stopping me.
I'm free, I'm brave, I'm out of my cave, shining my light so bright, bright, bright!'

Bracha Goldsmith – Astrologer

Table of Contents

Introduction 11

1. The Dark Agenda – Part One 18

2. The Great Awakening - What the Spirit Guides Say 20

3. Spirit Guides Speak of the Unfolding Age of Aquarius 202

4. The Dark Agenda – Part Two 226

5. Truth Tellers on Earth 233

Summary and Final Thoughts 293

Reference List of What the Spirit Guides Say in Chapter Two 296

Links 299

Introduction

This is an incredible time of change, one that is taking us into a "New Age", a new era. This is such a special time, a time like no other; so much so that the day may come when people, who are here, living upon Earth at this time, will one day consider that they were fortunate to have been here to witness the very beginning of the Great Awakening. **They will especially be happy if they played their part in the awakening of humanity.**

So much upon this little world of ours will be changing, upgrading, and ultimately transforming for the betterment of humanity and for all life upon this planet. This includes animal life and all in nature. All will be evolving to a higher level of consciousness, whether we recognise this or not.

Life on Earth will forever be changed by events that are unfolding here and now, and will continue to unfold over the coming years and decades. These events and the higher level of consciousness to which we can attune ourselves will in time bring positive changes that will encourage greater love, harmony, peace and understanding between all nations and people.

Although, overlapping with this coming 'golden age', there will be times and degrees of chaos, and destruction; as the old systems that no longer serve us will crumble and fade away, to be replaced by systems that are in keeping with a new Aquarian Age.

The 'New Earth' that will ultimately emerge will be one that embraces greater kindness, generosity, equality, fairness and a willingness to share.

All of these qualities will be part of the new world energies. The future will also bring a more caring nature forward, when people will show greater respect for nature, the environment, and animals.

New and improved ways of healing will come to the fore. Ways that will replace pharmaceutical chemical based drugs. All these things are already beginning to emerge, and have been spoken about by the spirit guides, as readers will find within this book.

To help usher in the new Earth we currently have support reaching us via many highly elevated and advanced sources from spirit life guides, angels, archangels, and extraterrestrial beings from other galaxies and star systems. These beings are all helping by sending loving energies to assist in the transformation of this planet. They truly are our cosmic and intergalactic friends, our brothers and sisters, and they are around us in great numbers.

There have been many spirit communicators who have confirmed the exciting fact of help coming to Earth from so many different sources. Although the majority of the communications that I have included in this book come to us from our 'human' spirit guides and teachers, and what they have shared with us about these times of change and the Great Awakening. (By the way, the spirit guides are continuing to share information, and encouragement, and circumstances permitting, I may well publish a second awakening book next year).

Within this book I have done my best to focus on the positive guidance and revelations of truth we have and are receiving from our spirit friends. However, I feel that it is also necessary to include a certain amount of information on what I call the 'dark agenda'; and about the Great Awakening to the realisation that we have for many years, and some say centuries, been dominated, controlled, managed, manipulated, lied to and ruled over and by those who have claimed authority over us.

In the main these 'dark agenda' people are and have been those with vested materialistic interests; people who, more often than not, are in total ignorance of the true nature of eternal life. People who think that life and how they live it carries no consequences or repercussions because, they mistakenly believe, "when you're dead, you're dead and cease to be". How wrong they are!

In many ways we should feel sorry and sad for them. They behave like little children who want to grab all the sweets, and to bully all the smaller and physically weaker or less able children. It gives them a sense of power, supremacy, control and strength. And this is what the dark agenda is all about, "Control, Power and Money". To the extent they wish to dominate and direct exactly how everyone else lives, and even if they live. Some of them are not adverse to murder, causing conflicts, wars, torture and abuse (physical, mental and spiritual), on a monumental scale. Many, it seems, have no moral compass or conscience.

It may seem to those amongst us who haven't researched the darker agenda, or received input from spirit teachers, to be impossible to believe that seemingly vast numbers of people are pushing in the direction of an agenda that is dark, and not for the benefit of the population at large. Yet this is the case, although I'm sure that not all who, effectively, play a role in 'pushing or selling the agenda', are themselves seeing and fully realising the possible future consequences of their actions.

People have become used to governments and politicians directing society, making laws or introducing legislation, and systems that more or less tells them what to believe and accept. The result being, that there are many people co-operating with, or implementing, nonsensical orders; despite gaining nothing by doing so. Some may be employed by 'the system', the politicians, civil servants, police, doctors and NHS staff, and so forth. Many, who are seeing the truth, or just suspecting that all is not right, are afraid to speak out. They stay silent because they know that if they speak out it is likely to cost them their jobs, which has been the case for many honest people.

People who haven't done any research mainly fail to realise just how many doctors and nurses and others have been sacked for daring to question and speak out about one or more aspects of the dark agenda. The mainstream media (MSM), TV, Radio, and Newspapers, and so forth, in almost all cases, refuse to report information that in any way challenges the dark agenda, an agenda that supports globalist, corporate, interests.

Even when those in the MSM are informed by highly respected scientists, professors, medical specialists, doctors, nurses, barristers and countless other fully qualified professionals, with expert testimonies from people in many fields of study and practice, that lies are being told, and problems with 'the system' and government endorsed policies exist, what happens? **Their 'expert witness testimonies' are ignored and censored. They are blocked, so that they are never reported to the general public.**

In practically all cases the MSM refuse to question or challenge the 'dark agenda' that governments worldwide are attempting to impose upon the people. And "impose" is a fair word to use. They have attempted to gain as near to total compliance to their 'recommendations' (that in some instances have effectively been mandatory orders) as they possibly can. Despite this being in violation of all natural and common laws, and also against the human rights of the Nuremberg code. While in the USA they have attempted to ignore the rights guaranteed to the people in their Constitution and the amendments in their Bill of Rights (of 1791) that guarantee free speech and so much more.

How can this be?

What people need to realise is that most of the MSM worldwide is owned by those high up in the dark agenda pyramid of power. The generals, one might say. While those below, the lower ranks, are only told what they need to know and do. The further one moves down the pyramid, the less and less of the bigger picture is seen. Those at the top of the pyramid direct policies to ensure all that might expose them, or the full extent of their dark agenda, is hidden from the everyday view of the average person. It certainly remains hidden from those who only take notice of what the MSM tells them. **(But it is clearly seen by those in spirit life!)**

Those below the so-called 'elite' at the top of the pyramid and their generals who 'disobey' or fail to 'follow orders', are sacked. Or worse, in some cases, selected individuals have been murdered, as mentioned earlier and will be again later in this book. (Naturally, they go home to spirit life, because we are all spirit beings, temporarily occupying a physical body).

This has been the fate, to be murdered, for some who were deemed a threat to the proposed 'new world order', also called 'the great reset' that they plan and are trying now to instigate. It has also been the fate for some who wished to reveal research discoveries (as revealed within) that would have made life better for the average person, but would at the same time have greatly reduced the massive profits of one of the significant major globalist corporations.

I realise that it is difficult for many people to 'wake up' and realise just how corrupt so many people in this world have become. As a writer of spirit/spiritual teaching books, I long ago realised that the majority of people in this world are happy to give no attention to centuries of overwhelming 'afterlife' evidence. With this they have effectively 'stuck their heads in the sand' and ignored the subject, or worse, considered it as nonsense, and all who believe in it, as gullible fools.

So the widespread dismissal of all suggestions that the governments of the world, the politicians, establishment paid scientists and doctors, and many others would tell lies for personal and corporate vested interests, seems to such people impossible to believe. This, despite the fact that many, many past historic cases of corruption, lies and greed have been exposed, and one might say are still being exposed in relation to politicians and others of today. It truly amazes me that anyone still places an ounce of trust in absolutely anything said by a politician. As one teacher has in recent times said, 'the bigger the lie, the more it is accepted', because most people believe that no one would tell a lie that is as monumental as the lie (or lies) that we in recent times have been told.

Declassification of 'official secrets' showing historic cases of government lies have been revealed. There is also a 'mountain' of official secrets that have never been revealed to the public. One should ask, "Why not?" Then think again, if they still believe that governments and the media are always honest and truthful. Indeed, only recently, in January 2023, a UK TV programme on ITV titled: *"The Stasi: Secrets, Lies and British Spies"* showed us that Stasi (East German) spies, who were effectively a branch of the KGB in Russia, operated in the UK for a number of years and enlisted a number of British people as informants. In Germany 30 years or so ago records kept by the Stasi were opened for public scrutiny. Yet in Britain they remain secrets. The implication being that the Stasi records would reveal one or more British politician, or high profile influential people, that would 'embarrass' the establishment.

Why would anyone believe that time has changed such people? They tell lies or cover-up (censor) anything they do not want the public to learn about.

Leaving aside for now the awakening to material exposures, one must above all else remember that life on Earth has a purpose and that it is a temporary experience that we have likely undertaken multiple times before in other lifetimes. So no matter what nonsense we are presented with 'down here' we can in due course look forward to a brighter future in spirit life, as well as to a more enlightened, new Earth, that will unfold around us over the coming years.

The promise of a new Earth has, for many years, decades, and even centuries, been spoken of in communications from a number of spirit world guides; and it seems what they have been speaking of is this time in which we now live. The time of the "Great Awakening" that is unfolding evermore as each day passes.

Some of the spirit guides have also informed us of our necessity to stand-up for our fundamental rights of free speech, and freedom of choice, as the free spirits that we truly are. It is necessary for us to do so in order to help overcome the 'dark agenda'. This is an agenda planned by those who, these days, as I have loosely mentioned, are often termed, "Globalists". The ultra-materialists and morally corrupt of this world.

It is with the help, the efforts of spirit guides, and their mediums, and all who share spiritual and earthly information to help enlighten us, that we, collectively, will be enabled and encouraged to assist our own and the Planet Earth's transition to a higher frequency of consciousness.

All life upon this planet, as mentioned, is transitioning to the fifth dimension. This is a degree of consciousness that will encourage a higher degree of morality, honesty, kindness and compassion; and a greater universal love for all life. I realise that I am somewhat repeating myself here; I do so because I do wish to emphasise that the Great Awakening will, ultimately, lead to a better world.

In the meantime, even though there may, and likely will, be some difficult times for many of us to face, it is worth knowing and reminding ourselves that our efforts now, at this time on Earth, are worthwhile, and will help usher in the new and more enlightened Earth.

I'd like to remind readers at this point that the communications from spirit guides that I have included are often only segments, abridged or shortened extracts of all that was said in audio or video recordings that I have transcribed. In most cases these recordings can be found if one follows some of the links I provide at the end of this book. I have naturally included what I consider the more important or valuable, and in some cases uplifting, or relevant, inspiring or revelatory parts of all the guides have said.

In Chapter Two, "What the spirit guides say", I have included quotes in chronological order from when they were communicated. However, since the spirit guides were sharing information that they obviously felt needed to be said at the particular time, this can flow from one speaking of the dark agenda and how we must resist and overcome this, to the spiritual awakening and how this will transform us and life on Earth. While some communications speak of both the spiritual awakening and the dark agenda; so what is said may appear to go from good or light to dark in nature and back again.

But of course, this is the reality; we do have both aspects running side by side. This is why we need to remain focused on the good, the light, and remain upbeat and positive, because this empowers and speeds the unfoldment of a better, new Earth.

We are immortal spirit beings and as such we can help everyone by ourselves remaining fearless, courageous, and happy and willing to stand our ground and speak our truth as the aspects of God we truly are.

I hope, trust and believe that readers will be informed and inspired through the reading of this book, for this is my intention.

Be happy, stay in peace, and never forget that we are all immortal spirit beings.

1. The Dark Agenda – Part One

This chapter is a brief introduction or summary of how I see things in regard to what I think can justifiably be called 'the dark agenda'. I do not attempt to go into the full narrative of the agenda in this book. My main objective within is to awaken those I can to just part of the story, and a part that is particularly relevant today in regards to health and climate.

The dark agenda of the so-called elite, who are often grouped under the term, "globalists", the "mega-wealthy materialists", has many depths to it. If one truly wishes to delve deeply into this, then many, many books are available concerning "the great reset" or "agenda 2030" and other such labels they give to their dark agenda. They do attempt to dress their plans up as good ideas for the benefit of all and the planet, and they are experts at doing so. But ultimately, if all their plans were successful, the world and most people would find themselves in a dark place. It is for this reason that I believe people need to be aware of certain things. If they are not, then they will be open to the manipulative misdirection and misinformation that is constantly expounded through the media by those with ulterior motives.

These ulterior motives, to be perfectly clear, do not have the best interests of anyone at heart other than the select 'elite' attempting to dominate the lives of everyone else on Earth. Their motivation is based on having, power, money and control over all.

Below are six statements to consider, I believe these to be accurate.

1. The so-called Pandemic of 2020 was planned, and the virus in question was little if any more 'deadly' than most previous seasonal flu viruses.

2. The so-called Covid Vaccine was unnecessary, it was not effective, and it was never safe.

3. PCR tests are totally unreliable and produce meaningless results.

4. Face coverings are dangerous to the health of the wearer and, given time, to other people.

5. There is no climate crisis.

6. Free speech has and is being censored and blocked. This is denying many people the opportunity and right to consider ulterior points of view and facts concerning the above statements presented by highly credible scientists, medical specialists, doctors, nurses and climatologists, and many other truth tellers, who speak with decades of expert understanding and experience.

The chapters in this book can be read in any order one wishes. So if any reader wishes to read all that I have included about the dark agenda and the chapter I have titled, 'Truth Tellers on Earth' before reading 'What the Spirit Guides Say', in my opinion they can do so without spoiling the overall reading experience.

2. The Great Awakening - What the Spirit Guides Say

I start this chapter with a statement, or reminder, that the Light of Love, both of which equate to God, or the Great Spirit, will ultimately always triumph over darkness.

We, none of us, should ever forget that we are aspects, or facets, of the Great Spirit, the ONE energy; the ONE life. As I once described it in one of my books, we, along with all else in creation, are like cells within, that collectively make the one body that is God.

Those who seemingly imagine that darkness can triumph over the light and love of God, imagine the impossible. Those with a dark agenda or a dark motive for their actions on Earth are deluding themselves. Any 'success' they have is illusionary, temporary at best, and can never be sustained. They are operating, living and behaving through ignorance. Their own ignorance, manifested as a desire for earthly power, and greed, and the need to seek dominance and control over the majority of us, in order to achieve their desires.

They may have some measure of 'success' in their own terms, by becoming wealthier in financial or materialistic terms, but at what cost to not only others, but ultimately to themselves. I say this because eventually, their actions, the energies they send out, must return or rebound to them. It is the law, natural law, the law of spirit, the law of God. It is cause and effect, and if it does not take full effect in the current lifetime then it becomes a negative karma that will need to be faced not only in spirit life, but also in one or more future incarnations.

The first guide I will mention here is Rudolf Steiner (1861-1925), because even though he was still incarnate on Earth when he communicated all that he shared with humanity, and there is a vast amount of this freely available to find on the internet (see Links), he was clearly a channel for knowledge that was beyond any reliance upon pure intellect. Two of the 'evils' of the dark agenda concern the attempt to jab or vaccinate, as they try to categorize it, "inject" is more accurate, all people, many times, with, in my opinion, no genuine desire to bring any beneficial health results. Another concerns climate, and the truth here is that there is no climate crisis. It is a lie, perpetrated for a dark motive; some of which is to enforce more restrictions upon us, our liberty, to say where and when we can travel. With more 'lockdowns' as though we are prisoners of the state. The "state" is directed by our would-be rulers, those who claim authority over our liberty, rather than those we think we have elected to represent our desires and ensure our liberty to live as the free spirits that we are. Natural law simply asks us to harm no other; at least not deliberately or with intent.

More than a century back Rudolf Steiner foretold some of the dark agenda. It is indeed quite an 'eye-opener' to find that he said, or predicted, events that those of the dark agenda are today attempting to 'roll-out' and force upon the people of this world.

I would describe Rudolf as a 'philosopher', while he was also considered an 'esoteric teacher' (or mystic) who it is said possessed 'second sight'. It was back in 1917 when his lectures spoke of a time that was then 'in the future', and I can imagine that some who at the time heard the lectures may have considered what he had to say as 'a little far-fetched'. But that time has arrived, it is now, and what he said has today started to become a reality – if we let it. (And I am confident that collectively we will not).

What he said can be considered a forewarning, not a certainty, for nothing is 'cast in stone'. Collectively, people have always had the power to overcome any adversity.

Although, I must say, that the very fact that he was receiving or accessing such information over one-hundred years ago, shows us that all is known to those sufficiently advanced in spirit life. This, I'd say, is a very good reason to pay attention to what the spirit guides are today saying in regard to current world events.

In his lectures Rudolf spoke on 'vaccines' (experimental injections) of the future. This, in the language of the day, is what he said:

1. Rudolf Steiner – October 1917
The Fall of the Spirits of Darkness – Part One

'It will be the main concern of these spirits of darkness to bring confusion into the rightful elements which are now spreading on Earth, and need to spread in such a way that the spirits of light can continue to be active in them. They will seek to push these in the wrong direction. I have already spoken of one such wrong direction, which is about as paradoxical as is possible. I have pointed out that while human bodies will develop in such a way that certain spiritualities can find room in

them, the materialistic bent, which will spread more and more under the guidance of the spirits of darkness, will work against this and combat it by physical means.

'I have told you that the spirits of darkness are going to inspire their human hosts, in whom they will be dwelling, to find a vaccine that will drive all inclination towards spirituality out of people's souls when they are still very young, and this will happen in a roundabout way through the living body. Today, bodies are vaccinated against one thing and another; in future, children will be vaccinated with a substance which it will certainly be possible to produce, and this will make them immune, so that they do not develop foolish inclinations connected with spiritual life - 'foolish' here, of course, in the eyes of materialists.

'The whole trend goes in a direction where a way will finally be found to vaccinate bodies so that these bodies will not allow the inclination towards spiritual ideas to develop and all their lives people will believe only in the physical world they perceive with the senses.

'People are now vaccinated against consumption, and in the same way they will be vaccinated against any inclination towards spirituality. This is merely to give you a particularly striking example of many things which will come in the near and more distant future in this field - the aim being to bring confusion into the impulses which want to stream down to Earth after the victory of the spirits of light.

'The first step must be to throw people's views into confusion, turning their concepts and ideas inside out. This is a serious thing and must be watched with care, for it is part of some highly important elements which will be the background to events now in preparation.'

When Rudolf spoke of 'rightful elements' I interpret this as referring to those trying to speak their truths, such as those on Earth exposing corruptions, and also those following more spiritual pathways and teaching others of spirit truths. The 'spirits of darkness' and those on Earth pushing the dark agenda have and continue to attempt to confuse people with their conflicting statements; or their nonsense, as I think it can quite justifiably be called.

Rudolf also said that those pushing the agenda on Earth will be under the influence of the spirits of darkness - in whom they will be dwelling – and people generally have no idea just how true this can be. In spiritual terms, like attracts like, and those from the darker spirit realms can be attracted by equally 'wrong-doing' people on Earth and can literally "obsess" them and sometimes fully possess them. This warning has been given by a number of spirit communicators and the reading of my book, *Escape from Hell*, warns of the dangers of a lifetime lived purely for self gratification, greed, and worse, and the consequences to be faced when one eventually returns to spirit life.

Rudolf further said:

2. Rudolf Steiner – October 1917
The Fall of the Spirits of Darkness – Part Two

'The time will come, and it may not be far off, when people will say: It is pathological for people to even think in terms of spirit and soul. 'Sound' people will speak of nothing but the body. It will be considered a sign of illness for anyone to arrive at the idea of any such thing as a spirit or a soul. People who think like that will be considered to be sick and, you can be quite sure of it, a medicine will be found for this.

'The soul will be made non-existent with the aid of a drug. Taking a 'sound point of view', people will invent a vaccine to influence the organism as early as possible, preferably as soon as it is born, so that this human body never even gets the idea that there is a soul and a spirit.

'The two philosophies of life will be in complete opposition. One movement will need to reflect how concepts and ideas may be developed to meet the reality of soul and spirit. The others, the heirs of modern materialism, will look for the vaccine to make the body 'healthy', that is, makes its constitution such that this body no longer talks of such 'rubbish' as soul and spirit, but takes a 'sound' view of the forces which live in engines and in chemistry and let planets and suns arise from nebulae in the cosmos. Materialistic physicians will be asked to drive the souls out of humanity.'

In other words they will, and I'd say have been 'at it' for years, to convince people that all mediums are fakes, and that only the gullible believe otherwise. And if anyone thinks that Rudolf was amiss about the materialists setting their sights on effectively attacking babies from birth, they'd be wrong. Part of the dark agenda involves micro-chipping from birth. And they want to grow babies outside of the womb, and I am not making any of this up. These people would make Frankenstein far less scary.

Big changes are coming though, and these will not all be those we will welcome. We need to recognise that this planet is a living being, believe it or not, and partly at least in response to human behaviour and way of life, the planet will respond in an attempt to rebalance her energies. As the spirit guide Magnus informed us, via the medium Colin Fry, a couple of decades or more back, when he answered the following question.

3. Magnus – circa 1990's-2000's
Q. Can you tell us a little bit about the Earth Changes?

'There have been seers in times before your own that have predicted and spoken of having seen a time of Armageddon, an apocalypse of darkness and the burning, and despair, we have heard of these things. You would also know that there are seers that had spoken of a dawn of a new age, the time of Enlightenment and love, you have heard these things as well; and you would say to me, "Magnus, they both can't be right", but I tell you my friends they are.

'For those that have had the gift, they have seen how the negativity must fall. They have seen the darkness, and they have seen the fire, they have seen the lands move, the fire rage from its belly. Those that have been inspired by love and truth and God within that understanding have seen what would come.

'You would accept my friends, no doubt, the world is ravaged by negativity, then I tell you this, you shall see, many of you, in your times upon the Earth plane, great governments fall to their knees, you shall see established religions crumble to dust, you would see your world split and ravage and change as she strives to evolve, you will see great financial institutions fall to nothing, you will see commerce, industry, become nothing at all, you will see confusion and chaos, but if you remain true to the spirit, your spirit, the spirits that guide you from our side of life, and the eternal spirit that is God, however you comprehend God, then you shall go through the fires of change and, you shall come into the light of**

your world as it should be, as a plane of spirit that was always intended.

'It is the case my friends that this is one instance where you can be like Nero, you can fiddle while Rome burns, and I say to you, let it burn, all that is not conducive to life of your world, or that is negative and corrupt, let it fall. It is rather like a forest fire, how does one control a forest fire, do you not let it consume of itself, and burn itself to exhaustion?

'No more must the human spirit feed the force of negativity of your world, let it consume itself. You do not and should not be fearful of the times of change my friends, you should rejoice that the time of change is upon you. So many of you have looked to our side of life for the paradise, God's Eternal Kingdom, and yet in this, you fail to recognize the truth, that is, transition to our side of life is an inevitability. Just as you are born to your world, so you are born to our world; that is a truth undeniable. But you look to our side of life for the spiritual paradise, and yet my friends' your own plane of existence is also, underneath the grime and the negativity and the cloud, is the paradise that you search for. As much a plane of spirit as any that you shall progress to, it's time to chip away that which has tarnished, polish that which is of your world, it is time to evolve my friends.

'It is not evolution that has evolved the spirit upon the Earth plane, no, no, quite the contrary; it is your desire upon the Earth plane to progress your spirit that instigates evolution. As you strive for greater spirituality so your form shall change accordingly, this is not just true of humankind, but this is true of all life on your world. And also, your world, does she not have the right to evolve?

'Therefore I say to you my friends, fear not the time of change, rejoice that the time of change is upon you, the Garden of Eden, whether it be mythology, whether it be an ideal, or a faint and distant memory of what was intended of the Earth world, shall once again be. But it would be the new Eden, not as was before, but evolved and greater for progression is an onward march my friends, not a repetition.

'The time of change is upon you, and if you call yourself Spiritual Beings, if you accept that God is beyond and around and within, then move with the change, flow with the tide my friends, do not fight against it. You will only exhaust yourself, and physically, emotionally and *spiritually, drown. Swim with the tide, and rejoice, in the time of change.'*

Next I include something from the wonderful spirit guide, *White Feather*. This guide has always been willing to speak of the 'dark agenda', as well as a vast array of spiritual teachings. Many are contained in a number of excellent books.

In one of them, *'The Enlightened Soul - Wisdom from White Feather'*, first published in 2008, chapter nine: A glimpse of the future, White Feather said as follows.

4. White Feather
A Glimpse of the Future – circa 2008

'You cannot cage the spirit. You cannot imprison the soul and yet in many ways, this is what some are trying to establish in your world as they tighten their grip and their control through various means. Brother is set upon brother. Wars are created. Lives are lost in the physical sense. The landscape is obliterated. The beauty and harmony that should prevail in your world is replaced by pain, suffering and darkness. The light of truth is obscured by the clouds of ignorance. You are offered 'solutions' that create only more problems. You are offered answers that only produce more questions and until mankind as a whole begins to turn inward to the subtle planes wherein lie truth and understanding, love, harmony, light and oneness, will this state of affairs change.

'You have to realise that you bring into being the reality that you see and sense around you. Those who are your manipulators and would be captors recognise that if they feed and stimulate the senses of man in a certain way, then they can achieve certain results. The wise soul sees through the illusion. The wise soul recognises the illusion for what it is because it can see the greater reality that lies behind it. It is a fool who follows fools. It is a wise man that follows his heart. Within you lie the answers to all things. The immediate future of your world and of mankind is difficult. I wish I could paint you a rosy picture of a century that stretches out before you, bringing increased harmony, co-operation and love between individuals and nations, but from where I view the opposite is true. There will be wars, there will be darkness, there will be confusion, there will be fragmentation upon many levels as the ignorant

have their day. But I want you all to recognise that in these times of difficulty the divine light of the spirit which has created and continues to create the boundless universe with its myriad of forms, which keeps the stars and planets in their orbits, which brings life and light to the darkest corners, is aware of this situation and is watching over events. As I have said, man can hinder and delay, but he cannot prevent the plan of the Great Spirit from outworking itself. Man thinks he has great power, but he has little power in true terms. Compared to the real power of the spirit, of the divine intelligence that created everything that is, mans' power is very, very limited.

'I have said sometimes in the past that it is darkest just before the dawn. You are entering into that time. There will be periods of great darkness when you will be fearful, when you will be filled with despair and hopelessness, but I say these things not to frighten you, but to let you know that in the midst of this turmoil will come peace, will come light and will come truth. This will not come in the form of a saviour God or any individual sent to your Earth to create miracles. It will come through enlightenment of man as a race. Even now change has begun. Even as I speak there are many who are turning inward, who are questioning, who are searching and looking deeper within, beyond their material form and its limitations. They are finding and recognising the divine and the infinite that lies within them.

'This is a sea change. It is a change of enormous proportions. Energies will come to mankind that will enable this transformation of consciousness to take place, but it won't be overnight. It won't be in a day or a week or a year. It will be over generations of time. Slowly and surely the darkness will be replaced by light. The sun will rise and shine again and man, captivated and controlled through his own ego state, will be released and will set himself free as the divine power of the spirit is realised within.

'So when you ask me to speak of the future, these are my words to you. What I am offering you is a double-edged sword. On the one hand you have the unfolding of events that have already begun, on the other you have the deeper, more profound spiritual change that also has begun.'

In a further White Feather book, *The Collected Wisdom of White Feather*, first published 2010, the guide, once again displaying his foreknowledge of events to come and presently unfolding on Earth, said the following.

5. White Feather
From: The Collected Wisdom – 2010

'Well let me say there is a great darkness which is yet to emerge upon the Earth and I don't wish to frighten or disturb any of you. But there are minds of the lower order which, even as I speak seek to manipulate thinking, to direct humanity into ways of manipulation and control that would deny the divine heritage of the spirit, which is the rightful heritage of all of you. You have to be vigilant and aware of any form of control of your thinking and actions, anything that erodes your freewill and freedom of thought.

'You often think that you live in a democracy but you do not, because even as I speak to you, you are controlled and manipulated in ways of which you are not always aware.

'So you have to learn to be wary of the propaganda that is given to you and to use your reasoning mind. Because certainly what you are fed through your media, through your newspapers and your television bears little resemblance to the reality of things.

'There needs to be, as I have often said, a revolution. Not a violent, bloody revolution, but a revolution of thought and of action where you as individuals can take power back to yourselves, not be controlled and hand it over to governments and companies who manipulate and whose desire is wealth and material possessions. That is not right.

'The real power in your world lies within you as individuals and when humanity collectively begins to realise that, then and only then will there be any radical changes.

'But I am afraid that there will be a darkness which will come upon the Earth before there is light. But do not despair because there is a plan which is unfolding. These things are known and even though man can hinder and delay and even destroy to a point, he cannot prevent the outworking of the plan because always remember this; the universe and everything contained within it has been devised and continues to exist through perfect mind; the mind of the Great Spirit. Always remember that matter is servant, spirit is master.'

In 2011 White Feather spoke to a group of spiritual seekers and answered their questions. Again, he demonstrated the fact that he knows about the corruption and darkness on Earth, and of the agenda planned by the spiritually ignorant globalists and their allies. The following are a couple of the answers given in reply to questions.

To begin, one seeker of truth asked whether a cure for cancer would ever be found.

The reply of the guide confirmed what many people have for years said, that cures are known, and that they have deliberately been withheld. Covered up, for financial gain; and, sometimes good honest people have been murdered to keep the secrets.

If this does not 'ring alarm bells' in people's minds about the pharmaceutical industry; and bring their integrity and honesty into question, into the light, to exposure just how corrupt and totally undeserving of anyone's trust they are, then nothing will.

The following, in his own words, is what the guide said in reply to the question as to whether a cure for cancer would ever be found.

6. White Feather - Speaking in 2011
Cancer Cure Deliberately Covered-Up for Financial Gain

'This might shock you, but there are those in your world who don't wish man to have a cure, because there's far too much money to be made out of finding a cure, and that is a devastating indictment upon your world. Let me say that cancers take various forms, even though they all seem to be gathered together under the umbrella of the word cancer; but there are various types and forms, many which are viral in their origin, even though this is not always apparent on the surface.

*'The cure is known by a few in your world and certainly by some in my world, it is known, **but like many cures they are withheld,** they are withheld from the general population, and this is a terrible, terrible, indictment upon your world, or some in your world, not all of course.*

'As to whether this will become common knowledge one can only hope, we do strive, we do inform people, we do work with scientists and doctors.

'But such is the corruption in your world that there are those who have this knowledge, who are, shall I say, destroyed, taken out of their position. Even have had their physical lives removed from

them by those who have vested interests in perpetrating the myth that cancer has yet to be cured.

'I know this is a shocking revelation perhaps to some of you, but it is a truth nevertheless. There are many who work within the scientific fraternity, microbiologists, I think you call them, and others, who have mysteriously disappeared. Who have mysteriously died in strange circumstances, and if you bother to investigate these you will find that there are suspicious circumstances, more often than not, because they're getting too close to the truth.

'It's quite a statement isn't it, but I can only say it as I know it, and understand it.

'But addressing your question, the cure is known, it is known.

'But it is being withheld; having said that, let me say also that you've witnessed and heard of those people who have entered into what you call spontaneous remission, how does that come about?

'It comes about because something changes within them, their intent, their belief; their mind power changes.

'Change your thinking and the world changes. This is being withheld, you are not little helpless people, you are not victims you are all powerful. You are the Great Spirit, you have immeasurable power within you, but this is being held back from you like some great secret that is denied.

'And this change, this paradigm shift, has begun in your world, and there are certain groups and individuals who know this, and so, they are struggling and striving ever greater in their methods to control and manipulate man and prevent man from realising his true nature. That is the struggle that is ongoing, so it's a complex issue, but I try to present the truth, or the picture, to you the way I see it.'

Most people reading the above, or who have, or at some time do listen to the recording of White Feather, will I am sure be appalled to learn that a cancer cure (*"like many cures"*), was withheld from the public. There is little doubt, in my mind at least, that this 'cover-up' was perpetrated by some of the same 'players' who are pushing the dark globalist-materialist agenda. Those who want to 'run the world' and control the lives of all others, as they see fit.

Although White Feather informs us that some of the 'baddies' (as they could be termed) do have some spiritual knowledge and are withholding it from the general public, it seems to me that many more of the greedy and power hungry would-be dictators have no spiritual understanding. This is sad. Because they do not realise that life is eternal and that there will, as previously mentioned, be consequences to follow for their actions on Earth. It is of course easy when one has some spirit-spiritual understanding to condemn and judge when one sees the wrong that so many on 'the dark path' are taking. But it is not our place to judge, this is why, in more rational moments, I feel it is more appropriate for us to feel sorry for these perpetrators of the dark agendas, especially when one has some awareness of the fate that has befallen others of this kind in the past. To highlight this is why I published my book, as mentioned previously, *Escape from Hell.*

During the same 2011 meeting White Feather gave confirmation of the dark agenda plan for what is termed, 'The New World Order' (NWO), and also confirmed that man (humankind) did visit the Moon (whilst also confirming that even with these historical events, there had been some tampering with photographic evidence, as well as the manipulation of information by the authorities).

Incidentally, in the guide's response to a question asked about the NWO and the Moon, he also confirmed what I was saying above, that consequences will follow for 'poor' choices and actions taken on Earth.

This is some of what he said:

7. White Feather - Speaking of the NWO in 2011

'You are sadly right in your summing up of the direction in which your Earth is going, and what is termed 'a new world order' and those who are the perpetrators of it, a very sinister motive.

'They operate behind the scenes in secret groups and societies to manipulate global events and everything that you see unfolding has been planned by those who are mad with power and seem to think that they have a right, as some kind of elite, to rule over the masses; sadly misguided, they will pay the consequences of their ignorance, that is the natural law.

'I only wish that there were more who could understand and see clearly the events that are playing today, because they are so manipulated, to the point where they don't even realise they are in prison, and that is one thing, secondly, yes man has walked upon the moon, as far as I know.

'There are many in my world, let me tell you, who know the score, who know what's happening, and we are doing our utmost to enlighten people. And, as I said earlier, there is a sea change taking place, there is a paradigm shift, but it hasn't fully emerged yet, it is still some way beneath the surface.

'The problem that you have in your world is that what you call the media, your televisions, your newspapers, your radios, and so on and so forth, and even your film producers, are all working to the similar agenda.

'People tend to believe what their eyes tell them, what their ears inform them; they tend to accept as the truth, they don't think for themselves. All that you can do in your small way is to influence those who come into your orbit, and try to put the other side, to give a balanced view.'

"What their eyes tell them, what their ears inform them; they tend to accept as the truth", White Feather rightly said. Meaning people in general have too often believed what the media want them to believe and accept as truth. When, all too often, it is either a complete or partial lie, a distortion of the truth or true situation and reality. I could easily, again, compare this to how often I have seen in UK TV productions stories that portray a medium as a fraud. It is on rare occasions only when we are 'permitted' to see a fictional story that portrays a genuine medium.

Even when a genuine medium, such as Colin Fry (now back in spirit life), appeared on TV to demonstrate his gifts or abilities, the programme used to say, 'For Entertainment Purposes only'. The media (the majority of which is owned by those pushing the dark agenda), 'nine times out of ten' do not like anything that enlightens and empowers the public. And awareness that life is eternal is empowering.

Next is a communication from White Cloud, via medium Al Fike. Al and Jeanne Fike are true examples to us all in their dedication to raising awareness of spirit life and the teachings of advanced spirit communicators. They freely share a vast amount, including complete spirit communicated messages at their website (see Links). They kindly gave me permission to use all that I have included from them in this book. To them, I say "Thank you" and God bless you.

8. White Cloud – 2nd December 2016
The World Needs Your Prayers

'Blessings to you brothers and sisters, I am White Cloud. I have heard your prayers for my brothers and sisters who struggled mightily in this world, and for this planet, that also struggles to retain its equilibrium.

'I tell you that those who are resisting, and calling out the truth, do so because in their hearts they know the truth, and there will be many more in this world who will gather together and speak the truth; and this may cause division in the world.

'But there needs to be a voice crying for truth and love in the world; for too long the world has suffered from the abuses of man, the greed; the inability to love.

'**And for you, my brothers and sisters, who know the truth of God's Love, it is for you to shout out this truth to the world, to give this truth to the world, not in an insistent way, but in a gentle way, a way in which you demonstrate and carry the truth within you, and act upon the truth as you live your life each day.**

'And there will be times when you will have the opportunity to speak, to bring God's Love as an acknowledged truth in the world. Pray for those opportunities to come to you, beloveds, but most of all pray that you, each day, will come closer and more fully into the truth of his love.

'That you may shed all that is within that is not of this truth and love. That you may walk with a dignity and a purpose in the world that says "I am a child of God and I am a channel of God's love and I love you".

'**For all of these abuses in the world stem from a lack of love, my brethren, they stem from a lack of love and each of you have struggled with this very issue, for the entire world struggles with this and you have overcome much. You are coming into a new awareness, each one of you, as to the power of God's love, the glory and the joy of God's love, and you will shed whatever mantle of pain and error that you carry and walk forth in this freedom, and**

33

this liberation of your souls, as your souls awaken to this truth more fully and more beautifully.

'Continue to serve God, beloveds. Continue to live the truth and continue to speak the truth when that opportunity arises. And yes, pray for your brethren who also seek to express truth, to bring healing to this world, to bring change that is of healing and light.

'For all need your prayers. This world needs your prayers. The children need your prayers. The lost souls need your prayers. The hungry need your prayers. Those in pain need your prayers. All need your prayers, my beloveds, for what will save the world? Not violence, not insistence, but love, and the strongest man and woman is the one who can express love, the most powerful agent for change in this world, in the universe is love.

'Seek to express love in all that you do. Seek to serve in love each day. Seek your Heavenly Father to receive His Love so that it may flow through you in all aspects of your life and be humble, be gracious, be gentle, be strong. God bless you, beloveds. I am White Cloud and I am with you in your efforts, in your prayers, in your struggles. God bless you.'

Another lovely communicator from spirit life is Dr Peebles; the following comes from a transcript of one of his talks, a collection of which Summer Bacon, the medium for the Doctor, kindly sent me. And to remind readers, all the messages so far included in this chapter came through from those in spirit life before the so called pandemic of 2020, which, as I have said, is part of the dark agenda.

9. Dr Peebles - May 2018

'Your world in general is going to be going through a tremendous transition period, and for all of you it is more important than ever to stay steady in love. Know that you need each other; know that you count for something in this world. With every thought that you have in your mind, every word that comes out of your mouth, you are creating energy in this life.

'As long as you are thinking in terms of a world that is filled with hope, not tragedy, not trauma, not going to be torn down but going to be built up closer to God than ever before, and always

remember this, you will see a divine experience unfolding in front of your very eyes in the next ten years.

'You are going to experience, first hand, some tremendous changes upon the planet. People are going to become closer to each other, they're going to embrace one another in ways they have not done before.

'The planet Earth will return to this beautiful, sensuous, glorious Garden of Eden that it once was, and you my dear friends, you are going to be a big part of that through your thoughts, through your prayers, and through your awareness's.

'It is a magical time period for you upon the Earth, this is the beginning of the ending of many things, but it's the beginning of new beginnings as well. There are going to be, if you will, grand and glorious movements and communications between governments and such that will be tremendous in transforming this school called planet Earth.

'It will become, shall we say, in your words, a bit of a trend now to be nice to each other.'

I'm sure we all look forward to the day when governments are genuinely and with no darker co-operative motive, 'nice to each other'. In the meantime, this is something we, individually, can aspire to be. We know that in many cases those who have 'gone along' with what those with darker motives have 'encouraged' only did so because they either trusted what they were repeatedly told, or through fear. The fear itself having been promoted and driven into the minds of many by the non-stop media campaign of repetition. A bombardment, which itself is a form of torture, hypnosis or brainwashing.

People were presented with information they were told was factual, and claimed to 'follow the science'. When the truth was that people were being presented with a corporate materialistic profit based story intended to bring people into line with the ideas and plans of the 'new world order' and effectively under the control of the 'elite' would-be world rulers.

As I have said before, those in spirit life know what is going on, having foreseen what was coming decades back, and spoken of this well in advance of its most obvious 'power grab' of 2020.

The following message being another example of how our spirit friends see what is coming; this communication came through the medium Al Fike.

10. White Cloud – 1st June 2019
You Must Stand Up and Speak the Truth

'Every creature, including all of humanity, suffers here because the Laws of Creation, the harmony of God's Creation has not been obeyed nor recognized. Humanity continues to trample the Earth with no feeling or reverence for what God has created. It is for each of you and many, many more who must rekindle your understanding, your perception of what life truly is, this gift that God has given you.

'You must use your understanding, the insights of your souls to share truth with others, to help open their eyes, to help open their hearts with gratitude and awe and wonder of what is in your world. What is in all of God's great Creation, this understanding, this knowledge, and this Love for all that is, is the power that is required to change the world.

'**Each of you in your own way understand this and know this truth. I say to you, my friends, stand up and speak your truth wherever you are or whatever situation you may be in, in the world. Stand up. Be brave and walk your truth in every way that you can. For change in the world, the healing of the world, my friends, will not happen because someone has waited and not taken action. It happens because each one stands for truth and will not sit and wait.**

'God needs strong souls, souls that are awakened to truth; souls that are persistent, souls that are wise. In this way, God will guide each one of you in whatever way is part of God's plan to awaken and heal the world. For too many are asleep. Too many passively wait for something to happen.

'My friends, God calls each one of you in your hearts and beckons you to that place where you are aware and awake; that you, will not sit idly by, and allow your brothers and sister to trample upon this planet, numb and unaware of their actions. You must speak, you must reach out; you must talk in ways that are of love but also in ways that are of truth.

'**To do so, my friends, God will put the words in your mouth. God will guide you upon a journey that is of service that will awaken**

humanity, and where you will join many, many others who also feel the call, who also have awakened, who also are brave and speak the truth, unflinching they speak the truth.

'This will not make you someone who people adore. But it will make you someone that people respect, for they will feel the power of the truth that you speak. Something within them will be stirred. Within this call that you make to your brethren, there will be an answer that will come that will bring peace and balance to your world.

'This begins my friends, this great change; this great transition is in place. God has ordained and has come to sanction these changes. For without intervention, your world will crumble and fall into great chaos. God comes to save His children and all creation. You must listen. Listen to that call. Listen to what God has to say to bring you into alignment with this changing time that you may speak your truth and live your truth, and bring others to a place of knowing and understanding why all that is in motion is important, and necessary.

'Seek out your Creator, my friends. Seek God into your hearts. Come to know the Love that God has for you and all His Creation. Love exists. For every soul that walks this Earth, God's Love can be given and can awaken the true sight, the true understanding of life. It is for the asking, my friends. It is for you to ask and to receive, to seek and to be awake within.

'I thank you for listening to me today. I thank all of you for your efforts, for your light, for your work, for your time that is given to God. God will continue to pour His blessings upon you all. It is a never-ending cascade of Light that you may all receive and bask in and be changed and healed by. The Light of God's Love is for you and is never, ever restricted. Its bounty is endless. Its power is beyond your comprehension, my friends. Seek it. Come to seek it within your hearts and it will show you the way.

'Those of us who live in the Realms of Light come to assist the children who seek Love, Light, Truth, and great blessings for this world. God bless you. I am White Cloud and I know you. Many of you know me in your hearts for I've been with you as your friend. God bless you. Thank you.'

Incidentally, White Cloud, whether the same White Cloud I do not know, is the name of my brother, my main spirit guide in this lifetime. So finding communications, perhaps from him, was particularly a delight for me.

The following message also came through the medium Al Fike. Although it doesn't directly relate to the Great Awakening, I feel it is worth including for two reasons. Firstly, I find it an informative description to help us grasp the concept of time on Earth compared to time in the spirit realms. Secondly, because to me, it in a sense highlights just why those in spirit life may say that an awakening is happening and yet to us, on Earth, it may seem that progress in the awakening sense seems rather slow to manifest. In other words what may be coming soon, from the perspective of those in spirit life, may be weeks, months or years in coming to us on Earth.

11. Copernicus – 2nd December 2019
The Measure of Time on Earth is Very Different
Than in the Celestial Heavens

'I am Copernicus. I believe that you all know of my history in your world. I have come to talk to you about the measure of time. For the measure of time in your world is very different from that of which it is upon our world. Within your world the measure of time is very precise. There are many aspects and elements of your existence in the world that are parcelled out by the flow of time as the Earth makes its revolutions. The Sun and the Moon appear and all is within the harmony of which God has created in this physical universe. So time is easily recognized and you all live by the ebb and flow of night and day, of year upon year. So you acknowledge each year that goes by as you have done today.

'But within our world, no such markers exist. There is no night and day, only for those who live very close to the Earth plane and are still living within that rhythm but in essence do not belong to that physical world. Yet they do not realize that they are no longer physical but in spirit. For those of us who are not caught in that delusion, the world of spirit does not truly recognize time. Though in many ways our existence is linear as is yours. There is progress forward as it is in your world and yet that progress cannot be easily delineated by segments of time. Instead it comes with the sense of our own Light, our own being gradually edging towards greater Light.

'Even with those who are in the dark spheres, there comes a time in their existence where they come into Light. This may take aeons of time and yet in their perception, it may not seem so. Although for some, it may seem greatly so; it is a matter of perception. But once a soul has found their way towards Light and begins to learn about the nature of their existence and the nature of who they are, so time becomes a fluid part of their existence. One may spend many, many hours of your Earth time, even days, contemplating a Truth and yet to them, it may seem an instant, a very short time indeed because they do not consider time. They consider existence of being in the moment and knowing in all of their being that they exist for this very moment and that existence is a natural part of their being in the reality in which they exist. This sense of being can stretch what you call time, or shorten what you call time, for there are no markers as I have said.

'It is the choice of the individual marking their existence how that existence in relationship to time may feel. That feeling and sense of time then is dependent upon the individual. When one progresses into the higher spheres of life, even such a marking, a sense of time becomes more diluted in the flow of time, of existence, of progress forward.

'In the Celestial Kingdom, the souls who are there within this special realm are very far removed from your sense of time. It would be difficult to explain to you what their sense of time is except to say that when you wonder of the patience of your angel friends, how they mark your progress and how in your perception of your progress, it is very slow indeed. I tell you that to them it can feel very quick and not erratic but a beautiful flow, as if they are watching a flower in the sun open petal by petal. So they see with each of you an awakening that comes with the opening of each petal at a time. With the perceptions of the angels, that marking of your progress is a beautiful witnessing of your soul awakening like a flower. So the angels do not fret or worry about timing. Merely the angels are within the flow of God's time and the eternal time that exists in the Celestial Heavens.

'They must mark your time in as much as when they come to Earth they must acknowledge your times together, when you pray, when you ask for their presence, so they must come at the appropriate time. Yet for them, the only sense of time truly is when they are with you upon this Earth plane. Otherwise, they are within a great river of existence, an experience that is never ending. They and we feel and recognize the joy of existence in a way that you never can beloved souls upon this Earth. It is a great joy, an expansive understanding of existence of a soul in relationship to God, in relationship to the entire universe, in relationship to one another, this beautiful dance of existence.

'If you might think of molecules that are spinning and interacting with one another, so it is like with souls in the Celestial Kingdom, all interacting and touching one another, sparking joy and insight and acknowledgement and many more things that are beyond your understanding. So the existence within the Celestial Heavens is indeed very different, very different from the Earth plane. It would be hard for you to imagine what this is like, the consciousness of a soul redeemed by God and continually fed by the stream of His Love growing and expanding evermore, experiencing and awakening to evermore Truth and Knowledge, Joy and Love.

'This is what you will come to in time, my friends. I hope that I might have explained to some degree the differences between your existence on Earth and the existence of those spirits in the higher planes and those Celestial Angels in Heaven. You are aspiring to something magnificent, beloved souls. You will come to those magnificent understandings and experience. You will come to know the expansive joy of a soul awakened and redeemed by God's Love. All comes in time, and yet in time you will feel that time does not exist. And so I contradict myself as is the case when one uses words to explain the infinite Truths of God's Creation.

'May God bless you, my friends, and keep you in His Love. I am Copernicus and I too am a Celestial Angel and wish, dearly wish, that I could convey to you more of this understanding of the ways of the universe that is in harmony and operates fully and completely within the Laws of God's Creation and Love. But we try, we try, my friends, to help you understand, to help you to wonder, to ask for yourselves to God "May I come to know these truths from my soul." And in this experience of soul, you will truly understand. May God bless you and keep you in His Love. God bless you, beloved friends, and my love is with you. God bless you.'

The following message also came through the medium Al Fike. Again, I will remind readers, all that has so far been included from the spirit guides, and the following message, came through before 2020 when the dark agenda began to come more into the open for us all to see.

12. Augustine – 3rd December 2019
So Goes the World, So Goes the Catholic Church
A Variety of Souls, Some Light and Some Dark

'There are many within this church which you call Catholicism that have had a touch of the Father's Love within their souls. Yet there are many within the church who have not. There are a good portion of those within the church who are not motivated by Light but have political intentions for power and control. So with your world, so it is in this world, this little enclave of belief in the world.

'Is it often that the humble soul rises up in the ranks and becomes the leader within the bureaucracy of this church? No, it is not likely, for their work is "on the ground" as you would say, with their brothers and sisters who are earnestly seeking truth. Though they may speak error, their hearts are filled with Love and this is the potent touch and power of their ministry amongst the children of the world.

'They are drawn because they feel the strength and they feel the love and they know of that individual's wisdom and courage and caring and loving. They are an instrument of God. There are many in the world, humble and unknown, but they are blessed deeply for each effort that they make, each action and expression of the soul given in their daily lives is rewarded by God. Those who are in great power are often not in harmony with God's Will. For what is ambition rewarded with but the rewards of a material life, the rewards of ascendancy and power and control. These motivations do not garner the rewards from God.

'**So it is in your world, so many, whether it be a church or whether be in the political realms or the commercial realms of your world are dominated by these individuals who seek power and control, whose great motivation is to be puffed up within their minds with the sense that they are important, that they have control over others, that they may make decisions that affect the lives of others. These individuals create a very dark condition within themselves if they are not motivated by love. So they are contrary to the Laws of God's Creation and the Laws of Love. This contrary action and life may bring its material rewards but as you all know,** *these rewards are very temporary indeed in relationship to one's life that carries on in such a long, long road of existence in spirit.*

'So those individuals who are motivated by the human desires and predilections must face the consequences at some point in their existence. There are many who have lived a life of great power on Earth and have found a condition of great diminishment in the world of spirit.

'So, beloved souls, when we ask you to be guided by God, to follow the desires of your soul, to express the Truth as a humble child of God, to be in harmony with God's Laws of Love, to practise this each and every day, to discipline your thoughts so that they are elevated, to be aware of your motivations that you may nurture those motivations that are in harmony with God's Laws and Love, this is true leadership. **This is true awakening.** As you continue to nurture this Light within you, receiving the blessing of God's Love then that desire, that motivation to be a teacher, a healer, an instrument of God in the world and with the intention of reaching many souls with the good news of the Father's Love available for all, may come to be in your lives depending upon your light, your motivations, your actions, who you are in the world.

'That includes humility. Humility is when you are willing to listen to God's Will and not supersede God's Will with your own. So it takes a great deal of effort, as you well know, in your world to put aside the human condition, the human motivations, the desires for things other than awakening the soul and spiritual life and those things that are not in harmony and in balance with the spiritual, when these things are predominant within you then the possibility of leadership manifests not with intention but as a natural outcome of your soul's progress and your willingness to allow your soul its place within your being as a motivating factor of your life, hearing and knowing and feeling the presence of God with you always.

'These religious organizations, if they were led by such individuals, would be very different than they are today. All the rules and edicts, dogmas and creeds that are superfluous to a spiritual life would be eliminated, falling away revealing the golden Light of Truth within each religion. When that can happen, when humanity is willing to let go of this deep desire for dominance and control and power and give way to God with a sincere desire within their soul to know God's Will and to acknowledge God's Will in a truthful way, then religions will melt away. Instead there

will be a life that with each soul born into this world will have a natural component of spirituality to it.

'Those innocent children will not be corrupted by darkness and error but be nurtured and will grow in Love and Light. God's Hand will be upon each soul, guiding that soul, bringing a greater harmony to all the world. In this, this world will be elevated. As the world becomes elevated, so the world between us and the material world will be less of a barrier. There will be greater communication and rapport between all the souls in all worlds coming together in harmony and light.

'I know this sounds very utopian and quite distance from the vision of what is today but I say to you as there are greater numbers of those of you willing to step forward with this simple truth with humility and grace and true power, that is the power of love, then it comes closer. You add your light and your efforts to the forward progression of humanity towards greater harmony and closer to God and God's intention for the world.

'So I say to you, beloved souls, do not be like those who have risen to great power through their own wilful actions and desires. Rather be as God's children knowing and obeying the desire of God, His Will in your lives, and you will be surprised how you are guided and become acquainted with many of power and have some influence, bearing upon them, through your beautiful gifts.

'May God bless you upon that journey and may you come to know your true selves and take every advantage that you can to continue to grow within your souls and become strong and free of all conditions that are not in harmony with Love.

'God bless you. I am your teacher Augustine and I come to you with humility because I was one who sought power and control in my life on Earth and continue to this day, many, many years past, to help rectify those mistakes and actions that I made in the light, or should I say darkness, of power. May God bless you so you will not make these mistakes but continue on as God's humble children. God bless you. God bless you, beloved souls. My love and encouragement and prayers are with you all that you may indeed walk forward in this world of yours and bring the Truth with all humility and grace and beauty and love. God bless you.'

As Augustine said, *"There are many who have lived a life of great power on Earth and have found a condition of great diminishment in the world of spirit."* This is a point I have been making for a long while. To this end, to highlight how awful the consequences of a lifetime led, on the dark side, I'll call it, my book, *Escape from Hell,* can be read. Those on such a path should take heed, for it is far better to change whilst still on Earth, and it is never too late to at least begin the process of changing oneself.

Additionally, we should all recognise that division is an age old military tactic, 'divide and conquer', get the 'enemy' fighting amongst themselves. In this case it could be those who have been jabbed against those who have not, black against white, heterosexual against homosexual, 'royalists' against 'cavaliers', man-made climate change believers against non-believers, and whatever else might cause division and conflict. One might even say that those of us who believe (or know) in the reality of spirit life have in a sense been 'fighting' against the lack of awareness of non-believers for a very long time.

What we need to recognise or remember is that we are all One, all aspects of God. Even those people who are promoting or aiding the dark agenda; those who, sadly, have allowed themselves to shut off their moral compasses, and be swayed by power, control and greed. They are us and we are them, for all of us are facets, aspects, of God.

The following White Cloud message also came through the medium Al Fike and highlights that we, the awakened, need to stand together at this time rather than allowing those with a dark agenda to divide us.

13. White Cloud – 16th February 2020
It is Time to Come Together as One

'It is time, my friends, for all peoples and nations, all philosophies and religions, all perspectives and perceptions to come together as one. The time for individuality is coming to a close, where you will give up something for the benefit of all, rather than guarding your own individuality so closely and so firmly to your bosom.

'It is time to love and accept your brothers and sisters. It is time to go to the Source of All that is Love and Light, peace and healing, and to ask for a blessing. That you may shed those skins that keep you from love,

that keep you from light in the world, and walk boldly and lovingly in your true nature and true selves which God has given you.

'This is found in your hearts, beloved souls, not in your heads. In that deep place of feeling, and knowing, that your dear brother and sister have opened their hearts to you. They are an example. We must reciprocate with our hearts to them and to all you meet, all cultures and ways that you may encounter in your world. Open your hearts. Embrace them in love. Ask for the Creator to put this love into you, the power of this love to transform and bring unity to this world.

'Blessed are those who are meek and humble, who seek to serve in love. Blessed are those who are strong in Light. Blessed are all the children of this world who seek to be in the Grace of God. May you be blessed, beloved souls, in this search and journey for all that is true, all that is of love, all that is of the Creator.

'You will find your way, given your desire and effort to do so. This will come to each one of you, an opening, an understanding, a blessing, a sense of truth and peace, as God puts His Hand upon you and awakens you to Love. God bless you.'

At the beginning of the most obvious roll-out of one of the dark agenda plans, one that managed in large to subjugate and more or less imprison many people around the world. A time when people were told to 'be afraid', to hide themselves away, stay home, see no one or as few people as possible, to stay clear of others when it became absolutely necessary to venture outdoors, and even then to wear a face covering when entering a shop for essential groceries, what were spirit guides telling us about a so-called virus. The following will enlighten those unaware that so much of what they were told was utter nonsense, lies, or gross exaggerations of how 'deadly' the manmade 'virus' was or is.

Like all the guides "Sanaya" knows the truth of how humanity has in recent times been misled by the 'establishment' (Governments, media and so forth).

In the following, Sanaya, who communicates through the medium Suzanne Giesemann, confirms that Coronavirus was never anything to fear, this is part of what Sanaya said:

14. Sanaya - March 2020

Coronavirus Perspective from the Spirit Realms

'It would be remiss if we did not address that one item that is on everyone's mind thanks to your media. It is that virus which all of you have heard so much about, and the reason we bring it up this evening is because it is so vibrant in the collective consciousness of humanity at this time that is seen by all of those in what you would know as the heavenly realms.

'You can see it like a grey blanket that blankets your Earth, but we are not speaking of the virus itself, but of the fear that accompanies it, and this has built upon itself to the point where it has gone viral, the fear.

'And so we wish to bring a bit of reason back into this, this evening. Not that we are the sole voice of reason, your heart knows the truth, and we wish to simply remind you not to get caught up in what others are saying.

'We are quite aware that you can now find on your computers, statistics that will show you, you have far more to fear getting behind the wheel of your cars, than from a virus.'

I would add that Sanaya did also suggest we use our God given common-sense. In that if someone has flu or anything else that is considered contagious, or if they are already in less than perfect health or run down or in a frail condition, and so forth, then they ought to take care of themselves as well as around others. Just as most sensible people have always done.

But generally, any reasonably healthy person had no more to worry about from the latest well publicised virus, than from any previous flu virus. There never was anything vastly more 'deadly' for them to fear; and it is fear itself that is potentially harmful to us.

Spirit guides have for years been saying that fear is a negative emotion that can cause suffering, pain, ill-health, and so forth. Immortal souls, which all of us are, should fear nothing.

We should face every wrong that is directed towards us, and say, "No". And never comply with anything that our inner knowing feels is wrong and out of alignment with good.

Next is Dr Peebles, a short extract taken again from a transcript kindly shared with me by Summer Bacon that echoes the previous statement concerning fear.

15. Dr Peebles - March 2020

'Understand my dear friends that there is never anything to fear, because fear is the place where-in this particular virus can attach itself, in the deep and fertile soil of fear.

'It is not to be feared my dear friends, the virus wants to do nothing to you. It is not mean, it is not intentionally trying to hurt anyone, it is doing as everyone else upon the Earth has done, for centuries, it's striving to live and to thrive and by being in fear you're giving it that grand opportunity.

'She is a very sensitive little virus, a very sensitive little virus wearing a very thin coat, and this very thin coat can be shattered by lasers of love.'

'Essentially, the attempt here, to create mass panic, of fear to control the many, rather than the few, is not working. It's back-firing, it's going to create a stronger sense of community than ever before. You are going to know that you need each other upon this school called planet Earth.'

The following are some extracts from a longer communication delivered through the medium Al Fike. I find it quite wonderful, and exciting, just how many different evolved spirit teachers speak through Al, and there are many more communicators and messages than I can include to be found at the website.

16. Keea Atta Kem – 15th March 2020
Changing Earth Conditions

'Beloved souls, I am Keea Atta Kem and I resided in Egypt many hundreds of years ago, and now reside within the Celestial Kingdom, a redeemed soul and angel of God.

'The world is in great change and shifts beyond your understanding. Massive shifts within the world that will bring change to each of you here and all of humanity. Nothing can stop this, beloved souls, and nothing will stop this.

'As you ride upon the changing Earth, so you must learn to keep your balance and to be in harmony with God. It is those who are in harmony with God, in harmony with their own souls, and able to reconcile their minds with their souls, and their souls with God, who will carry the answers, and the key to the next awakening of the human race.

'This is all being orchestrated, my beloved friends. God has a plan for the salvation of humanity and I will assure you that there will be upliftment and progress upward rather than dissension and chaos; for it is in the present trajectory of humanity's intentions that this will come about; that much pain and suffering will be realized through the intentions of men. But what is happening now is the result of God's intervention, and in this way, many spiritual blessings and awakenings and manifestations will come with these changes.'

'God is seeding many souls with truth and a desire to serve and be uplifted in light. This is part of His plan for the unfolding of higher truth, of deeper purpose, of soulful recognition of the true nature of humanity. It is evident that if God left this awakening to mankind that it would destroy itself before the possibilities of this recognition. God's intervention is required, a redirection if you will, of the flow and actions of humanity away from the delusions and the distractions of materialism to a place of truth and simplicity and harmony.

'Many in your country and in what you call the western world are content with the way of life that is essentially built upon sand and not the rock of truth. Because of this unsound foundation of belief and way of living, much of what you enjoy and much of this illusion will fall away. Challenging each of you to find a different way, a way that is in greater harmony with God's Truth and Love, of what is truly meant to be in this world, which is a harmonious interaction between humanity and the creations of this world, the diversity and beauty of this world.

'This great gift to humanity must be acknowledged. The Earth itself is a deep blessing that nurtures you all. Because of the potentials of humanity, you have learned to manipulate the Earth to your own benefit. Some have fared very well in your world and have come to a place of comfort and pleasure and abundance while some have suffered greatly and in great deprivation.

'This is not God's plan nor Will for humanity; for God's plan ensures that all will be provided for, that needs will be met, that what is required

for a soul born upon this planet be available to each in equal measure and beautiful harmony.

'Humanity has come to a level of consciousness that they may intellectually understand this, but unfortunately their souls lag far behind. The understanding of the soul is very weak and feeble in most souls. In order for balance to be struck in the nature of man, God is providing those blessed souls who have great potential and gifts, to be aware of this truth of the soul and to awaken, to be nurtured and uplifted to the point where this wakefulness may be present and may be expressed in many different ways through those individuals who within their souls have chosen this work and this role in the world.

'Many of these souls that God has seeded are beginning to wake up and are beginning to feel a deep yearning for things spiritual and for God. In this way, God is orchestrating that many of you may meet and acknowledge one another, that those who are a little further ahead than others may come and help this birthing of new perception, of new truth and new potentials.

'Each of you will be called upon to do your part, though some of you feel unqualified in this regard. I say to you that the potentials of your souls go far beyond your minds capacity to understand and within the soul you must put your focus and trust that it will awaken, but must awaken through your yearnings to the Creator of all who will provide for each of you the spark that will bring this awakening and open the great potential of the soul.'

'There will be great upheavals as the world which you call Gaia, responds to the apathy of humanity which has built in numbers to such a degree that it is a great force upon your world. A force not for good beloveds but a burden, actions that are destructive; that are self-serving, that are unwise and unloving. The world in response will always bring balance and harmony back, that all life in this world which continues to suffer, as many creatures leave this world, must come back and be a part of this beautiful tapestry of life.'

'There are disruptions and eruptions that are taking place with great intensity and this will continue as your Mother Earth awakens to the dangers imposed by you. You have done so through your free will. You have done so because you do not know what else you might do. You have not done this out of malice or a desire to be destructive. It is difficult for you to see the picture that is present in the actions of* *humanity all around your world. We who come from far off, who see you from that distant place, see clearly how there are such great waves of disharmony, energies of destruction, desires and intention of humanity that are inharmonious and do not agree with the laws of God, and the laws of life, and the laws of love.*

'Many continue blindly down these roads of darkness, destruction and in-harmony, and as I say, many do so innocently, asleep, trusting in the powers of men to ensure their safety and their well being in the world. Unfortunately, this trust is very misplaced. The powers that be in this world do not consider the well being of their brothers and sisters, but only of themselves. Those who are presently in power, who presently control the life in this world will lose that power and lose that control. The structures of your world are crumbling. You see this now as plans made and ideas of future plans seem unlikely and impractical as the world changes.

'You must live day by day in faith and trust in God, the true power of all things. In this way, you will find your way through and be used in surprising ways. Not all will be lost, there will be communication amongst you; there will be ways and means to support one another that will be simple in nature and expression but more in harmony with God's Creation. Unfortunately, after all is said and done, there will be fewer of you upon this world, and many will enter into the world of spirit so that there may be a recalibration of the way in which you may live.

'In that time there will be great assistance given from many different avenues and possibilities. Forces of good and truth and love will come and teach humanity the new ways within this new era of peace and harmony.

'These changes are a great gift. I urge you, when you are in the midst of difficult times to remember this, as this is happening for a reason and has a purpose and outcome, to uplift humanity and bring the world back from the brink of destruction to a place of harmony. These are tough lessons, difficult lessons, but necessary so that all may find their way into greater light and deeper truth; that harmony may be with your world as it is with ours.

'May God bless you on that journey.'

Another spirit guide that has been forthcoming in speaking about current affairs and times on Earth, and the Great Awakening, is Jonathan.

The spirit guide "Jonathan" speaks through the trance medium Elaine Thorpe. In 2019 (if not before), he started mentioning that something was going to happen in 2020. As far as I am aware, he did not publicly say what.

As can be gathered, it all depends upon how one perceives what did begin to unfold. If one's focus is on the purely physical side of life then what unfolded could easily be seen as negative and bad news. On the other hand, although a dark agenda exists, many spirit guides also see that what has and continues to unfold is generating an "awakening". The awakening will gradually expose the dark agenda. However, perhaps more importantly, it will also bring an awareness of spirit life to many people who previously may have given their true nature no thought. Basically, all people should with absolute unshakable certainty know that we are immortal spirit beings who temporarily occupy physical bodies. (We should, also, know a vast amount more about our spirit nature and our "home" world).

Furthermore, collectively as well as individually, we are being helped to 'awaken' by higher frequency energies that are flowing to this planet at this time. Some call this a 'cosmic upgrade'; this as mentioned before, will shift our planet from a third dimensional planet to a fifth dimensional one. The quicker and more successfully people respond to these incoming energies, the sooner the effects, of a more enlightened world, will come into being.

With the above in mind, here is what Jonathan shared with us during April 2020.

17. Jonathan - April 2020
Reasons for Spiritual Awakening

'One of the reasons for spiritual awakening is for you to connect to yourself, and to our world once again, you see, it is a sort of a little reminder of where you came from.

'You live in human worlds, in human society, and you carry on as you do, but some of you forget that there are other existences beyond your world, and we want you to know that they are there. So the reason for the spiritual awakening is the fact that it is connected with unconditional love, as well as the connection with our world.

'So the spiritual awakening has many phases to it; it has a test, where you go through a particularly testing time, the dark time, and then from that you will go to many other phases during the spiritual awakening, where you will question things, and you will wonder what is happening to you. Will wonder the reasons why it has to happen, and you start to question all of that, until you have a total spiritual connection with yourself, it is about going back within, to yourself.

'You will go through the maze of life, and you will live a human existence, but then, sometimes it gets a little too human, and you seem to forget about your spiritual side of yourself. So, many of you will experience different things with a spiritual awakening.

'Some of you will begin to perhaps see visions, some of you will experience seeing different number sequences that will give you signs for other messages from the spirit; there are many different ways to experience it. Some of you may experience vibration from within your being which is where your body will vibrate, many different ways to wake up spiritually. But the reason is that we have noticed in our world that you have all not been having time for one another.

'You say, "Well, we are so busy with our lives we don't have time to connect with each other". So this wasn't particularly done on purpose in order for people to suffer, many people chose to go to the other side in mass, you see, for the reasons being that they also wanted to teach the Earth about unconditional love, so they chose to go home in mass. So you have what you call the mass exodus, and many people are passing to the spirit world each and every day, but nobody notices that, they don't really notice it; it is happening every second of every day.

'And there are incarnations happening every second of every day, but it is not particularly recorded for everyone to experience it, it is just something that happens without you even noticing.

'But this, had to come to a point where everybody would stop and take stock, and everybody would notice that something different was going on, the truths had to come out in your world, and they are going to come out, and there is going to be all of you coming together and being at peace with one another and the Earth actually being at peace itself too.

'The way that you are perceiving life to be, the way that you are treating one another, we see that there is a lot of negative going on in the world, and it has to have negative alongside positive in order for you to coexist together. So sometimes the negative gets a little out of balance and it tends to try and go into the positive a little bit more, and overtake it, so it needs rebalancing again. That is happening at the present time, but I should think that if you're all going to stop and experience something so profound all over the world, does that not tell you something, it is teaching you how to come back to your families, how to come back to yourself, and find unconditional love with all of them and each other.

'You go through what you call the dark day, you see, and many people will be tested in their lives, before they have a spiritual awakening they go through a dark period in their lives, where they perhaps come to a dead end in their lives, a full stop. They don't know where they're going, they cannot find their path, and they look in all sorts of directions to find out where their self is going to be.

'But if they go within, it is already there, it's just a matter of knowing how to go within. Just a matter of knowing what is around you, how to appreciate it; and how to love you.

'It would happen on many scales, it would happen with an individual, it would happen with a group of people, it could also happen in a great mass. So you see not all viruses are about spiritual awakening. Some of them are just particular viruses that are able to evolve and travel from human to human and unfortunately it would take one's life, and others would survive.

'But there is something different about this one, isn't there, and many of you would perhaps have felt it. Some of you would be angry and bored and stay at home and you would think, "I want to get out, I want to go out, I'm human; I need to go outside, I feel a little bit trapped in here". But if you take stock and look at what is around you within your house, maybe you are on your own, or maybe you are with your families, you have time for each other now, don't you. You've all been complaining that you haven't had time, look at the time you got now.

Question: Did the souls that are leaving now, choose to do so before they incarnated?

'Yes, they would have done, and every single soul that incarnates to this Earth will choose the lifetime that they have, and then they will choose when they pass.'

The following message came through the medium Al Fike.

18. Josephus – 27th April 2020
Free Will and Its Impact on Earth

'I wish to give a message for all those who are willing to listen. It is on the theme of free will and that God does not interfere with the lives of mankind. God does not manipulate individual souls, mortals in your world, for to do so would be to contradict the Law of Free Will.

'Each individual in your world is given the privilege of having the opportunity to make their own choices, choices that at times contradict the Laws of Creation. Humanity above all other creatures on your world have this gift, and can act freely in the world. So the conditions of your world are created by humanity. Humanity has free reign, although still subject to the Laws of Creation, such as the Laws of Cause and Effect. Yet, the will of man is free to move, to act, to be in the world without the interference of God.

'The will of man, in what it has created in the world, will bring about a response in relation to the laws in which mankind is subject. Every action will bring some response. If that action is in harmony with the Laws of Creation, God's Laws, then there will be a positive response and greater light is created. The atmosphere around the individual is lightened and purified to some degree. It is the thoughts as well as the deeds of each individual which determines this outcome. So we encourage you to have positive thoughts, to consider your actions, to be guided by God, to bring within yourself the great blessing of Divine Love which purifies the soul, thereby influencing individual thoughts and actions.

'The journey of soul awakening is an important step toward understanding the responsibility and the power that the individual has in regards to free will. Rather than stepping forward in the world expressing oneself without the wisdom and understanding of the Laws of Creation, and thereby creating often negative responses, one has the opportunity to step forth in wisdom and responsibility to create greater light and harmony. But God will not interfere with that choice. God does not interfere with the workings of humanity's continued existence in your world. This would contravene the Law which He has placed in regards to your existence.

'It is up to each individual to understand this, rather than what is the case of so many, who step forward in error, creating conditions in the world that are inharmonious with God's Creation. Then turning to God and blaming God for the response to these actions. Indeed, many innocent individuals are victims of the collective actions of humanity. Unfortunately, this cannot be avoided in the realms of this Law in action. It is suffering that ensues when humanity acts without true knowledge or the higher intentions which comply with God's Will. Therefore, all are subject to the harsher conditions and responses that come with the world whose existence and what you call vibration is low and unresponsive to the higher blessings of God. So your world continues to react to the actions of humanity in ways that are harsh and definitive and not ameliorated (made better) by the gentle touch of God.

'I know this is difficult to understand and it is a complex matter but the Earth has its own consciousness and in fact, is subject to its own Laws of Creation. But it is also subject to the conditions which humanity has created on the surface of your Earth. Humanity does not understand its own power of influence, its energetic touch upon the world; for most of humanity sleeps. It does not have the capacity at this time to see beyond its own daily interactions with life. A deeper understanding is possible but the choice of humanity is to ignore this, often in ignorance of its existence, often in a desire not to engage in deeper thoughts and perceptions which complicate their daily lives rather than complement them.

'So the Earth reflects the harshness of humanity and the ignorance of humanity. In God's Creation, energies interact. Conditions, as we call them, elicit responses in a way that encourages greater harmony or at least healing of that condition toward harmony. Unfortunately, the power of the free will of humanity is confronting the power of your Mother Earth, creating friction and response that is, in itself, often harsh and decisive. So within this interaction, as humanity grows in numbers and power and influence, on the Earth, the power of response of Mother Earth will intensify. Humanity will indeed suffer the consequences of its actions. God is not condemning or punishing humanity for God has, to some degree, an arm's length relationship with humanity. God is allowing humanity its own course of action.

'God is offering solutions: love, healing, peace; all things that are good, and of light are being offered to each individual. Those who are listening to this message are often benefitting from these blessings given. But humanity on the whole is sleeping, yet acting out of self-desire, and cannot see clearly the consequences of such actions. The power of culture, a nation, the world, is immense in its capacity to limit the choices of humanity and carries all towards a certain trajectory that is not in harmony with God's Laws.'...

'You have trouble understanding how you may play your part in this global situation of conflict between Mother Earth and humanity. This is why we have assured you that there is a plan so that the outcomes of Light and harmony, of Truth and Love, of wisdom and peace will come to your world. There is indeed intervention, but it is not how you perceive God's influence and effect in your world. It comes from the Laws in action, those things that God has created for all eternity coming into play in response to men's actions and expressions.

'With this comes the help of spirits, high spirits and angels helping to guide each one of you in the way of wisdom and light. Even we cannot countermand the power of free will. We may only advise and assist where there is an opportunity and invitation from the individual to do so. Yet, we work with many, many souls on your world. We make great effort to influence many. This influence is coming to bear upon the minds of men. Many individuals are beginning to see the bigger picture as you call it.

'So, we continue and we seek the guidance of God, to continue to enact this plan for the salvation of humanity. It unfolds with each day, as the overriding conditions of humanity, continues to be enacted with each day.

'The antidote to this darkness is also being expressed with each day and grows with each day until the light that is focussed upon your world is greater than the darkness that is proliferated on your world. This is the plan, beloved souls. It respects the free will of men. It respects the Laws of Creation. It respects God's Will, God's desire for humanity to entreat light. So you will come to resolution, beloved souls.'...

'Although the resistance is great, the ignorance is overwhelming, and the lack of love gives us great distress. Yet, the power of all *the elements of your world and our world and God's Will, will win the day, in time.'...*

'This is a very crucial time. You sit upon the cusp of great change which brings great opportunity, and great enlightenment, provided humanity chooses this path towards light though their expression, and journey towards such a path, is of their own choosing and expression.

'We do not wish to set forth dogma, mental rules, and paradigms that are to be applied universally. No, this is not the way of free will. Each will be given the opportunity to choose and if they choose light, they will do so on their own accord and in their own way, but they must elicit the wisdom of their soul in order to do so. This gift of the soul, and the wisdom of the soul, is given to every individual, yet very few understand its capabilities and blessings and power to bring deep insight. So many walk in ignorance and are asleep to their own potentials. The coming times will bring an awakening, will cajole humanity from its slumbers and will insist that each individual comes to the truth of what is of light, what is important in their choices and desires that will bring light.

'So much awaits humanity. You are on the verge of a great revolution of thought and deed, of desire and of the soul. May each of you continue to prepare yourselves for this event, or shall I say series of events, that will help to awaken humanity, bit by bit, to come to the Truth.

'We are all on a powerful trajectory; this great plan that God has initiated, to bring this awakening, to bring the deep change that is needed in the world, may each of you consider the need for greater prayer, for greater awakening, for greater strength and love and light, for it is up to you, and up to all those who are beginning to awaken, to enact their part in this great revolution that will bring light to the world.

'Be attuned to God and be attuned to your own soul. Know yourself. Know yourself well, and be in the flow of God's Will and Light and Love and all will unfold in miraculous ways, in wondrous ways, in beautiful ways. There will be harmony, in time, great harmony and peace that will last and last. You will be the forerunners of a new world that will have in its existence, great Light and peace, Truth and Love. Your future generations will benefit from your efforts. When your time comes to be in spirit and you look back upon your efforts, your time here on Earth, and the

choices you made, you may have great joy and acknowledgment of these efforts and choices for the benefit of humanity.

'May God bless you, beloved souls; I am Josephus. I am happy to have come to give you this message in hope that it will clarify, encourage and inspire your efforts in the coming days, and weeks, months and years as the Earth changes, and becomes what it is meant to be. God bless you.'

The following is more from one of the transcripts that the medium Summer Bacon kindly sent me.

19. Dr Peebles - 8th July 2020

'Look forward to the days and months and weeks ahead my dear friends, and certainly find that this world is not disappearing; it is not dying, human beings are not going anywhere; you are going to learn from each other and expand the love upon the planet Earth.

'Be careful with your words at this time, because your words mean so much; they carry a heavy energy within them. It can be heavily laden with love, or heavily laden with hate, you, my dear friends, decide.

'When you speak your truth from your heart, you will find that your words are spoken with love. You will find, truly, that the truth within yourself is love. Love prevails. Love is the only thing that is everlasting, and it the only thing that can heal your planet Earth at this given time. Raising the vibrational frequency of love is what we are asking for you to do.

'You can strive, if you will, to change the planet Earth through your science's, your medicines, and all sorts of activities that you engage in, but you cannot do anything if it does not have love in the equation. It does not work. You cannot move a mountain just through faith alone, you move it through love. You ask the mountain itself to simply move aside and it shall, if you have love in your heart and you ask in a loving fashion, it can move mountains, literally in your life.

'And in this world, the way that it is, in the condition that it is in, it is time to move mountains, mountains of hate, and certainly hate is nothing new to planet Earth, it's been around for centuries. You will find that hate is just something that is finally being acknowledged, and seen and heard and felt, in ways that have not been done before. So it's making

58

you all more acutely aware of what is occurring upon the Earth; and what you don't want any more. That you want to join together, that you want to understand yourselves as a collective upon the Earth.

'You human beings are a very special unique bunch and we love you so very much. You have so much within your heart that you can do to make changes that are grand and glorious upon the Earth.

'You will find in the days and weeks and months ahead, that your planet is going to change remarkably. Barriers, borders, and boundaries will come down, and with that, yes, there is a bit of chaos.

'But do not say that there will be civil war, do not say that there will be disturbances, do not say that it's going to be a scary time, do not say these things that are creating and generating more fear in your world. Speak a greater truth, and speak from your heart. That every day the sun is rising, the birds are chirping, the animals are awakening, and sometimes they are making babies and making love beyond your wildest dreams and imaginations, bringing new life into the world.

'Your world is a beautiful, beautiful place and human beings are beautiful, once they find their heart's they will realise this more than ever before.

'The world is moving in a new direction now, and it's fantastic. It's going to have a remarkable outcome. Love will prevail ultimately my dear friends, and you're not going to go backwards.

'It's never going back to the way it was my dear friends; and thank goodness for that! You are moving forward, you are expanding in awareness of each other. You are expanding in your awareness of the boundaries that have kept you separate in so very many ways.

'It's a remarkable time to be upon the Earth, it is not an easy time to be upon the Earth, however, one of the more alive times that you will ever experience upon this school called planet Earth.'

What follows is also taken from one of the transcripts sent to me by Summer Bacon.

20. Dr. Peebles - 3rd August 2020

'Beautiful spirits, students of the Divine! Wonderful creators, each and every one of you, my dear friends! We celebrate you here today. We love you so very much. You are a beautiful spirit upon this school called

Planet Earth, and it's a tough place to be sometimes, but you're doing a beautiful job of making it a beautiful place, by living from your heart, by allowing for yourself to be heard with compassion; by being as gentle as you can possibly be in terms of your abilities as the listener for others to vent their concerns, their fears, their expectations about life at this current time upon the planet.

'We celebrate you! We are applauding you. You are all doing beautiful work. You're really striving to live from love and we want to thank you so very much for this, because it really makes a difference. It really does. Not only on the Earth, but we feel the resonance of that where we reside in the 16th Dimension, because we are all connected. That's why we care so deeply about you.

'We want for you to be uplifted. We want for you to feel joy within your hearts. We want you to feel freedom within your soul. We want for you to live life without any barriers, borders or boundaries ever again. We want for you to come together as the collective that you are; the beautiful spirits; the human beings upon this Earth, striving to understand your right to receive and to give abundance in this your chosen lifetime.

'You chose this lifetime for a reason. You came here knowing full well that you would be around during this time on the planet Earth. You came here with a desire to study love, to study freedom, to study joy, to study how to release yourself from the pains and ills of others by looking inside of yourself and creating a reality there, starting on the inside rather than on the outside.

'You came to this planet Earth at a particular time to celebrate self in a variety of ways. This is a place that is a school. It is intended to be a little bit hard sometimes, because that's how you're going to grow here. You're going to learn by hard work sometimes, and that's alright. It doesn't have to always be carefree. Life is not always one big party all the time, but you can certainly strive to experience it as such on the inside by celebrating the love that you are; bringing more and more of that to the surface. You are a beautiful spirit upon this school called Planet Earth. We cannot emphasize this enough.

'As you come into this next period of time in your life on the planet, you're going to find that there is going to be a series of events. It's going to be one after another that are going to be challenging; short and sweet and to the point, but very challenging for human beings to *get through. You're going to find that no longer do you want the adversity. No longer do you want the pain. No longer do you want the wars. No longer do you want the control.*

'People are going to be coming together in uprisings and saying, "Enough is enough! We want to celebrate our freedom! We want to celebrate the fact that we are a collective upon the Earth."

'You are going to find that this is happening around the world, because human beings are by nature people who love to be within community, and by nature you love to hug each other. By nature you are intended to be social creatures. By nature you are involved in relationships, not only within self, but within life, with each other, with the world, and this is a time period where people are going to come together more than ever before.

'Human beings are going to come together united, and you're going to have very interesting times ahead. But, remember, as you go through them they aren't going to be easy, because it's going to be one thing after another after another, but short and sweet and to the point so that people come together. It's intended to bring you closer together, because you are going to see the division is not going to work anymore. You're going to have to be together. So, remember this.

'This is a little bit of a heads' up for you for the next several months ahead of you. But, you're going to come into a time period where you're going to realise that your pains are going to dissipate, because of the very fact that you will start to celebrate each other; you'll find the truth will be revealed.

'You'll find that the illusions of separation are going to start to melt and fade away. You will find that it's going to be an extraordinary time to be alive. So stick around why don't you!

'There's going to be a flurry of activities with human beings saying they want to leave the Earth, and they will in droves. Some through Earth changes that will be occurring; some will be leaving by their own hand, and that will become something that is rather fashionable for some, but we don't suggest it for any of you.

'You are beautiful spirits, and you've got a great soul, and you've got a great desire to see these grand and glorious changes that are about to happen upon the Earth.

'When you see others going through pain, when you see others who are going to leave the planet Earth, it is a choice that they are

making. They choose this for themselves. It is their journey. It is not your journey, it is theirs. This is what they have decided. They can't stick around because they just simply don't understand; they are in fear, they are in panic, the classes are too tough, and so they want to go home, and they want to get off the Earth. They want to get away from the chaos and such that they are feeling.

'But you are going to stick around to see this time period through; to realise within yourself that you are here upon the planet Earth to experience the unity within the diversity of life.

'Now, we want you to understand something here. Your planet is certainly experiencing tremendous arguments and contentious behaviours and upset, and there is a lot of finger pointing and that sort of thing.

'There's a lot of divisiveness; lots of individuals who are being divided here. This is a period of time where there is clearing out and cleaning out of old, old, old karma that has been around for centuries, some of which that you were part of.

'There were times upon the Earth where slavery abounded in the United States of America. It was something that was very tragic for the many, rather than the few. Individuals who were enslaved were oftentimes treated in unbearable conditions, not given enough food to eat, and they were required to work hard hours without much in return at all.

'Many times this involved horrific behaviours on behalf of one human being to another; such as rape and other things. Yes, it was a terrible time upon this school called Planet Earth, a very sad time; and, some of you were involved in that period of time in a previous lifetime.

'You are intertwined and united by all sorts of experiences that you have had, in not only this lifetime, but in other lifetimes. You are carrying inside of you memories of old. And, so this is a time period where there are going to be uprisings, because it is a clearing out of karma.

'There's a little bit of tit for tat here. It's something that is going to happening very quickly, very rapidly. There's going to be one event after another, but it's going to happen quickly and rapidly because it is just simply a clearing out of karma. If you can see it as such, then perhaps you will not fear it so much. You'll realise that the people who are involved in these different scenarios, it is their choice, and they are doing it because this is part of their karma that they want to clear out.

'So, they are working in terms of getting rid of old stuff upon this school called Planet Earth, and sometimes it doesn't look very pretty. But, it is a necessary step in this journey of life, wherein the expansion of the universe is happening regardless of whether or not you feel you want to go along with it; it's happening anyway.

'In the process of the expansion of the universe, there is always going to be some upset. There's always going to be a little bit of fire. There's always going to be a little bit of pain. There's always going to be a little bit of rain. It's going to be something that is going to happen no matter what, because it is a necessary part of the process of this tilling of the soil so that you can now grow.

'The events upon your Earth are very frustrating. Of course it is! You don't want to see anybody hurting. Never! You would not want to see anybody ever pinched with pain, and there is a tremendous amount of pain upon the planet Earth, no question about it. But, it is the way it was created, because it is the way in which you are learning to get back to love; to labour in love and to see very clearly spelled out in front of you - everything that you see, hear, taste, touch, feel, and smell - you start to see clearly what is love, what is truth, what is that which works, what is that which is good, what is peace, what is prosperity, of the soul.

'You are beautiful spirits, you are in this physical form called "human being" and it can be very cumbersome, because in truth you are a spirit; a free spirit.

'You are never under anybody else's control. Ultimately you are only under the control of yourself. You have that decision inside of you as to what you believe or experience in any given moment. You are the master of your universe. That's the way it works, regardless of what is happening around you. You are the master of your own universe, and you make the decisions that create your reality in this given moment.

'In your human form there is a lot of concern, people are asking in their prayers, "How can I increase my immunity? How can I strengthen my immune system?"

'Well, we are going to tell you this my dear friends, it's not going to come from any vaccination or anything else. It's going to come from a process that happens inside of you. If you're going to inject

yourself with anything, inject yourself with hope. Inject yourself with faith. Inject yourself with trust. Inject yourself with peace. Inject yourself with love. Inject yourself with all of those things that build up your immunity to fear, hatred, loathing, anger and what you believe and perceive to be death.

'You have a chance to grow beyond your wildest dreams and imaginations. You'll become more awake than you've ever been before. Awake to truth. Awakened to love; the love that you are. You will start to see the magnificent creator that you are. You will find that you are spreading joy and peace and love through your own energy everywhere you go. Can you catch yourself when you are thinking and speaking words that are less than kind, and bring more kindness to the surface? It is more important than ever before. It truly is.

'Right now upon the Earth there is a shift happening, and it is a tough shift. But, you are going to find that the more you settle into peace, faith, hope and wonder about beautiful things in life, in the future that is exactly where you will end up.

'Those who live in anger and hatred are in fear. They are sad. These are just other ways to express that. They're afraid of being seen as vulnerable. They're afraid of being seen as sad. They're afraid of being seen as fearful. So they put on a big nasty face and they come out with some really good nasty words, and they strive to stand on top of the mountain and preach to the masses to make people believe that they are right. And that goes for everybody. You have all done this at one time or another in your life. It's natural. It's human of you. There's nothing wrong with it. It's just that, in truth, when you look deeper inside of yourself you'll discover that these are ways in which you are just simply trying to hide your fears and your vulnerability.

'You are not the victim of this time period upon the Earth. It is not a matter of crying out, "Why me? Why now?" But coming to the understanding that you chose this. "Ah, this is the time period I chose to be here for. That's why I'm still alive. I wanted to see what's going to happen next. I wanted to be a part of the upliftment of planet Earth. I wanted to be a part of that raising of the vibration of love."

'And you bring that into yourself, my dear friends, because you don't want to censor yourself anymore. Look inside of your heart

and find your truth and speak it; find your truth and live it. Don't censor yourself.

'These are part of the events that are going to be occurring upon your Earth. There's lots of censorship that is happening. It has always happened; it's as old as time, and as old as the beginning of your media, such as newspapers and other things where people started to censor others. And it happened even before the written word. People were censoring others.

'Take time for yourself to sit and relax into the part of you that knows truth. The one that knows that only peace can create peace; only love can create love. You cannot force anybody to comply with either one of those. They must find it within themselves, and it will take some centuries. Some will return to the Earth over and over and over again. Some will strive to find it in a variety of ways. Some will strive to force things to fit, not realising that everything already fits perfectly, beautifully.

'You are an energetic being in body on the Earth temporarily, and there is no death. When you leave this body, you will feel a lightness of your being beyond your wildest dreams and imaginations, and you will feel the love that is in the universe. You will return to source, and you will feel it tremendously. But, you can feel it on the Earth as well, and that's what you are here to explore, because it is a school, and you're a student, and you're really good students, we must say.

'Those of you who are listening to us, we thank you for all that you are doing in the world. This is an important place you live upon, this planet Earth. It's a real focal point for the universe. It really is. Because it's a place that's hurting, and just as in your body you might have an ache or a pain that's asking for attention, and asking for love, that is what your planet Earth is like in the universe. It's a place of pain and sorrow, and it's asking for love. And many of you have come to the planet Earth to be the healers; to bring that light. You got down in the trenches to help and to assist the many rather than the few.

'There is so much happening upon this planet Earth. So much more than what you hear about from your media, from your politicians. Stop allowing for your mind and your heart to be shaped and moulded by these things. You are the creator of your own reality. You shape and mould your own heart. You are the master of your own universe.

'When you are watching your media, such as your television news, what are you watching? What are you hearing? You are hearing one form of truth. You are hearing something that is being shared because it is being very carefully calculated and shared with you to evoke a certain response. Some, certainly, yes, some news is true, honest, direct. But, that's for you to decide within your own heart. It is time to awaken to the energy that is being thrown at you. Thought forms of hatred. Thought forms of fear. You choose to either take that within yourself, or you choose not to.

'You can by all means watch the news all day long if you want to. But, if you're going to buy every single bit that they're selling, that's where you are going to get entangled in a terrible web of deceit. You've got to learn to discern.

'There are wonderful people upon the Earth, speaking truth. Some are speaking truth on your television. Some are truly telling things honestly. Listen to your heart. Does it feel like a yes or a no inside of you? That's where you create your reality. And we suggest that you prune back anything that wants to put fear into you, because that's the last thing that you need right now.

'Enough with the fear; enough with the anger; when you are seeing riots in the streets and such, go back to what we shared earlier. Remember that those individuals are the creators of their own reality. They are clearing things out; there is a massive purging of old, old, old karma.

'It is a scary time for some to watch this happen. But if you can understand from an energetic standpoint that it is necessary, that that which has been hidden is going to be revealed, that people are going to start to speak their truth and demand attention, to say, "We are hurting, and enough is enough with being divided! We want to be seen and heard and felt, despite our skin colour or anything else." You're going to find it happening more and more.

'It's going to be very interesting because you're going to find that there's going to be lots of different sorts of groups that will be rather fun. There will be individuals that are going to say, "You know something? I'm rather liking working at home."

'And there will be people petitioning to say that they want to stay at home and continue working from home and not have to go back to work.

'There's going to be lots of children saying, "I love learning at home. I'm really enjoying it." And, they're going to petition to not have to go back to a public school. There's going to be a lot of different things happening, and there will be people coming to surface saying, "You know something? It's most interesting, I was unable to go to the doctor because of everything that's happening upon the Earth, and it turns out that I'm healthier than I've ever been, because I wasn't going to the doctor! I've found ways to change things in my life to make myself feel better." You're going to find that there are some really remarkable things coming out of this time period, and it's all going to be really wonderful.

'Some of you might say, well it's not so wonderful for those who died! Well, you don't know that necessarily, do you really? You're not there where they are now. You're not seeing the vast array of incredible magnificent colours and feeling the love and the warmth of God, and the peace that is there within their hearts, being free from the physical form.

'You are a beautiful spirit, a student of the Divine, and we love you so very much, God bless you, indeed. Look for the goodness in your world. You'll find it. Look for the joy. It's there. Look for the love. You'll experience it. Why? Because, it's all there, inside of you, to begin with. Put your attention upon that which matters, my dear friends, and know that you are a beautiful spirit and that we love you so very much.

'Go your way in peace, love and harmony, for life is indeed a joy, and all you have to do is you enjoy the journey to your own heart, and to your own enlightenment'

The next contribution below comes from the spirit guide *Monty*, who communicates through the medium Warren James. In this he gives us some good advice that follows on and basically agrees with what Dr Peebles said during the same month (as above), and the reasons why it would be for the benefit of all, if we can take heed of this advice.

21. Monty - August 2020
Concerning Emotions

'The biggest virus in your world right now, my friend, is an emotional one. What you must remember is that what goes out from you is absorbed by others; and that is a fact.

'That is a fact. In your world, if you feel hatred, you give off hatred, you do not even need to tell somebody you hate them, for them to know. They in their head may not realize it immediately, but their body does; their senses, they truly know that they are hated.

'And that creates a second reaction. And that is one feeling of hate, just one vibration of hate. Other vibrations from hate to worry, to concern, paranoia, they are all vibrations. They all have a frequency unique to themselves, all the way up through love and balance.

'And I would say, my friends, to truly change the world in some respects, you need to rise above the emotion of the matter, approach the matter head on. Never be ignorant of the truth. The truth is the truth. Never be ignorant of the truth, my friends. If you believe something is wrong, then it is wrong. But the important thing is to rise above the emotions, because the emotions will keep you giving off the wrong one. Whilst those emotions fester within you, the vibration of that emotion will leave you, it will impact on those around you, and they will react with an emotion in accordance to the one that is dominant, that you feel.

'If you give off anger, frustration, irritability, you will receive from the people around you anger, irritable response. You understand? It is so hard when I say this, but it is true. I cannot change the truth to make it fit any other way.

'And when you give off a different vibrational emotion, when you yourself rise above the anger and hate, but not being ignorant of the matter at hand, when you know within you, I am not ignorant, I know the truth, but I am capable of rising myself above those emotions. And I give off a different emotion now, immediately, because you no longer resonate with what is happening, you allow it to become weaker, within you. You control your emotions. You are in full control of them. You are in control of you. And I am not allowing sadness, anger, frustration or even hatred to come into the equation.

'I know what is going on in the world. I recognize it. I look it in the eye, dead on. But I do not react with that. I do not fight the fire with the fire. I

68

will fight the fire with water. I will use water to extinguish the flames. Therefore, when you rise above and live and learn to rise to a level where you are no longer stuck in the same misery that other people are putting upon you, you no longer pass it on. Other people cannot, as I've said before, they cannot cease to be moved by it. They won't know why. They will tell you, "You seem different, you seem a different person. What's going on? Can't quite see what the thing is. It's happening, but I can't understand it".

'And that's because you now emit a non emotional output. And even better, if you can learn to find the love and the peace, then, try to emanate that, instead of.'

Below is some more from a transcript of a Dr Peebles communication. Speaking generally, few people realise that we, especially collectively, are very powerful creators, whether we create with intention or unintentionally. Either way, we contribute to what is called the "Collective Unconsciousness" of planet Earth. This can have an effect on so much, including the weather we experience.

22. Dr Peebles - 12th August 2020

'Realise that the movements of the Planet Earth are created and generated by a collective community called human beings. You create this energy together no matter what comes about in your day; no matter what sort of weather you are experiencing; no matter what is happening within your neighbourhood. You are creating that reality collectively together. What are you putting into that equation from your heart? What role do you want to play?

'Feel inside of yourself as to what you would like to contribute to the world, regardless of what anybody else is doing. What is it that you desire to contribute? Do you wish to contribute pain? Do you wish to contribute hope? Do you wish to contribute love? Those are just choices you make. Sometimes you're just in a rage. Sometimes you just don't like what's going on. Sometimes you spew expletives like venom. Sometimes you stomp your foot. There's lots of ways in which you choose to express yourself.

'And, sometimes the only way to really know who you are is to go into who you are, and feel it, and experience it, until eventually you come to understand that hatred and anger are really things that can't hurt

anybody unless they choose to allow for it to hurt them. Most of all it hurts the person who's doing that. If you are feeling anger or hatred about anything, it's hurting you. How long do you want to hold onto that? You're in charge there. You make that decision, as to how long you want to hold onto those things that hurt. It's a decision you make. Or, do you want to bring into your life beauty and wonder?

'Every single solitary person upon this planet Earth is important because God loves you. You are the children of God. God does not forsake anybody, but loves you all equally; wants for all of you to know yourselves, to explore yourselves, to come to the surface, to feel his love within your heart, and within your day, no matter what is happening around you.

'How do you do that? By knowing that that is within you; that love is already there. It's been there all along. It's for you to decide to bring it to the surface; to experience it, to breathe it, to express it, to give it in a variety of ways. If you are to just simply tie the shoelaces of a child, your day has been important, because you gave of yourself to life. If you can lift one robin unto its nest again, you shall not have lived in vain.

'Human beings have a tendency to think very lofty thoughts about self; that you must become something. That you must be highly educated; that you must be well read; that you must learn a skill and master it. Those are all beautiful things, but it is not necessary in order to be someone great in the world. You are already great, right here and now. There is no there to get to, where suddenly you are given a badge that says, "You're great! You're a success!"

'No, my dear friends; by the very fact that you are on the Earth still, that you are breathing, you are a success. You are courageous because you chose to be here at this given time upon the Earth.

'With this constant bombardment about this pandemic upon the Earth, constant news, constant sharing, constant conversation about it, stop for a moment and realise, that something is happening, yes.

'It is a condition that you've been put in, in order to learn about yourself. But, it does not have to hurt you. It does not have to hinder your growth. Stop waiting around to have a happy day! Stop waiting around to find joy and peace and wonder. Stop waiting for this to be over to feel movement in your life. Find creative ways in which to create that reality within yourself. Go

inside of yourself, and enjoy the journey there. You might find that you really like yourself. And, you might find that you really love that freedom and flight of soul. You might find that you prefer to be in meditation more often than not. And you might find that you stop waiting for the right moment to sit down and talk to God. And you may find that that becomes your greatest obsession; to have conversation with God all day long. It is there that you are released from your struggles and your pains; going inside of yourself and acknowledging who you are. No longer living your life for everybody else, but living your life for you.

'Show yourself authentically, so that people know who you are, and who they're dealing with. Watch your reality change. Watch your life become an exciting exploration. New friendships; new family; new lovers; new relationships; you may find your life changes in remarkable ways.

'This is a time period on the Earth, as we've said before, where the reset button is being hit. Time to start that business that you've been thinking about creating; time to tell that guy or gal that you love them; it's time to make that movement happen in your life. It's time to not be afraid; it's time to be bold; to get to know who you are, and to allow for that to be expressed.'

The following is some more from Jonathan, via the medium Elaine Thorpe.

23. Jonathan - October 2020
The Great Spiritual Awakening

Question: What is happening on 21st December? (Solstice 2020)

'I think that you will find that it is, you know, officially very much a winter time of year, solstice, but that is when you look towards the New Year don't you, you prepare yourself for leaving behind the old, and you begin with the new, but I would say that this is part of the Great Spiritual Awakening.

'And with what has been happening or what is happening on your Earth at present, many consciousnesses, many thoughts, of people are going to come together, and they're going to start to bring the light to the world, the angels are drawing close to your Earth to create a great *healing, to create and help with a Great Awakening. So many of you will become very much curious, and are wanting to know more about this connection to spirit, and more about the awareness of it, and so this will cause a mass of people to come together, and start to become more curious and wanting to know.*

'So you will all be feeling it, that your Earth is going to rumble, I will tell you, a great shift is going to take place within the Earth, you would probably want to call it a pole shift, but it is not going to be quite like that, there are going to be many movements of Earth, shall I say. Partitions of Earth happening again, as it has done over many millions of years, but this is really much more prevalent, it is happening on such a great scale, but I would say that man will not have any power over it, the Earth has always changed herself, and evolves herself, over millions of years, and she will continue to do so, of course, but with great velocity.

'So all of these strange sounds that you are hearing in places are the Earth's great vibration from within, and of course, from the heavens and of course from the outer beings that are also in communication with your world. They are not about to invade it, they are knowing that your world is in distress, and they are wanting to help in some way. They are also saying to you, tune into your higher self, your intuitive self, your consciousness, because it is the most powerful tool that you have in life, if you are spiritually awakened you may go through many different emotional states of mind that will confuse you, and you will think, "Well, why do I feel like this, this isn't me, I don't understand what is going on with me, why do I feel depressed today or why do I feel so excited today"', you will go through many different phases of a spiritual awakening. Every journey that you make in life, through different relationships that you will form with friends, partners, family members, pets, doesn't matter what it is, that is what you call the maze of life.

'You will take many avenues and those avenues will then teach you something, then they will come to an end. You will find that many people that you have previously circulated with in life, it's not that they don't any longer have any meaning to you, that they start to draw away from you. They take a different path to yours, you have not outgrown them, but your soul has progressed on its path. So these people are no longer a requirement to you, although you would care about them, they are not any longer needed on your pathway. So each journey, each relationship that you form, is the journey back to yourself; and once you

awaken and go within, that is the most fantastic time that you could possibly experience, because you are happy and elated with yourself. You are no longer condemning yourself or blaming yourself for things. You are only human of course, it is not to say that every day is going to be fantastic and you are on top of the world, what it means to say is you have found us, you have found yourself, and you have connected yourself to the consciousness of the universe, and it is the most wonderful feeling that you could imagine.

'And then it is time to give it to the rest of the world, isn't it, there are always going to be people that don't believe in it, there are always going to be people saying well, "What are these people, are they mad", but perhaps they haven't chosen to experience it in this lifetime.

'Mass consciousness awakening is on a huge scale, that you could never possibly imagine, because you are going about your daily lives. We watch you, you're doing your shopping, you're doing your living, aren't you, you're living the human life, and a lot of you don't even think anything about it, you have no idea, absolutely no idea what is going on in the heavens. Some of you don't believe in it, and you think to yourself what a lot of poppycock, a lot of nonsense, they're all mad, until you pass away and you get to heaven yourself, you think, "Well, I regretted not understanding or believing in it, because I could have learned so much more. Maybe I will have to incarnate again to experience it all over again, and try and get to it again".

'We choose to have the human life, but it is time now to start Awakening, to start discovering what is so beautiful and so limitless that you couldn't possibly fit it all into your consciousness, but you are it, you are it, you are that Consciousness, you are that limitlessness.

'Why would you begrudge yourself something so magical, so beautiful, why would you doubt that; that is human minds isn't it, doubting that is what you call the ego, you do not have an ego in heaven you lose that when you pass, it is only an earthly requirement, but the ego will teach you many things although it'll sometimes say, "Well, don't go over there, because that's not the place to go, we want to limit you, we want to test you"; perhaps you will overcome the test perhaps you won't. Perhaps you will listen to other people's conditioning, and other people's opinions, don't bother getting involved in it; it is a total waste of energy, if they want to argue and bicker amongst each other let them get on with it, you have your path.

73

'I would say look onwards and upwards, you will see what is coming; you see all of the negative has to be drawn up to the surface. If you stir muddy water with a stick, it'll show you all of the dirt; it will all make the water look dirty and misty. Eventually it dies down, and goes back to the bottom, but this time it's not, this time it is coming up, and all of it will surface, it will seem like a dreadful place to live in, and you'll think, "Is there any end to it, why are we all so angry with one another, why are we all bickering and having differences of opinion, we cannot come together".

'But the people that are bringing the light to the world will teach you something, how to be at peace; you could carry on with your daily life, you could keep going on as you were, but would it ever change anything. Did you think that nothing was ever going to change; how long did you think that it could go on for before something had to give, how long did you think all of these lies could go on for before they would be surfaced? How long did you think that you could keep it going before something had to put it to a stop, and if you weren't completely stopped, all of you in this world, would you ever have listened? If you were only getting the minority of who it was happening to, for instance, if it was just one country you'd say, "Well, that's on the news, that's old news now, let's just get on with our lives; let's just carry on the way that we were". But because it stopped the whole world, you had to begin to think about something, you had to begin to look for your truths, and so you searched and you searched, and you argued and you searched more, and you're still doing it; and you will probably keep doing it, but it will bring the truth to the surface. You'll see all of this negative that you see on your computers, you think that's awful we don't want to get involved in that, but that's truth that's thrown in your faces as truth, you will see it, you could ignore it, carry on, do what you like, but it is still happening, it doesn't mean to say that you have to watch it every day and get involved in it, to become angry and upset and opinionated.

'We want you to be happy, but in order for the world to awaken, it had to be slowed down, so to speak. It had to be cleansed, and that is going to take time of course. There are millions and millions of people of the Earth, do you think that they are all going to listen at once. If your God, your Jesus, was to come out of the sky now, you would say, "Goodness me what is happening", you would all stop and look out of your windows in amazement, and it's not how it is going to be; he is in your hearts, and it is absolutely nothing to do with religion, control, fear, nothing, it has to be going inside of yourself, and seeing who you really are.

'**You are all a part of that multifaceted dimension that is Earth, the universe, and everything, you have the power, each and every one of you, have their power within you; you are all limitless, but you only see up to the wall and not past it, you are not even prepared to climb it, to see what is over the other side.**

'If you just take that one little moment to say, "Well, I am limitless, my consciousness is absolutely powerful and limitless", it is not about being above another and saying, "Well, you are no good, who are you, I am better than you; you can put me on a pedestal and you can worship me", it is not about that. It is about coming together as that Collective Consciousness and creating the most powerful healing that you could ever imagine, and seeing the light and the colour within you. Many people take drugs to experience it; and they will say, "Well, I had the most wonderful experience I want some more of it", because they are inquisitive they are empowering themselves, but it is not to say that it is a good thing to take a drug, and you may think, "Well, that's just hallucinogenic"; but certain drugs that would give you an expansion of mind that would make you see what is beyond this, that you would see the Earth as just this. The Earth is not just this, look at every single detail in it right down to the last grain of sand, that is the most amazing thing, it is amazing how it all fits together and it all works, the flower that grows in your garden, you just look at it and say, "Well, that's a pretty flower, there are more of them where that came from, could grow next year, die growing". Again, take a closer look at that flower, the life of it, the absolute intricate beauty of it. You will see your consciousness expanding, taking in those details, taking in the absolute beauty of everything that works together, even underneath your Earth, do you not realize that there are things going on underneath that, even that helps the Earth above to work, all the little insects and all the little worms underground are all doing their job to keep your Earth going. They're all surviving, but they're all making a difference; don't even think about it do you; you just walk above it and think, "Well, that's the ground, that's it". When you tread upon the grass or the ground you're earthing yourself, you're grounding yourself, think about what's underneath there, don't see it as a lot of muck, dirt, see it as beauty underneath there, as well as the above, the whole lot of it is connected. Creatures that you haven't even seen or discovered are everywhere, you haven't *even noticed them; you can't notice them, because they're not in the naked eye for you to see.*

'Progression everyone, it happens, and it is happening on a huge scale, your computers were deliberately invented, we knew all about that, did you think we did not know, we knew all about it; it was deliberately invented by these people, some of them would get greedy, but some of them would use it to seek knowledge or to give knowledge to others, that's the best part about it, isn't it, because if you didn't have this computer now, I wouldn't be speaking to you. I would only be able to limit it to one room and two people; computers, all over the world, now do you see how the light is spreading, the consciousness is awakening within you, that tool that you have in front of you, there that telephone, that computer, whatever it may be, is allowing you to do that, it's all part of God's plan, isn't it, you don't even know it.

'So this is what you mean about, not a particular date, it's the end of an era, the end of the whole way, the old habits, die hard; a lot of you think it's about the new control, that's an earthly thing, they can try to control you, perhaps yes, if you allow them to, but they cannot control this (pointing to the head), because if you think positive and think beyond that, beyond this Earth, they'll not even be able to grasp that.

'They can't get hold of it, they have no knowledge of how to, if they knew they had it within themselves as well, they would forget about all of this nonsense.

'Well, I will leave you to experience it. I will have much more to speak about that. I have enjoyed conversing with you all, and I'm sure that I will do so again, if there are people out there that do not like what I say, I'm going to say it no matter what, you can think of all of the hateful things that you like, but I am still going to come back and tell you all. God bless you.'

Next below is once more from a transcript of a Dr Peebles communication sent to me by the medium Summer Bacon.

24. Dr Peebles - 22nd October 2020

'At this time upon this school called planet Earth there is destruction of hierarchy, and you are watching and witnessing it on many different levels. Hierarchy in terms of the statues that

have been destroyed; hierarchy in the way in which the country is being run; hierarchy in the way in which human beings are speaking to one another; striving to understand that it is time now to come to the awareness that you are all equals, that there is nobody that is better than the other.

'There is no hierarchy in the universe; it is just a matter of growth. It is a dance. It is a point wherein you can laugh together, eat together, love together, and all the rest; and the need for hierarchy disappears. The need to laud anything over anybody disappears.

'It is time now for the collective human beings upon this school called Planet Earth to realise that you are a part of something together. That you are creating this reality together; you are the stewards of God's love upon the Earth, and it is time to share this with the world.

'When someone speaks, listen to them. Strive not to personalise it. Strive not to bring it into yourself as if it is against you or anything else. Rather, strive to hear it as a sharing of who they are, what they believe, how they believe it, and what they want to do with it, and how they'd like to enact it, and all the rest.

'But, you don't have to personalise it, or take it into yourself. Listen and learn. That is the primary task right now; to listen and learn. It is there that you find that the hierarchy begins to disappear. The need to be better than somebody else, to prove yourself or anything of the like, begins to disappear.

'There's no more need to get anybody to understand your opinion or perspective at all, but rather you will live your life more as a demonstration to the world as to what is possible. You will begin to realise that you are a demonstrator of God's love upon the Earth.

'You will say the beautiful things that you want to say in any given moment, no matter what everybody else is saying. You will speak truth of love in this world, and your life will begin to transform in remarkable ways.

'You will find that you do not need to engage with the energies of separation. You do not need to engage with the energies of hierarchy. You do not need to engage with the energies that say, "I'm better than you."

'This is a time upon the Earth where the playing field is going to be levelled a bit. Everybody's going to start to come to the awareness that you are human beings upon the Earth that need each other, absolutely.

You are all made of the same stuff no matter what your nationality, sex, skin colour. Whether you own a business building an empire, or you are living in a car homeless, everybody is the same. Everybody is experiencing life on the inside, and everybody wants to find love. That is the point of the journey.'

Next are some selections of communications received from the spirit guide "Zac" (Zacharia, from a lifetime in Syria) who speaks to us through the medium Janet Treloar. He is an aspect of the Ascended Master Djwal Khul, often known as the Tibetan and comes to us, he says, from the 26th dimension.

Incidentally, the Tibetan used to share enlightenment with the world through the mediumship of Alice Bailey, and books of his teachings can still be obtained via the Lucas Trust website. (See Links)

25. Zac - October 2020
Truth Revelations

'You are living at the moment at the time where people are more cynical and distrusting than ever they have been before on Earth. Now I do not say that to upset anybody, only the last few years especially, your time on Earth, so many things people all around the world have been promised by people who are, you could say, trusted, in power, whatever, and whoever the person is, whatever age group, they've come to realize that often these are empty promises.

'Often things do not actually happen; I'm talking very generalized here, of course, but because of this, some of these revelations that you speak of, that are very likely to be coming to the fore, because you are living in a time of truth. This happened a few years ago, the alignment of truth into the Earth. It allowed another level of energy so that suppression could not happen anymore.

'Now what this actually means, that for a very, very long, period in history, what you might call, dishonesty, a lie, a falsehood, could be buried deep and go on for maybe hundreds, if not thousands of years.

'When the alignment of truth (that has come through to Earth) was most through the Dragon lines (Ley lines) of this Earth, it is very subtle in people's energy field and it went across the Earth. Moving up through

the vibrational rays, as we move through, it was possible for this, let us simply say, for it (truth) to be bestowed once more upon the Earth.

'Slowly, slowly, like a sieve saving out truth, nothing could be hidden forever. Now I say, forever, because some truths started to come to the surface very quickly, others would take time, not so much about how much people try to bury them, but how many layers are on top of them.

'But now, of course, this truth is running, running, running. So it is highly likely that in all walks of life, truth comes out, and this is where the more grounded we are, the more in our own hearts, and in our own wisdom, we are able to take the barrage of truth. To have the freedom of expression, whatever that means for us.

'But as I said, this is the flip side of the cynical mistrust that has come from people being there (on Earth); that they had been lied to, or things being buried, information not being there. When people hear these things, the majority will say, "Well that is shocking".

'In their hearts with this truth, they know that it will come to light. Now, some people will be aware of big changes, big revelations, they may be quite distinct, in science, as well as in places of power. With this, it can also be to do with ancestral truth, other historical truths, what we are saying is this is a time of uncovering, it is to do with the breaking down of the old; the chaos that goes with that. Go into your hearts and see, but also, know that people are resilient, people are adaptable, people will have their own connection to it, but don't push them necessarily to come to a conclusion and feel accepting, until they are ready to do so, because everyone will get there, just some quicker than others.'

The following communication I have included more for its revelation. It truly does show us that this universe and spirit life is fascinating in the extreme and that there is always more to discover and learn. It is an adventure to behold; and in eternity to experience.

26. Zac - October 2020
Time Travellers

Hazel: A question now about Time Travellers. Zac, I'm wondering if we have time travellers amongst us, people who have come from our future to help to ensure we get through all of this. For example, was Nikola Tesla a time traveller?

'There are many time travellers, more than you would know, (I'm not supposed to tell you that, the collective are not so happy).

'They go very much underneath the surface, unlikely you will find them in your general history books, with them they cannot draw too much attention to themselves, they would give themselves away. What they often are, is the aid to another, particularly an aid or a teacher or a lecturer who has inspired someone to take a different course, to do a different thing. Now these Time Travellers exist, let us call it, a loophole within Divine laws, well it sounds like they are bobbing about all over time dabbling in things that are naturally going to get sorted out, they are more, how to put it, they're more like engineers.

'What I mean by this, they see how an engine is working, and then they go in and fix something that isn't working so well, sometimes to fix that, they need to go into the past to do it. So they are not changing a future, but they are making a future better, and they are doing it, as I say, they are going with the blessings of those such as ourselves, and all of the universe, but they do stand a little bit outside of a Divine Law.

'Saying that though, they had their own laws and practices, to ensure, what they are not allowed to do is to procreate in another time that they were actually born in a human, because this sets all sorts of very confusing situations.

'Now people time travel the whole time, in essence of their energy, but in true manifestation of physical and living for a period of time in another time, yes, this is happening. This becomes possible, do not think in the future the strongest future everyone will be time travelling, could you imagine, if you're living in a boring year you all went to a different year, suddenly you would have a place that wasn't populated at all. So of course, that is not, as they say, on the cards. But for a few initiated, and you could see them more as disciples of source, they're not doing it for their own ends, they are doing it for the greater ends of the universe.'

Hazel: So would that not then include Nikola Tesla?

'Not with Nikola Tesla, but certain people that you will not find in the books, I know this is very frustrating, but who had his ear, because he tweaked and he changed some of his blueprints. Where did that information come from? But remember, people that are often seen as ahead of their time are simply very much more in tune with the other dimensional selves, downloaded information, Alien information,

'That one act of putting within you Aluminium and Mercury, causing your cells to become inflamed, we're not talking about one muscle or joint, one muscle or joint would be bad enough within the human structure, but here we are talking about cells, billions of cells, inflamed in order to trick your own immune system to react and react and react to exhaust it. That is not correct, that is not good.'

Question: Can you see it becoming mandatory?

'I can see, if you do not intervene, I can see many things becoming mandatory, but only if you don't intervene, which brings me right back to the beginning, the true way to make people become aware, to come into awareness, is to live freely. So that what they are told and what they observe become conflicted within them. You understand, what they are told by your so-called media, yet what they see, does not match up. Your media is telling you everybody's dropping dead; their eyes show them something completely different. By living your life freely you will impact other people to live their life freely, I assure you.

'The slave did not just throw off his chains, one day, did not happen that way; you have to live your life freely with love, with good intent, be out there and seen doing what you know to be right. And the purging must come in your world, where you destroy the very structure that has imposed itself upon you, and that is vital, you must tear down the structure that imposes it on you, but only once enough people are aware of it.

'I've entered awareness, and they will enter awareness by seeing you live freely, truthfully, lovingly, embracing your families, not conforming, ducking and diving to avoid and evade, doing that, they too, like all those other slaves that I speak about in the story of old, will become cocky, like the slave they will become confident, and then they can break down the wall, the wall is the fabric of the structure of society that has held you in servitude.

'Once that purging is taking place, the lancing of the wound, the removal of the puss, only then can freedom, a new type of freedom, be rebuilt. A freedom that works for you all, a freedom that does not discriminate the old, a freedom that sees the elderly as wonderful people who have given and should be looked after, a freedom that sees the young as wonders of the new world, who should be encouraged, supported in love, the freedom that sees a

structure that supports one another, but does not set about to destroy one another in order for the system to survive.'

Next, is more from Jonathan, via the medium Elaine Thorpe.

28. Jonathan - November 2020
Knowing Yourself & The Awakening

'I wish to discuss with you about your Awakening and your spirituality, which I have previously discussed, there are many subjects from the spirit world that your guides will come and talk to you about, but the Awakening is the biggest part at the moment. The healing of the people of the world, the healing of the world, because the world has an Essence, the world has a soul, as most of you will know.

'So I will say that at this point in time when most of you are sitting in your homes and not doing as much as what you would normally do, you are beginning to appreciate your lives, you are beginning to think more and have more time to look at life as it is. Some of you are angry because you are shut away, some of you are happy because you find peace, and some of you are Awakening spiritually, and you are beginning to know truths, not only truths about the world, but truths about your inner self. It begins to show you things that you would not normally think about, you would be rushing about and doing your daily things before all of this happened, so you see there is a greater purpose, because out of the negative will come the positive. And the world is always going to run by negative and positives, that is the way that it goes, but of course you would think the more positive that you have the better it's going to be, well yes, that is wonderful, but there are many things to go through before all of the peace will come.

'For instance, say that there are lots of things that you have discovered on your internet, and a lot of people tell each other different things, well, I did say to you that your world and yourselves are in for a change. Some of you will remain the same, some of you won't be spiritual, maybe your soul has not chosen to go that way in life, but those of you that are will understand what I am talking about; there are many emotions to go through with a spiritual awakening, many tests that will be given to you, or you will put yourself through, this period of time in your life.

'You may become more empathic, more understanding of nature, more understanding of people's feelings, become more forgiving perhaps, or you may go through dark times, where you do not know where you are. You take a crossroads in life, and you are standing there thinking, "Well, what shall I do with my life, what direction shall I take, because it seems to have come to a halt". Well the reason it has come to a halt is there is a different direction for you to take, there is a purpose and a reason for that halt, for you to decide whether or not to take the right journey that leads you back to yourself.

'Yourself is the important self, you see, it's not about being selfish, it is about loving yourself from within, and experiencing everything that is within, that has the answer there for you all along, but you never took any notice of it. You just carried on and thought, "Well, I will look for the answers outside of myself, I still haven't found them after all of these years, and then all of a sudden I had a spark within me, that told me to look to my higher self for the answers", well, "What answers you say, answers about what", well the answers are about you yourself, your essence within, and how you would love it, how you would learn to love it and understand it.

'So I will say to you at this time use the time that you have not to think about negativity and what is going on so much in the world, the more you attach yourself to that negativity and argument the more you will become it. The more you will think about it from the time you get up until the time that you retire to bed. If you get up in the morning and look at positive things all day, you will feel totally different, happy music, positive discussions time with your families. They are the times that are most precious, you see, because when they have gone there is no more of it to get back, for instance if someone was to say, "Well, I wish that I'd have had time with my family or time with a family member as such, because I could have said so much more to them, and there were things that we didn't say to each other, and habits that would get on each other's nerves, and not want to be around each other, and now they are gone, I want to be with them, I feel bad about it".

'So use that time that you have, use it as a preciousness, hold on to every moment that you have, appreciate everyone for who they are, because nobody in your world is going to be perfect, you will all make faults in your life, it's whether or not you want to forgive each other for it, isn't it.

'So that's part of what the Awakening is about really, it is the journey back to yourself, through the Maze of life; and each term that you take may come to an end, well that means that you are going to take a different direction at life, so you go back and you take another turning, maybe that will come to an end, each phase of your life teaches you something, it teaches you how to go within; and when you eventually through each lifetime reach the centre of the maze, that is you, you have met you, yourself.

'It's quite exciting meeting yourself, really it is. But then some of you will meet yourself and you will perhaps not like what you see. Well look to changing it, look back over every part of your life and say, "Well, what can I change. Although I love others, am I punishing myself if I love me, no I am not, I am giving myself the greatest gift of all, if I could give it to everybody else outside of myself, then I should give some back to me". You've heard of the words, 'give a little take a little', well that applies to yourself.

'When you are happy within you do not require another, it doesn't mean to say that you do not need to experience love with somebody else other than yourself, when you are happy within you are happy alone, you are not sad alone, you can enjoy your day being completely by yourself, for those of you that crave to have time by yourself, now, most of you will have the chance to have it, some of you won't, but it is finding time to make time for yourself.

'That is important, I would say, whether you're going out for a walk in nature or even being at home doesn't matter, where you are, stop still for a moment and capture you, who you are, doesn't matter about everybody else around you at that particular moment in time, we know that you love them, that you need time to love you.

'Not to punish you all the time but to love you, because you are infinitely beautiful, and as I always say, you are limitless, multifaceted, a being that is of an existence of love, and from a place of love, coming into a conditioned world that will take in all of the negativity, that if somebody doesn't believe in them or they hate them they will hang on to that, where is the hanging on to the positive.

'What about the you liking you rather than battering you and hating you, concentrate on that at this time, but I would also remind you to concentrate on praying for the people of the Earth and the Earth itself,

29. Abraham Lincoln – 28th December 2020
Lincolns Speaks of the Condition of America
And Implores Us to Reach for the Light

'I am Abraham Lincoln. Since this medium has been reading of my endeavours in spiritualism, it has drawn me close. As you well know, I am a part of the Celestial Kingdom and have had a great and meteoric journey through the spheres of spirit to the Heavens of God. I have come to know the power of Divine Love to transform me and make me a spirit of light and love exemplifying the truths of the beloved brother and Master, Jesus, who has taught these truths.

'I am interested in communicating with individuals on Earth, a place that has continued to degrade into darkness and on such a vast scale that it brings great concern to we in the spirit world to see how fast things have escalated, and conditions have worsened; that even those who hold the high office, which I was a part of when I was on Earth, lack integrity, and contribute to this degradation that is the human condition.

'Indeed, those who are elected to office often reflect the conditions of the electorate and reflect back to them their attitudes, desires, and perspectives of life. So it is not surprising that those who are elected to high office have demonstrated the baser desires of the human condition and sought further wealth and fame. Yet, this office within my country, the highest office, was meant to be an instrument of service to the people, of looking towards the welfare of all within my country and applying oneself with wisdom and love for all people in a way that uplifts and brings solution to the many dilemmas of life.

'Unfortunately, those ideals are long gone, replaced by a fervent desire for power and control, of wealth and prestige. Humility is nowhere to be found in these administrations of late, merely a tragic reflection of what is now the norm in everyday life, what is now a downward spiral of my country and many countries in the world. Because the morals and spiritual aspirations of humanity have gone down a dark tunnel of need and desperation, of hollowness and superficiality, whose goal it is to gain notoriety, to teach the common masses ways of behaviour, attitudes, and judgments which lack love, which degrade every individual rather than seeking to uplift and educate and encourage everyone to seek light, to have integrity, to conduct themselves in a way that

they may contribute to society rather than seek to gain as much as they can by ignoring the needs of others around them.

'This is not the American way. The American way was founded on edicts and principles and religion which taught that one must share, one must consider, one must seek to do God's Will in the world. Unfortunately, these ideals are long past and in their wake is a pathetic attempt to enact baser desires and goals. How unfortunate, and how my country suffers from its illusions, its pettiness, its inability to see beyond the superficial.

'It is my hope that there will be those in my country and in this world of yours who will seek to rectify these wrongs; to bring greater clarity and inspiration to the souls of humanity that they may see that their baser desires and materialistic ambitions will not satisfy the very core of the individual. Their souls are in great need and in great deprivation, not because they have wilfully placed themselves in darkness, but because they have listened and sought out examples of men in leadership, who are talented, who have the ear of the people, reflecting those things that are of wrongdoing and of a darkened soul.

'So, the common man pays a great price for their comforts, for their desire, for materialism and materialistic goals, and to be acknowledged in society. Many are downtrodden. Millions are suffering. Oh, how this country which was once mine and which I led, has grown to such a gargantuan size and population with so many currents of thought and ambition and expression making it into a huge conglomerate, a powerful expression in your world that is often admired and despised at the same time. These great currents, some of light but most of darkness, have come to alienate many in the world since the influence of my country is great upon this world.

'I beseech the people of America to put aside their distractions, those ideas and ambitions and structures of thought which cause them to not consider that all men are indeed made equal, that all are indeed children of God. Instead, judgment falls in the way of true brotherhood and sisterhood. Without a sense of unity, without the acknowledgment of every individual in our world, including the world of America, there is no strength and the core is rotten. That rot spreads out through the people and contaminates so many with anger and judgment and a lack of unity.

'This can only intensify as the polarisation of my country, that is the political and spiritual polarisation, continues to divide and conquer what once was a great country. I am saddened that so few see through these conditions, environments which conspire to denigrate this beautiful country of America. Yet, there are some, some who are wise enough, some who have enough love within their hearts and desire within their mind to walk the high road, and who see beyond the veil of human deception.

'My prayers are with those who are strong enough to see these things, who have awakened to the reality of the situation, that not only affects my country, but many countries. The world is in great distress. The peoples of the world are either deeply asleep or greatly concerned. There is very little joy, very little appreciation of life, merely the relentless ambitions for the material, for power, for safety, all because there is deep fear and a lack of spirituality. The mind and the soul continue to languish in delusions and deceptions, and a lack of love, a lack of the motivation of the heart.

'These things must come to the fore to be in the light of God's Touch, to find the Grace of God's healing and peace, to be truly a child of God and regain innocence lost, so that they may be strengthened in light; that they may see with clarity and humility and grace who they are truly, and who their brothers and sisters are, in the eyes of God.

'My prayers are for this world. You must know that there are many millions of angels who are praying for your world, who are poised to do God's bidding to help lift up your world beyond these degrading conditions and attitudes, to something that is sustainable and of light. God has a plan indeed to foster conditions of light and to dissolve conditions of darkness.

'We in the Celestial Kingdom and the bright spirits of the spirit world all conspire to help in this effort to save humanity from its own self, to be within the flow of God's Will and work within the framework of God's plan. To eliminate the darkness and suffering that continues to plague the vast majority of humanity even those who are well-ensconced within their comfortable world where they may sleep a sound sleep of the soul that they have found in the material that brings them comfort and distractions. Even they know that what is at this moment is not in harmony with what must be in a world created by God.

'That knowing is deep within them, within their souls, but so few are awake enough to recognise this inkling of truth, understanding that the world has gone awry because humanity has stepped beyond the path of true harmony to that of wilful efforts that are contravening the Laws of God.

'We will continue our efforts as I am sure will these dear souls and many others in your world who seek light, who desire greater equality and harmony in the world. Leaders are often born of necessity. I encourage each one of you and the many who are in association with you, to take up the mantle of leadership and speak the truth. I spoke the truth when I led my beautiful country. Yes, I paid a great price for this, but I have no regrets, no regrets whatsoever.

'Indeed, I did my part to help lift humanity up from error and darkness. Thus, you know of me today because of my efforts and because of my history. I tell you that each one of you has the power to stand firm in truth, to walk in the light, to demonstrate and speak of the Light of God's Love, the truth of expressing oneself with integrity, compassion, honesty, and love. This is what is needed in your world. This is what is needed to reverse the unfortunate direction of humanity which continues to spiral downward in a great effort from those who are dark and evil, to continue to degrade humanity with the baseness of human desire.

'Work against these dark efforts. Walk with your head held high in the light. Know that we in the Celestial Kingdom will walk with you, will gather about you, and insure that you will be protected and that God will insure that you will be a clear and beautiful channel of light and truth and love in your world, that someday when you speak, many will listen. That day comes, my brothers and sisters, that day comes closer than you might think.

'Continue to prepare yourselves in the Light of God's Love, to be in harmony with God's Laws of Love, to seek the great blessing of His Love within your souls, and much will come your way, my friends, many opportunities surprisingly with many avenues and doors opened so that you may reach many and speak to many of the salvation of Love that is available to all.

'God bless you; I join you in your efforts, will continue to forge ahead in this great battle for light, for love, and for harmony in the world. God bless you, beloved friends. God bless you.'

The following message came through the medium Janet Treloar, in conversation with Hazel Newton. Many video recordings of their full conversations can be found on YouTube. _(See Links)

30. Zac - January 2021
Cycles of Change

'The common goal here on a planet such as yours, is for there to be a majority, at least, a majority of energy, that allows for the good outcomes. When I say good, for a better outcome than what went before.'

Hazel: One of the benefits of the lockdowns that are going on around the world, and the restrictions, is that many people, for the first time perhaps in their lives are suddenly desiring freedom.

'Exactly, it focuses the mind, does it not. One of the reasons why in this month I have been saying, enjoy the solitude, make the most of the solitude, feel what your soul truly desires, so that you can manifest it, even though humans are naturally impatient, of course you are, you have a short time on Earth.

'Every time you come here it is in-built to be impatient, to a certain degree, and of course we do not like to have what we see as freedoms, being taken away.

'It is like a child who is saying at breakfast time I'm not allowed to have the cereal I like most, from the adults first point of view they think what does it matter. But for the child it is very important, and this is the thing, there's freedoms at the moment that people feel that they do not have, would give vast freedom in the future, if they use the time wisely, if they allow the solitude, to allow them to really connect in with their heart.

'To really desire, and to project, like filling up like an empty shell of what is best for the world, we can only really desire very high level, when we see ourselves as part of the whole. If we are desiring from a place where we are the centre of the universe, we do not get very far. When we see ourselves as an integral part of the universe, then it is a

different matter altogether, that is where the power comes in, that is where to focus and that is where we can move through.

'If you're in 5D (5th dimensional consciousness) and one in 3D the thing about the difference is where your heart is projecting, and therefore if you are 5D you can live with 3D no problem. The reason being is because in 5D you move past any individual judgment, and this really does follow on from what we were saying. To be in a fifth dimensional form you are really only about the unity of Oneness, and acceptance, acceptance of self, acceptance of others. If somebody, even a very close loved one, has completely opposing views from yours, it is not about bearing with it; it is not about thinking, "Well, when I come into the 5D I can explain to them", it is none of these things. It is saying, "Aren't they wonderful as they are", and they may change into 5D, they may not, most likely we're all going there, of course, in that way, but then there will not be any impatience to get them there. There will not be an impatience, they will not have to have an argument between, it will simply say, "I love you exactly as you are".

'**When you have a child growing up, you do not look at the child when they are six and think, I will love them so much when they are ten. It does not happen, ask any parent, they love them exactly as they are, and then, when they look at photos and they see how much they change, year after year, they haven't even noticed, because they haven't been loving the future, they have been loving who they are at that moment in time.**

'**So you could really say that this is more about a question of love, if somebody is around you that you care about, even if they have completely opposing views, do not worry about them, just love them.**

'We are not in the point of this universe where everybody is in 5D or everybody is in 3D, there is always a spectrum, and a far faster spectrum than anyone can think about. So we may feel one day we are in 5D, or we are 3D, I'd say just accept it, go with it.'

Hazel: I think that helps people who to be able to cope with maybe family members who are on a different mindset, or different set of beliefs, just to be loving towards them.

'Exactly, think about things, not so much the differences, don't worry about the differences, focus on what there is the commonality, commonality may not be a actual same likes, dislikes, commonality *may simply be a love for each other, a love for a sibling, a love for somebody else that is in your life, think about something that holds that person dear to you, think of that, not the differences.'*

The following (abridged) message came through the medium Al Fike. As with all messages I have included from this source they can be viewed and read at the website: https://divinelovesanctuary.com/

Under his name, **Albert J. Fike**, a number of books are also available, including *Awakening to Soul Consciousness* (containing 24 Lessons from Jesus, 2022) and *Our World in Transition, Messages from Jesus* (2021).

31. Jesus – 11th March 2021
Earth Changes

'I am Jesus. May the winds of change blow blessings upon your lives further awakening your souls and your minds to all that which is of truth and light and love, that those changes that are sweeping the Earth may bring its silver lining, its blessing to each one of you. May you come to see beyond a shadow of a doubt that what is happening in your world, those things that are manifesting in your world at this time, are both a reflection of the human condition and God's blessings upon this world in efforts to counteract the human condition and the destruction that this condition brings to your beloved planet.'

Question: Will there be more geographical upheavals like earthquakes, volcanoes, tsunamis, and more illnesses sweeping the world and economic consequences, war, civil unrest, or more an awakening of those involved with the dark forces who are causing so much pain, suffering, and inequality?

'The crust of the Earth is always moving and changing. Therefore, there will undoubtedly be more manifestations of this in the form of earthquakes, volcanoes, shifts of many kinds which will happen upon your Earth plane. Yes, the human condition does affect the intensity and frequency of these shifts for humanity does not realize the power of its own thought, the power of its own action to influence the surface layer of your Earth and to bring about consequences unforeseen. So even though the fluidity of change in the Earth's crust continues and will do so for as long as the

Earth remains an active and viable planet, humanity will indeed, given the opportunity and the means to do so, affect these changes and shifts upon the Earth.

'It is the only species on your planet that has such a capacity. Unfortunately, because this capacity and power is wielded in ignorance and a lack of true understanding of the consequences, so it continues to bring chaos to your world. It is so with the diseases as well, that it is the imbalance within this human condition that will continue to bring waves of disruption and challenges to the human body because of this imbalance and disharmony with God's Laws and with the Laws of Love. Consequently, a great imbalance has been struck because of what I speak of, the inability of humanity to see and comprehend its own power and how the choices which come with free will bring about consequences that are not easy to live with and bring about difficult conditions which limit humanity so that it may not thrive upon the Earth plane.

'With the combination of Earth changes and all of the levels and aspects of it, the world is a victim of the ignorance of humanity, its inability to see beyond material, mindful deductions of this material world and see that there are spiritual consequences to the lack of spiritual knowledge and the activation of truth within each individual upon this plane.

'So much continues to be a consequence of this inability and imbalance within humanity to see beyond its shuttered visions of truth and its scientific explorations which limit the possibility of seeing beyond the material. So as humanity grows in numbers, as the conditions which humanity has created continue to escalate into darkness, so the consequences will become more severe. The Earth indeed will shudder and try to defend itself from the onslaught of the human condition and darkness. Indeed, much comes that brings pain to both those who have initiated these conditions and those who are innocent.

'In and upon this Earth plane it matters not whether you are innocent, because these conditions, these consequences are felt over the entirety of the Earth and affect every being upon it. It is not that God will save the innocent for God cannot. God can only bring healing, protection, guidance, love, truth and knowledge to those who are receptive, who are in a condition of prayer, who align themselves with God. In this way, there can be intervention. In this way, there has been

intervention for many souls. But for those who throw in their lot with the condition that dictates that humanity is independent of God and wish to exert self independent of God, so these unforeseen consequences come forward with each day.

'Though humanity has great power, it is also very weak in its ability to understand the complexities, subtleties and power of God's Creation. The Creation that God has made for humanity to live and thrive upon this planet in order to obtain identity, in order to live a physical life, but along with the physical life, a life that is also spiritual, so that these two aspects of the humanity may be nurtured in tandem as one grows and experiences the many blessings and aspects of life on this world.'

Question: Will the energy that God is pouring into the Earth make the people in darkness more volatile, angry, or sad. Will it make people with a great deal of love more loving and compassionate? And why did God wait until this time, so long it seems, to make a correction?

'The vision of God is something that none of you upon this Earth plane can understand fully. God's sense of timing, God's sense of planning, and bringing forward His plans are from a perspective of not years and time as you know it but in response to the collective energies and expressions of humanity as it continues to progress along the lines of human evolution and spiritual progression in accordance to the Laws of Progression towards harmony. With the power of humanity to determine its fate, the power to choose with each moment, so humanity has to some degree dictated the timing of God's interventions.'

'One of the attributes of God's Great Soul is compassion and love. So with compassion and love, God is working with His angels and with the forces of the universe to bring about change upon your world that will ensure that the powerful inclination of humanity towards in-harmony and tinkering with forces of the Earth plane towards destruction, will be neutralized, so that there is an opening and an opportunity for humanity to consider the consequences of its actions, so to consider that indeed there is a better way, a higher way to express themselves upon the Earth plane.

'Yes, there will be those who will react in ways that are destructive, in ways that bring greater pain to themselves and to their brothers and sisters, in ways that are a reflection of their inner rage and fear and desire for control and power. These unfortunate, negative conditions

which reside within every human may be ignited given certain circumstances, and may ignite more severe reactions within those individuals who are very vulnerable, and who nurture these conditions.

'But indeed, the forces of change will become so potent and powerful that the ways in which humanity may express these dark conditions within them, and to do so collectively, will be greatly reduced because the instruments that humanity has created to bring war and destruction upon the planet will be neutralized by these waves of change.

'As the world is reconfigured by the Breath of God and the forces of the universe to bring ultimate harmony, so these creations of men will no longer be viable within this changing condition, the expression that is the changing world. You have not seen to any great degree a manifestation of these great powers that are being laid upon this world in order to heal and bring balance, equity, and harmony, but they are coming and they will be awesome in scope, powerful in their capacity to neutralize that which man has created and invigorate that which God has created.

'During these times of great change and turmoil and upliftment, there will be an opportunity for every soul to look within themselves, to reconcile the truth within them, to see that which they have created in their own lives; and to come to understand that they have a choice. God will infuse insight into every individual. God will ensure that every individual will see, to some degree, that which is meant to be, and that which is not part of God's plan for the salvation of humanity.

'This wisdom will be a gift to every soul. Because of the power of free will, individuals may choose to ignore this, to hide away, to insist upon their old ways of thinking and doing in the world. Because of the scope and power of the forces that are coming, those individuals who firmly reject God's invitation to inhabit a new world, and to enjoy the benefits and blessings of this new world, will surely perish as the old world fades, and the new world comes to be. So many within your world are asleep but will be awakened. This awakening may come to some as a gentle breeze of hope and love and understanding and inspiration; for others, it will become a rude awakening, one which is not sought after nor appreciated.

'But indeed, all must awaken. All will come to that place of understanding that the Will of God is greater than the will of man; that the Will of God dictates at this time that His Creation, this vast and beautiful world that is part of God's Universe, will indeed seek harmony for this is the law. In what way and to what extreme this harmony is sought will be determined by humanity in its responses and actions which it applies to resist the Will of God.

'For eons of time, humanity has lived with free will and expressed it freely and has applied its actions and responses upon this world in accordance to cultural and mindful precepts which deem certain actions as in harmony with the Laws of Man. But now humanity has been and will be invited to gaze upon the Laws of God, to come to see what is truly in harmony with God's Laws, and come to understand these laws, every bit and piece of these laws that formulate the great harmonious function of the universe; for harmony comes because these laws are enacted whether humanity is ignorant of them or not.'

'The time to reveal the truth is coming, beloved souls. The revealing of truth to humanity is a great gift from God. This is the outcome. This is the greatest outcome of God's intervention towards humanity to open the eyes of all so that they may see the truth of themselves, of their life upon this Earth, and of their collective imprint upon this beautiful yet vulnerable place that you call home.

'Yes, this truth and understanding is starting to emerge in different pockets in your world, different individuals, those who are of the light, those because of their souls' commitment to come to the Earth at this time are being guided and shown the way as activators of light and truth in the world. The power of their gifts and abilities to do so will continue to grow as the many influences from God come to this Earth plane. Many feel a sense of great change. Many souls feel restless. Many do not see that the status quo is something worth adopting or expressing. There is in many a sense of alienation from the cultures and edicts of your various societies.

'This is all part of the beginning of a great breaking away of many from that which is the human condition and discovering and adopting the understanding and awakening to that which God intends for each soul. Those who are undergoing this transformation and restlessness which comes in response to it may be assured that there is a bright future ahead and that each one of you who are willing to forego the

restrictions of the mind and the errors of the human condition and seek for something higher and brighter and more in harmony with God's Creation, and more in alignment with God, will see their way through whatever tumult may come as the world continues to change and shift and respond to the great energies of God's creative forces, which are bearing upon your world.

'Much will come, beloved souls, wave upon wave, like upon a seashore where a child has built a sandcastle and the great tides come and work their way upon that structure until there is nothing left. So this is how it will be.

'The illusions of men will be washed away with the Truth of God. So those who are willing to accept and adopt that which is truly of God and truly of God's reality will thrive upon this world and will build and reflect the great Truth and great harmony of God's Creation that will be so very different from that which you live today, so very different but indeed a world which will thrive in beauty, thrive in vitality, thrive in the creative forces that are a part of your world.

'Humanity will thrive in its understanding of its true natures, of the true forces that are within, and how these things will be married together, the physical and the spiritual, the mindful and the soulful in a way that will bring deep wisdom, powerful perceptions, understandings that will foster great inventions and possibilities for your material life upon this world.

'These things will reflect harmony and will not go against the great flow of the natural order but will indeed be a part of the great spiritual awakening of this planet of yours. So you will see, beloved souls, a wondrous transformation, an awakening; a doorway opening to a deep and profound truth, a hand proffered by God and His angels, and all bright spirits so that they may be assisted in this great awakening.

'Those who are willing to reach out, to be vulnerable yet sure, to be gentle yet firm, to be wise and accept the Will of God will surely find their way in this great transforming world and know that they are embraced by God and awakened by God. That their souls may come to be awakened by His Love, that their hearts may be filled with joy, and that all the fears and trepidations and worries of the material mind may be washed away by the great peace and Love of God upon them.

'Those who accept this gift, who yearn to be a part of the great journey of humanity guided by God, will know a fulfilling life, a life of harmony and peace.

'Though there will be much that will be lost, and much to grieve for because many will not survive this transition, because they are lost in the darkness and the illusion of the human condition.

'Those of you who are steadfast, those of you who pray for your loved ones and this world, those of you who are strong within your souls and come to acknowledge this strength, and put this awareness of the soul before all else, will be used as powerful instruments who will activate these changes in some way. Their loved ones who are willing to listen, to be led, who are willing to release their fear and replace it with faith, will follow in your footsteps and come to enjoy the benefits of this new world. Those who do not wish to follow will make their transition into the world of spirit where they will be given every opportunity to live their lives in this place.

'Either way, humanity will benefit greatly. It is God's great mercy upon humanity that is bringing change to your world, so as to neutralize the intensity and vastness of the suffering of your planet and of humanity. To bring, through God's Grace and great compassion to His children, a new beginning, an open door, an opportunity to thrive in light. So each individual will find their way to light. That light may be manifest in different ways, different means, but indeed it will come to each soul.'

'**Each of you has chosen your journey. Each of you has done so in unique ways. In understanding this, it is important that you have great compassion for your brothers and sisters. Replace judgment with love. Replace ignorance with the truth. Replace reactivity with wisdom and grace. You need all of these qualities, beloved souls, in order to face what is coming, in order to be guided by God so that you may reach out and pull your brothers and sisters towards the light, towards the understanding of what is and what can be in relationship to God's great plan for the salvation of humanity.'**

Next is another contribution from the spirit Zac via Janet Treloar. This is further confirmation of our ability to transmute whatever we might have taken in.

32. Zac - May 2021
We Have the Ability to Overcome Anything

'Within your system we have to remember that you have been built not just from this lifetime, but from many other lifetimes. You are constantly connected to your soul, you are connected to the light of the universe; you are the universe.

'Therefore whatever you take in, whether it be in information, or whether it be in physical into your body, would it be an emotion you take in, or thought to believe you take in, you have the ability within you to transmute it. **To do anything that you want with it, this is a power that is coming for everybody, but you do have that power now, you are never in a situation which is a finite of that, of nothing else can be done.'**

The following abridged message once more came through the medium Al Fike. The full message is included in the medium's book: *Finding Our Way Home* (2021).

33. Jesus – 19th May 2021
Life on Other Planets Poised to Help Us on Earth

'The universe does teem with much life, some of which cannot be readily observed or detected by the material senses, but are indeed present in many places in God's Creation. The evolution of humanity reflects a pattern that is often present in many other places and planets. Though, the direction of that evolution or that progressive expression and refinement of the individual soul may not be so convoluted, complex, and erratic, as that of those who exist upon this Earth plane of yours.

'Instead, many of these individuals and cultures have developed swiftly, and have chosen an easier way towards light, rather than expressing their free will, which they too possess, in a way that has created much disharmony and difficulty for the progress of God's children in the universe. These great struggles that you are engaged within your world are not present in many other worlds.

'The length of time in which these worlds have existed varies greatly. Some are very new and like tender shoots, they are nurtured by God and are not very far upon their path of development, while others are ancient and have continued to progress often to the point where their what you call, vibrational existence, their physicality, is not detectable by the five senses or material instruments that may indicate their existence. They are far beyond this lower level or vibration that exists in your reality. Thus, in order for humanity to perceive their existence, there must be a great leap forward in spiritual senses and perceptions in order to comprehend their existence.'

'There are those who have come in material form and transport to observe the earthly plane, for as I have said, and many of you well know, this Earth is in great flux, and is on the verge of great change. This brings those peoples who are curious and who wish to assist this Earth in its great leap forward, towards a higher level of consciousness, a higher level of expression, and a greater understanding of the workings of the universe.'

'Those brothers and sisters from planets and even galaxies far beyond this one who have come to assist are often seen or imagined as enemies and those who wish to do harm to humanity. This is a reflection of the inner psyche of humanity which is built upon fear and a deep reticence to be open and to accept that which is not known or understood. Yet, all of these beautiful souls who are present within God's great Universe are as you are; creatures of God, children of God. Once humanity comes to see this as a truth then indeed, the great floodgates of connection, of realization, of understanding will open to your world.

'Indeed, it is fear that continues to proliferate in your world. The baser desires of humanity are reflected in almost all that is within the endeavours and industry of the human world. Yet many truths have been discovered and to some degree, are known upon your world but are not acted upon unilaterally. Much is hidden away or ignored, often because a particular truth is not well-understood. Because those who are in charge of the economic aspects of your world are often reluctant to change the ways in which commerce is expressed and to shift focus upon other less invasive technologies and ways in which greater harmony can ensue.

'The motivations of those of you who are part of the material world is rife with fear, greed, misunderstanding, error, and a lack of love. Within your world are great opportunities to turn the tide of these dark conditions and seek greater harmony and opportunity for the betterment of humanity. These dark and light conditions which exists *upon your world, is a rather unique characteristic which is not common in other worlds.'*

'Those who observe our world, many of which we in the Celestial Kingdom have made efforts to communicate with and to collaborate with, wish to ensure the betterment of your world, and are poised to step forward and make themselves known to humanity. Unfortunately, the conditions at this time are not favourable for such an effort.

'As the world continues to change, however, and as God continues to pour His Love and transformative blessings upon your world, there will come a time soon when these efforts will be realized and the assistance from your brothers and sisters from other places will come forward.

'This will be a time of great change, upheaval, such great waves of shifting understanding and perceptions of life that there will be for many the disillusion of their old paradigms and perceptions.

'They will not feel as if they are walking on solid ground, and will be greatly confused and distressed. With this great shift of perception and experience in life, there will come many opportunities for the higher forces, and that which is in alignment with God, to bring about interventions, to teach, to awaken those who have been sleeping, so that the dark night of human existence will now come to light, and the possibilities of light and truth, of wakefulness and of love, will take its place as humanity awakens.

'So much is waiting and is poised to happen in very short order. Thus, we make great efforts at this time to communicate, to be with you, to pray with you, to influence and educate you, so that there will those prepared for the great changes that are coming. Understanding that you are not alone in the universe will be one of many great revelations that will come in these times of awakening. The greatest of which will be the possibility for every soul to come to know itself, and to know its true destiny, its true purpose in life. With this understanding truly becoming a part of the consciousness of humanity, there will be great strides in many ways, along many avenues of human endeavour.

'In this, many things will change as perspectives and priorities are shifted towards light, love, equanimity amongst humanity, and deep respect for all. The great disparity that now exists in your world will be removed. The many who are shackled to their fears

and error and pain will find these chains dissolved by love, by the revelations that will come, by the dynamic forces that will be predominant within your world.

'There will be no possibility of hiding away from these things as it will become plainly evident. The awakening of humanity will not, and cannot, be resisted, though many will try. Many will look in disbelieve. Many will be fervent with their efforts to disregard this new reality. The only way in which this may be done successfully will be if that individual's soul leaves their body and transitions into a plane that is more in alignment with their thinking and being. There will be those who will transition because they cannot live in a plane that is of such light and building harmony. They cannot accept the changes that are coming, and they will not see beyond their wilfulness and desire for the old comforts, the old perceptions and understanding of the world.

'It will be time of great choice. Indeed, these choices will be extreme in nature, and many will feel weak and unwilling to step forward, for they are the ones who are governed by fear, and are not willing to release that fear. But those who are attuned to their own souls, whether that be in an instant or has been cultivated for many years, will come to understand the wisdom of the soul, that which is meant to be and is ordained by God. These dear souls will readily step forward and come to adopt their new perceptions and understanding of what is truly meant to be life on this Earth, the sort of life that is reflected on many other planets in your universe.

'This rising up from darkness is the next necessary step in the evolution of your world. It is coming soon, and in many ways it is upon us now. Indeed, there will be material manifestations, expressions upon your world that will indicate the great shift that is unfolding, and continues to manifest, in the coming years. These manifestations will grow in intensity. With this will come deep inspiration to many souls upon your world; there will come revelations of understanding, of knowing, that will comfort the hearts of those who are receptive, and help them to move forward within this great momentum of change.'

'Yes, much will change, beloved souls, and with that change and great adjustment that must come with change, those other brothers and sisters who reside upon different planets will come to assist you, and bring to you great knowledge which will help to bring an easier transition, and help awaken a more harmonious way in which humanity *may live together, and share with one another, all that is required in life to help sustain life, to help bring an ease of life to this material world.*

'Yes, much is coming, my beloved souls. I say these things so that you may have hope, not fear; that you may see with the eyes of your soul that, what is coming, is a great blessing from God. In these blessings, many wondrous things will take place within your life, and beautiful awakenings that will help you to see more clearly life's true meaning, and life's true gifts. You will see that God has brought to you many things and God's great Creations are wondrous to behold, such a great treasure trove that may be explored and known to the individual soul.

'Know that you are loved by God and that God continues to nurture your world and everything upon it. God has a plan for greater life upon this world, so that truly it will be in alignment with all other worlds in light, in truth, in vitality and love. This is coming, beloved souls.'

The above was a wonderful message for us all to enjoy. I do resist from saying this too often, but on this occasion I could not resist. I do of course feel so many of the messages I have been fortunate enough to include herein are also wonderful and full of revelations and wisdom.

Next is part of what was said by Monty in a communication shared on YouTube by Warren James, but quickly deleted by YouTube from its platform. This being just one of many hundreds and no doubt thousands, not only in the UK where I am, but worldwide of videos they, like Facebook and media outlets, have tried to stop people from seeing, hearing or reading with blatant acts of censorship that attempt to deny us the right of free speech.

34. Monty - June 2021
With a Warning

'There are nothing like the numbers of people crossing into our world as you are being told there are; there are very few people coming across at all, compared to normal. I would like it to be said that that remained so for quite some time, but in recent times, there has been an uptake for those who have subsequently taken the concoction. I can confirm for you that there are now increased numbers of people coming across, I can confirm to you right now my friends that you have, and will have, documentation to show that those who you are told passed last year,

the numbers do not add up. You will have evidence of that, and further evidence will come in due course.

'I must urge you to stand your ground, my friends, I cannot stand your ground for you, nobody can, I should put this into very clear terms, every person in authority in your world is your enemy, that is merely how you need to see it, your enemy is anybody who is in higher authority.

'If they say walk left, I urge you to walk right, you are, as an entire species, you are at present under attack by those above you; you know this, it is evident, it is there. They do not have your well-being at heart, they never have and they never will, they do not care about your health, my friends; they care about themselves, their profits, their finances, their greed, their control, and most importantly their control. Their control over you, their control over your children, my friends, you must stand your ground, you must say "No", I cannot do that for you, it is your choice in the matter, it is your decision.

'Not everybody my friends is your enemy, truly, I assure you they are not. Every nurse or doctor is your enemy, they are not, they are misled, they are misguided, they are misunderstanding; they are foolish, they are ignorant, innocently ignorant; it is not their fault. But, my friends, the only sure way that you will survive, and go forward, knowing that you did your best, is to treat them all as your enemy. Treat them kindly, but do not take their words.

'There will be increased deaths to come, you will be told of increased deaths, I assure you they are not by the disease that you are told about, it does not exist in the way you are being told, your own immunity is being compromised my friends, your own immunity is being experimented with, you have been withdrawn away from bacteria, you have been drawn away from the very essence of life, bacteria, which is everywhere, and you have been encouraged to wipe it away, I assure you once you all come back into contact with each other, they will be blaming every illness, every mild cold, on something that does not exist.

'My advice, my friends, you must be strong, you must, but it is your choice, and I cannot make those choices for you. I cannot fight your corner, and I cannot stand your ground for you. If you so wish to follow the authorities' version of what is, that is fine, I understand, it is your

choice. But for the final time, I urge you treat all in authority, medical or otherwise, as your enemy.

'As far as the concoction is concerned, there are more people ill because of that, and there will be more people ill because of it in the future; and once they come for numbers one and two and three, you will have numbers four, five, and six, until you are swimming in it. Right now my friends, there are plans for a version of fascism that your world has never seen the likes of, right now they are planning, not only for your country, but for your entire world, to barcode people, to have you numbered, to have you under constant observation, technologically.

'They are planning on restricting your movements; there are plans afoot which are darker than Mr Hitler himself could ever have dreamed of. It is not ordinary to put a gag over a child's face, it is not normal behaviour to walk around in fear and suspicion of the person walking towards you because they do not leave enough space, it is not normal, but you are already accepting it as such, you are already changing, psychologically, it is as I once told you, long ago, a psychological game that they are playing, and they are winning.

'You must stand your ground, the future that is planned, is one of constant checkpoints, where you will be checked to see if you are conforming, that is the future for your children, your grandchildren, and all future generation. You must stand your ground, you must not comply; you must not allow what is planned, to be accepted as normal. You must not allow it, for once it is embedded and in place that will be the end of the freedom that you have ever known; it closes the door on a form of freedom that existed for so many millions of years. And you will be the generation who beckoned it in, you will be the generation who welcomed it with open arms, and you will be the generation who said, "Well, what can I do, there's nothing I can do", whilst accepting it.'

The above communication of June 2021 from Monty mentioned, *'They are planning on restricting your movements'*. To some at the time it may have seemed unlikely. But it is already in the pipeline to be implemented with a '15 minute cities' plan, starting in the UK with

Oxford. In chapter 5 "Truth Tellers on Earth" more can be found on this dark agenda.

Next, is part of another communication through the medium Al Fike. (And to remind readers, all of the messages through him can be found in full online).

35. Jesus – 2nd June 2021
Humanity Will Awaken with Coming Earth Changes

'Much darkness is perpetrated because there is great ignorance of the laws. There is great apathy regarding one's own soul and the progression of one's soul. This is so in the vast majority of cases, that most souls upon your world are ignorant and also apathetic. They have no inclination to stretch beyond their present ideas and mode of thinking to something higher and more pure in its nature and expression.

'Therefore we come to Earth in order to awaken those who are asleep, that they may rise up from their apathy, and come to a place of understanding and purity. Beloved souls, there are many, many barriers in the way of the progression of humanity in light and love. There is much that is perpetrated in the name of truth and righteousness that is not so, and is very damaging to many souls.

'It is this apathy that is within the souls of so many that allows the perpetration of darkness. Even though some may have the knowledge and understanding of this perpetration, they see no way or means to intervene, to voice their disapproval, to change their thoughts and actions that they may be more in harmony with love. This is the human condition of which we have spoken of many times. There is so much that needs to be changed.

'**Indeed, change is coming as we have also spoken of. God will bring His children to wakefulness in the unfolding of Earth Changes. The uncovering of unspeakable deprivations and sins that have been perpetrated upon the innocent will bring many to recognize this depraved condition. Much is coming to light and will continue to unfold and come to light in the world, for it is important for humanity to realize that each individual must take responsibility for their actions, and are also their brothers'**

keepers. All are required to make effort to protect those who are innocent, especially the children of your world.

'There is so much inequity in your world. There are those who can change the world if they were to use their wealth to help reshape the world into greater harmony, to bring equity and equality to their brothers and sisters, that they too may live a life that is in harmony; that is not so deprived, in the material sense.

'We see the world so differently from you, for our elevation of perception allows us to see the dark corners of your world; the great deprivation that exists, the ignorance and the strife, wars, inequality, and all that which is perpetrated upon your Earth that fouls and brings great disharmony to it. Humanity is at a tipping point where the power of their actions, deeds and thoughts are overwhelming this beautiful world that God has created. The time has come for a reckoning of humanity, that all of humanity may open their eyes and see for themselves what has been perpetrated, what is not in harmony within their own personal lives.

'The scales will be peeled from all of your eyes, beloveds; God will ensure that you see clearly. Whether that comes in great despair and recognition of a life not lived well, or whether one sees the goodness, kindness and love that has been expressed. Most individuals upon the Earth plane carry both within them. They have expressed some good and they have done those things that are not of light. When the individual sees clearly the difference between the two, and understands clearly the benefits of bringing light and expressing light in their lives, so they are given the choice and opportunity to change their thinking and their doing.

'To be true channels of love and light in the world, one must first begin with the recognition of that which is not of love and light. This we call sin. Indeed, every individual carries a measure of sin within them for no individual upon your Earth plane is fully in alignment and in accord with God's Laws of Love and Light. So humanity must awaken, choose, and gather within them the strength to change those patterns that are not in harmony with God.

'No one can do this for the individual, for it is their personal responsibility, and determined by their own choices and actions, in the world. Certainly, many can help their brothers and sisters, uplift them, teach them, and guide them in the way of light. Those

who are not ignorant of this carry a great responsibility to share these truths, to help others understand the journey that is required towards light. This is why we continue to strengthen you, beloved souls, and we continue to work with many others in your world to strengthen them, so to have upon this world a great army of light, a great coalition of those who bring truth and love and comfort to many.

'These things are happening at this time, and you are indeed a part of a great movement, a wave of light that is coming to your world. As the darkness is pushed back, as the scales are peeled from the eyes of so many, so will come your opportunity to step forward, and bring the Truth of God's Love to many. This simple Truth need not be changed or added to or predicated upon the minds of those who wish to bring to them power and recognition. Rather, it must be presented in its simple form, humbly so, without any pretence to carry the truth as some exalted being, and one who is above their brothers and sisters.

'This too is a sin, for I did not walk upon the Earth, and proclaim myself as one who is all-powerful; rather, I stated that I was the Messiah that was predicted who would bring the truth to the world. I did so with humility. I did so with love. I did not carry a crown or a mantle that said I am the authority and you must bow down to me and listen to me. Rather, I went to my brothers and sisters, many of whom were in great need, and told them that I loved them and asked if I could pray with them and teach them how they may receive a blessing from God.

'So you must also be those individuals who carry humility, who walk in grace, who are true to the simple Truth of God's Love and its redeeming qualities upon the soul. That measure of humility will bring others to you, for with this humility comes a sort of charisma that beckons those souls who are in need, and who desire relief from their pain and suffering to come forth and to seek you out. Indeed, in the times to come, there will be many, many souls who will be in despair and confusion, who will need comfort and clarity.

'God will guide you into their midst, beloved souls. God will use you as His instruments. This does not mean that God loves you any more than all your other brothers and sisters. Rather, God has given you the gift of service, the gift of truth, the gift of the way beyond your personal struggles to that of freedom and joy and love. So, you are not more loved than others, but you are indeed blessed mightily because you

111

have chosen to be blessed. Within your soul, you have recognized the truth and come to God in all earnestness to be blessed by His Great Soul to your needful soul.

'The great perpetration of sin and error upon your Earth is coming to an end. The time of reckoning is coming close. It will not be done in a moment or day, a week or a year but it will come as all things come in God's Creation, in a wave that builds and becomes more intense as time goes on. Many of you have felt this, beloved brothers and sisters, sensing this wave of light building, and you are built up and blessed by this changing condition, this blessing upon your world. You will continue to open to God more fully and be in harmony with God as you come to understand your Creator and come to know His Love for you.'

'The awakening of humanity builds, beloveds. It will come to a crescendo at the right time. You will all be called. That clarion call will be true and heard by all of you. You must come to prepare yourselves in prayer, to continue to awaken within your souls, to continue to forge your alliance with God so that all will come into alignment and truth and light.

'This is not difficult for any of you, beloved souls, for you have put your steps upon the Divine Path. In so doing, you have opened a great treasure trove of truth, a great power of alignment and the resources of God and His angels. Utilize these resources, beloved souls. Come to see yourselves as true children of God. Put aside self doubts. Put aside your guilt and your shame, and all those things that you harbour within your minds, that say you are not worthy, for truly you are worthy, beloved souls, truly you are worthy. Find freedom in God. Find comfort in His Love; find truth in that inflowing of His great gift of Love into your souls. In this way you forge the path forward, and will be able to lead your brothers and sisters who have freshly awakened to the truth and light and peace that must come.

'May God bless you on that journey, beloved souls. Though sin is perpetrated throughout the world, know that every time you choose light and take action in light, you are neutralizing this darkness and that you are helping God to wipe away all that is of sin and error. You are my true brothers and sisters for you carry the truth that I taught, and you are a part of this great effort to bring this simple truth to humanity.

'My love is with each one of you. My hope and prayers are that you may overcome the darkness completely and be resplendent in light. This can be your destiny and it can be your life upon this Earth if you so choose, but it requires your efforts and dedications, beloved souls, and the efforts and dedications of many more.

'We all travel together upon this road anticipating what God has to bring and what He will give to His children. We are all together within this great journey of awakening, of service, of love, of truth. May you come to know your true selves in all its glory and beauty. May you come to know God as your Heavenly Father who loves you so and has such a bountiful treasure to give to each of you. May you come to know your brothers and sisters in the Celestial Kingdom, for we too wish to be by your side, and to assist you upon that journey of awakening.

'May God's Love continue to flow into your souls. For those who are awakening, may they come to know the comfort and strength that comes from God for this is available to every soul. It is fervent prayer and desire that brings you to God. Allow this to be uttered through your lips, expressed through your minds, and emanate from your souls. In this way you will truly know God and truly come to know of those things which I speak of, leading you to at-onement with God.'

If anyone should feel that communications from highly advanced souls such as those of the Celestial Kingdom is in any way difficult to believe, let me assure everyone that, in my experience, this is happening far more frequently, and through many different channels, than in times past. Times truly are changing, and looking at the messages of each communicator I have managed to include in this book is, to me, further confirmation of this fact.

When I first started my journey of spiritual discovery and experience many people and spirit guides seemed reluctant to speak of reincarnation. While these days reincarnation is accepted as almost self-evident and an obvious fact by the vast majority of people seeking spiritual knowledge. This in itself is a sure sign that collectively we have progressed in our understanding and therefore are more ready to receive teachings from those in higher dimensions.

Continuing with the spirit messages, what follows next is more to enjoy from Jonathan, speaking via Elaine Thorpe.

36. Jonathan – 16th July 2021
Awakening and Earth Changes

'I will speak to you about what I feel should be said, it is about your world, actually, and what is happening in it at present, of course there are only certain things that I'm going to mention, because I do not want to mention things that do not need to be said, things that you really already know about. But as we are speaking to you we know that things are already happening in your world, it is changing, with great velocity, it is also changing along with you, and your situations on Earth that are happening at present.

'So if you look at 2020 vision the word 2020 vision, that was a vision for 2020 onwards, you see, it was the clear vision, that what was going to happen in your world from there on in; and of course, many things are going to happen in your world, to bring about many, many changes, some for the greater good.

'Because out of the negative comes the positive, and at the moment your world seems very much a place of turmoil, and with the great awakening happening, not only in a spiritual sense, but in an earthly sense of people coming forward to try to change things, there is of course, what I was speaking about, the exodus.

'This means that people will pass, as they always have done, it's not to say that you've got to worry about it, because it happens; and sometimes people pass with natural disasters, sometimes people pass in the way that would be more expected to be passing, naturally, or with some sort of health condition.

'But there are souls that have chosen to go in their masses, amongst all of this happening, and of course we're not going to sit here and tell you everyone is going to suddenly pass, because it is naturally happening. So in this time, with the mass awakening going on, many, many people are coming forward and telling people of their spiritual experiences, not only during their sleep state, but during their waking state, and that they are feeling a little different about life to what they did before.

'But I do understand that this is mainly come about more so during your time, when you were spending much of your time at home, because

you had to be, you see, and so people went about on their computers researching things, and delving into things a little bit more, not necessarily all spiritual, but some did.

'They wanted to know more information about the spiritual awakening, so they started to discover that, and discover themselves. So this is going to be happening on a huge scale, there will be people awakening in the Earth sense to come forward, and there will be many more awakening spiritually; that is true.

'I spoke about this around two years ago of your earthly time, I do believe, and before that; and other guides have also come forward and spoken about it, and many people have felt it, before it all happened, that something big was coming. Well it is, the big change is coming, you see, the big change in your world, and also the big change with the Earth. Because your planets surrounded, whatever they do is accountable to what happens to your Earth, and whatever you do here on your Earth is accountable, it makes a difference for your planet, doesn't it.

'So because the Earth is changing, that means that water levels can rise, and land that was once there will not be there, Earth has always moved its land, you see, that is nothing new. But it is having a bit of a surge at the moment, the Earth is erupting, the Earth is shaking, Earth, air, fire and water, are happening on your Earth.

'I have spoken to people about that before, Earth, Air, Fire and Water, and they are all happening at the same time. They will happen with grave velocity, and that will be the earthly changes, you see, land will separate, sea will cover, there's your volcanic eruptions that will change the shape of the landscape, as they always have done, but now with greater velocity, greater power.

'The whole planetary system is going to shift, a whole lot of it, in the way of your planets that are aligning with yours, Saturn, Jupiter, Mars are going to end up, in the future, lining up together, or almost lining up. That will be quite some time away, but of course it will come about in the end.

'So I'm going to go back to the subject of you awakening, this is a wonderful time to be living, to be awakening, this is a wonderful time to go within, and discover yourself, and discover all that is, and begin to appreciate life, the beauty of the Earth, and yourself.

'This is the time to begin to love yourself, this is the time to begin to forgive one another, no matter how hard it is, if you can find it in your heart then you will feel much lighter and better within yourself, and that is all part of the awakening.

'To become somewhat, I would say, empathic, to feel another's feelings, to step into their shoes for one moment, and imagine what it feels like to be in their shoes, and then you will become more understanding, and more forgiving, as to why they are behaving the way that they are.'

Next is the first of four more communications from the lovely Dr Peebles via Summer Bacon.

37. Dr Peebles - 11th August 2021

'The way in which you thought you're supposed to live your life, the way you thought it was going to be forever, has really broken down. It's changing rapidly, and you're being challenged on a variety of levels from the politicians, from your medical industry, and other things, as to what you're supposed to do, and how you're supposed to behave, and suddenly a lot of your freedoms have been taken away from you, and you say, "I don't like that. I want to be free, I want to be free to be me, I want to be free to understand who I am".

'They're not going to be able to control you, my dear friends; they are really, truly, not in a position to be able to do that anymore. You are in charge of yourself, and that is the part of the awakening that everybody is going through.

'As you move into this greater understanding of love, and the fifth dimension of understanding, you find freedom, and flight of soul. You start to realise that you are not going to have to comply with anything that anyone wants from you.

'God has given you all the gifts that you need in order to be upon the Earth. All of the gifts that can make you feel alive, and happy, and thriving in this world. That's what everybody's being asked to see, asked to feel inside of self, God has already activated that within you now. It is up to you to acknowledge that, so go inside, deeply in yourself, and find out who you are.

'What did God give you, what gifts were you given when you came into this life, what beauty is there inside of you, that you have yet to acknowledge? Perhaps it is just simply your ability to put words to things that other people can't. Perhaps it is your ability to be silent, when other people really need to talk, what are your strengths, and realise these, my dear friends.

'This is also a time period upon the planet Earth where the energy that is here is also inviting you to please, please, please, discard that which no longer works for you. It is not necessary to carry old damaging thoughts about yourself, it is not necessary to carry any grief, or guilt, or shame, about anything, move forward from this.

'Release yourself from the confines of the Earth, the body, and the mind, that tries to keep you trapped in the past, in old ways of thinking, because this is a time on planet Earth where paradigms are breaking down.

'**Human beings are going to try to create new ones, but it's not working, it's not going to work. Human beings are going to find themselves in more expressions towards each other, in terms of massive uprisings. There is going to be more and more pressure for everybody to have vaccinations and such, and vaccination passports, and human beings are going to up-rise against this, and say, "This is not fair, this is not for us; we are not going to comply". It's going to be on a massive scale that can no longer be denied or ignored by your central media that is sharing information with the world, because it's going to be right outside a lot of your doors. You're going to see it, you're going to hear it, you're going to feel it, and you're not going to be having to dig too deeply, as it comes closer and closer into your life.**

'You're going to see this happening around you, indeed so it's going to be an interesting time period, but don't live in fear, don't be afraid of any of it, it's a fantastic time of growth, it's a difficult time of growth, there are times where the storms are raging on the oceans and such, and that's when you've got to sail your very best, and this is one of those times my friends.

'But it doesn't mean that the ship is going to sink, the oceans are beautiful, and they are absolutely remarkable when they are raging, when there are storms in the air, and you see the fantastic electricity that is in the air, it's so beautiful. The lightning bolts, the sound of the thunder, the torrential down pour of rain, and that sort of thing, it's a beautiful thing. That is a beautiful expression of emotion on the planet Earth, it is something that happens for a reason, it stirs things up, it moves things around, it takes the seeds of understanding and plants them elsewhere, as they are swelled around in the wind and deposited on other parts of the Earth.

'It is a magnificent thing that happens, people are afraid of everything a lot of times, but if you can just simply imagine a beautiful storm that is happening, that is raging, and you're just simply watching it, and enjoying it, and it's beautiful, and you know that there is a reason for it. All the electricity that's in the air, and the tornadoes and other things, that are there, they're fascinating, truly, and we understand they have the opportunity to tear things down, so that people have to then rebuild and such and it does create a lot of change in the world.

'Changes your lifestyle and such, having to go inside when you wanted to go out and plant a garden, or whatever it might be, but it is important to know that these things are important to the growth of the planet Earth, all that is happening right now upon the planet Earth, all of the judgments that people are casting at each other, all of the hatred that is there, all of the demands for change, and growth in a wide variety of ways, when it comes to acknowledging different races, different forms of sexuality, different ways of living in different lifestyles, wanting to be acknowledged for who you are, for the authentic person that you are upon this planet Earth, and without judgment, is an important part of this process of growth.

'It is an important part of stripping down old paradigms, it's an important part of awakening to each other, and eventually just as with any arguments that happen, eventually everybody calms down after a while, and it will happen, and human beings will come closer together, and will say, wow, look what we learned from all of that, and our world has now changed and rearranged itself, and human beings are moving around the planet Earth and it's going to be more of a mixture of human beings in all countries.

'There's going to be a wider variety of people from different countries moving in together, different nationalities, different political perspectives coming together, there will be lots of people who are now of different races coming together, modern marriages of this sort, different sexuality, and other sorts of things coming together, there's a lot that's happening my dear friends.

'In this process there's also going to be a greater and greater awareness of love, greater and greater awareness once again as we've shared so many times, that you need each other, God bless you indeed, there's no question about it.'

38. Dr Peebles - 7th September 2021

'You are a courageous adventurer, courageous for being upon this school called Planet Earth. We love you so very much, and now is the time upon the planet Earth where, 'hang on to your hats', things are going to be accelerating quite quickly in terms of the energetics.

'This is a positive upswing in a very beautiful way, but it's going to look like chaos for a while. It's going to be beautiful because more and more people will rapidly be coming into their hearts. They will rapidly come into knowing themselves in such a way that they will have awareness. An awakening inside of self, and will suddenly realise that they no longer want the control over their lives, but rather want to have control over their lives themselves.

'They are going to come to understand the great creator that they are. There are going to be a lot of, if you will, experiences upon your planet Earth. Where people are going to come together in uprisings, there will be all sorts of strikes that will be occurring within the airlines, within the political system. There will be as well within the teachers, doctors and nurses and others, who will be standing up and saying, "We no longer want to be controlled. We never ever want to have our rights taken away; we want to make our own decisions here about what we want to do with ourselves, with our bodies and everything".

'There will be an uprising on many different levels, many of which you will not even hear about, unless you scout around a little bit for it. Some you will see with your own eyes right there in your own neighbourhoods where people will no longer be willing to lock themselves down because of the virus, so called virus; the virus truly being the admission of fear in your world, and the administration of it (fear) in your world. It is very, very finely created, my dear friends by the many who are organizing themselves to keep people suppressed upon the planet Earth.

'And we want for you to understand that you have every right to feel a bit indigent about it, and say, "You know something, I want to be free, because I want to be free in God's will. I want to live my

life according to what God wants from me, not what somebody else wants from me, outside of me. Not what a government wants for me, but what God wants for me, for my heart, to be living free and understanding myself, and learning about myself. And finding my way through life, and experiencing life, and dying when I do in whatever way that shall be, and understanding that, that, as well, is part of this journey upon this school called planet Earth as a human being."

'So, you my dear friends, you have entire charge, control over your own destiny here, by your choices and perceptions in which you create your own reality. And this is going to be coming up, not just for a few but for the many upon the Earth, who will say, *"I want to take charge of my life, I no longer want to be told what to do or how to do it. I want to share of myself with the world. I want to be authentic; I choose this direction in my life."*

'There will be some of you who in the past have not really wanted to express yourselves, a little bit afraid to find your voice in the world, a little bit afraid of what people might think of you, suddenly, overnight, change and say, *"It doesn't matter what anybody thinks of me, it's what I think of myself now. It is me taking charge of me, listening to my heart, listening to that still small voice within, listening to the God light that exists within me, listening to the voice of Christ within me, understanding that every answer that I need to understand who I am, and to awaken in this world into greater consciousness and awareness of the greater love that is coming to the planet Earth, this is what I desire now more than ever before".*

'It is going to become increasingly important as to making the decision, taking a stand, as to which side you're going to be on in your heart. Are you going to allow yourself to adhere to the light, or are you going to find yourself succumbing to the darkness?

'Are you going to allow your own voice to speak your own truth, and not worry about what others say to you in return, but rather allow for them to have their voices as well? Are you going to allow for this light to shine in the world, in whatever way it wants to emerge through humanity?

'You, my dear friends, have that choice now. It is going to be a decision again, an awakening within the many rather than the few.

'There are people who are again, going to be coming together in uprisings, going to be striking, who are going to find ways to collectively stop the madness upon the planet Earth and allow for the love to shine through.

'There are going to be movements upon the planet Earth where human beings will gather together quite deliberately putting their arms around each other, holding hands to create change around the world, and other things that will show that human beings' hearts are really, truly the strongest thing that there is upon the Earth. There is no weapon stronger than the human heart. There is no weapon stronger than the, if you will, the adherence to love and the giving of that to the world.

'That, my dear friends, is what's coming up, for the school called planet Earth. And here you are upon it, the courageous adventurer that you are.

'You are standing now in a time period where it is important to remember who you are, and what really matters to you, God bless you indeed.

'Because right now on your Earth there's going to be a lot of topsy-turvy things happening, and there will be more virus's being brought to the surface, and there will be more mandates occurring, and there will be more lockdowns occurring, not in all countries but in some, not in all states but in some. And there will be more arguments and such in a desire to persecute those who are not vaccinated and other things to vilify them and such.

'But people are going to start to catch on because those who think they are in charge here are starting to make some very, shall we say, fatal errors in their judgements.

'They don't understand how really smart human beings are. They don't really understand how many of you are willing to listen to your hearts. They don't understand that there is an energetic force at work here called love, and that God is really the one in charge.

'They don't understand this, but they are striving to create a world where they can design it according to their own will.

'But truly my dear friends, human beings are going to catch on, and human beings are not going to like it, and human beings are going to rebel, and that is why there will be uprisings, and that's why there will be strikes, because human beings are going to get tired of living in fear.

'Human beings are going to get tired of being separated from each other, human beings know in their heart of hearts that they need each other, they need the hugs and kisses, eventually human beings will say, "We don't care if there are fifteen thousand virus's", which of course there are all sorts of things in your world that can kill you, but they're just there, and it's a matter of whether or not is that your destiny? Are you going to create that reality?

'Human beings are going to say, "I don't even care anymore, I just want to live. I want to live a quality life, I don't care about quantity anymore, I care about peace, I care about love, I care about trusting people who are guiding me in this world, I care about people who have, if you will, love in their hearts who are helping and educating my children. I care about things that really matter now.

'And this is the grand and great and glorious awakening that is happening upon this school called planet Earth as you are all moving into the 5th dimension of understanding of love.

'And that, of course, again, comes with a bit of topsy-turvy energy. But the reality is that which has been hidden is now being revealed. Human hearts are being revealed, human anger is being revealed.

'Human tendency to want to dominate is being revealed. Human beings are showing their true colours in a wide variety of ways. Human beings who are egomaniac are showing that to the world, demonstrating it, on a daily basis, in a wide variety of ways.

'People who are strong and loving and sincere and authentic in the world are showing their true colours in a wide variety of ways, and it is so magnificent to watch. And everybody is working hard to get to know thyself, God bless you indeed.

'You are a beautiful spirit, know thyself, be gentle with thyself, and then be gentle with others. You are a beautiful spirit and only you truly know who you are. Nobody can tell you anything about you.

'You have every right to be yourself, to be expressed in this world in any way, shape, or form that you desire. We, of course, always suggest that you do that from love within. Always, when you are looking in your heart and you are finding out who you really are, you will find that you bump into love everywhere you go.

'But really remember this, as you are moving along in this very, very, strong current of energy that is coming to the Earth, remember my dear friends that everybody's going through it. Not

just you, not just some, every single, solitary person is feeling the vibration on the Earth. Every animal, every creature, every cell of your body is feeling. So, remember this as you are riding this current, relax, release, surrender, strive to take a deep breath, slow down a little bit and understand that this too shall pass.

'Human beings are really starting to say, "I want to know who I am and I'm going to live and abide in this, I am going to take a stand. I'm standing in my truth. And I'm going to see what happens next, and things might change, things might not work out the way that some human beings want it to work out".

'There is a choice that each and every person upon this school called planet Earth has made, and masses, of course, have decided to follow what is being directed, as to what their direction ought to be and such. There are many who are complying because they feel that it is necessary, and they feel this way because of a terrible fear, a terrible fear of death, a terrible fear of endings. A terrible fear that they won't last for another day upon this school called planet Earth.'

'You are not going to die from something that you are not intended to die from. You are not going to be infected by anything you're not intended to be infected by. If you so choose to believe in it and attract it to you and want to experience it and love it in that way, that is entirely up to each and every person upon this school called planet Earth.

'God created human beings so beautifully, each and every one of you are remarkable in your ability to change self, to change your body, because your body is at the mercy of your spirit, and your spirit in God is so strong that things start to change rapidly in your physicality when you are adhering to the life, to the reason, to the love and voice of God within yourself. Everything begins to change, and you begin to manifest a greater and greater and more beautiful reality than you could have ever dreamed of having before.

'You are a beautiful spirit, you are a student of the divine and you can stand up and fight for your freedom if you like in whatever way you like, but we suggest that you always choose the path of love. Strive to remember that that is why you are here upon this planet Earth, to live, to learn, to grow into greater and greater love for self and for others around you.

'You are all beautiful spirits, all growing beings, all striving to understand your right to receive and to give abundance in this your chosen lifetime, and you are a beautiful spirit.

'So we suggest that you take a stand for yourself and realise what you are fighting for in your world is really to be alive in a way that you want to be alive, by allowing yourself to be seen and heard and felt by living life authentically, by not fearing humanity, by not feeling that you have to hide yourself away anymore; not hide your passion, not hide your truth of any sort, not hide your love, your loving nature.

'Goodness gracious my dear friends, once you come to life like that there is no turning back, once you come to life like that there is no fear of anything, because you are standing in pure love and in that love all sorts of things can dissolve.

'Cancers can disappear overnight; all sorts of things can dissolve once you are adhering to what is the greatest truth about you. You are an energetic being in a physical body over which you have charge.

'Can you now take that very same principle and direct it at the world around you, the human beings around you. They are just other cells of the universe. And if you can love them, then you will find too that they might dissolve and disappear as well; some of them who are acting like cancers upon the Earth.

'So you have the opportunity here to realise that giving love to the world and to human beings of all sorts, shapes and sizes, all colours, all nationalities, all religious perspectives and in a wide variety of ways, is a beautiful gift that you can give to the world.

'Why not live life without fear, without expectation of bad things happening, terrible things are happening, and the world is falling apart; perhaps it's all just falling apart to be rebuilt closer to God, to be rebuilt stronger within each and every person upon this school called planet Earth?

'Stop waiting on life to be a particular way in order for you to be happy. Stop waiting for your rose garden to bloom in order to be happy, enjoy watching the growth, enjoy the experience of the pruning and such that needs to be done in order for it to look its very best. Enjoy everything about your life and if there are things that you find that you do not enjoy whatsoever strive to find ways in which you can create change there.

'You're a beautiful spirit, again, as we say, there's going to be certain interesting happenings on your planet, uprisings and other things, some of which you will hear about, some of which you will not, lots of which will be according to what the news media wants you to hear.

'Why not turn that television off, why not start listening to your heart, your heart is much, much better in terms of giving you truth than any news media channel has ever been. Why not learn to listen to your heart in a world where you just don't know sometimes who to listen to or who to believe.

'Why not turn to God? Why not believe in God? Why not believe in what's happening inside of you? It's not random. You have little senses about things. Trust those senses, even if it seems to go against the entire planet, trust the senses that are happening inside of you. Trust it, and that is where miracles begin to happen, that is where miracles occur.

'**There is always going to be manipulation, that's what happens upon the Earth, we've said it many times. There are governments and people who are truly wickedly greedy, incompetent, and uncaring, except for themselves. That is where they have yet to understand what it means to love self. That is where their egos are driving them in life. Thinking that they are going to acquire power through a variety of means, not knowing that the power that they are really seeking is the God light within, and that is where the true power is.**

'My dear friends remember not to run away from yourself, during this time; this is the time to run straight into your heart. Trust you first and foremost with anything and everything that happens. Remember who you are, you can't go wrong with that, because God created you in His image, and you are perfect, God bless you indeed.'

39. Dr Peebles - 29th September 2021

Question: This question is about Australia and all of the strife and tension, and discord going on in that country, what can we do globally to help?

'*Really, it's about praying, giving love and praying for the upliftment of all involved and praying for clarity for the many rather than the few. There's a lot of panic, a lot of mayhem, there's a lot of control, there's a lot of judgment. There are a lot of things.*

They're teetering on the edge of certain tyranny, and it is something that doesn't have to happen if human beings can awaken in their hearts.

'So globally pray for those who are in Australia that they open, and open their borders simultaneously, that is what needs to happen in order for them to move on. Otherwise, it's going to be a really, rather crushing, energetically crushing, time period for a while in Australia.

'Human beings need to stand up and say what they want, and ask for their freedoms, and there are many who are rising up who are willing to take a stand, and to be very clear about what they believe in, and that sort of thing. And it's taking a lot of guts; so there is an educational learning within Australia itself that is awakening in Australian hearts.

'All of those who are there either as true residents or not, those who are there at this given time, are there for a reason, because it is one form of collective consciousness, Australia itself, that is awakening and growing in a different fashion. But, we want to say, pretty smart cookies they are, and we see it all coming out to be a very good. It's going to have a very good result, ultimately.

'And there's a lot of truly, truly beautiful human beings who have truly open hearts there in Australia, who really want the country to come alive again, they don't want it to be squashed and such. They don't want any more fires, they don't want the anger. There's a lot going on there.

'Each country, in and of itself, does have its own consciousness, just as each family has its own consciousness. Each family has its own personality. You have a personality, your family has a personality; your city has a personality, of which you are a part, your community and such; your country as well. You are a part of that personality. You chose to be in that country at a particular time, in a particular lifetime, in order to experience the educational system that it provides for you.

'And again, that is the tip of the iceberg. But if you think about it in those terms you will start to realise, "Why I am here, what is it that I am choosing to learn in this experience by being in Australia", or wherever you are at this given time.'

Comment from Liz: There's certainly a lot of interesting energy on the planet.

'There certainly is, and a lot of it we know is difficult, but there is a lot more than you know, there is so much love on your planet Earth, there *is so much awakening happening, there are so many people who really want the world to be made whole again.*

'There are so many beautiful prayers that we hear every single day, all the time. There are those who are praying without ceasing for the planet Earth. There are those who are giving of their hearts, their time, their money, everything, to the upliftment of the planet Earth.

'There are those who are helping those who are hungry, those who are without shelter. People are absolutely remarkable in the ways in which they are learning to express love in the world, because love is really the only thing that creates true movement, ultimately in a direction where you feel at long last that peace in your heart, and closer to God.'

40. Dr Peebles - 13th October 2021

'It's an important time upon the planet Earth where there are going to be, again, more things coming to the surface, a tilling of the soil, revelations about certain politicians in your country of the United States of America that will be coming to the surface. There will be other relationships that will be exposed in terms of different politicians around the world and their relationships with each other. There will be lots of controversy around it because people will deny it, people will not want to accept it, people will not want to see it or hear it, and others will say, "But this is the way it is". It is what it is, no shades of grey anymore.

'So it's going to be a wonderful time for you to open your hearts more than ever before, to realise that every single person, even these politicians and others are just simply growing persons upon the Earth.

'You're growing into greater love, the light of understanding of love; some a little ahead of the game, and so to speak, but not better than anybody else. It's going to be an interesting time upon the planet Earth, as you move into the greater light of understanding of love, a deeper vibration of that, bringing it into yourself.

'Don't give up on love, but always remember that that is the constant, that is the thing that remains forever. When all of the other stuff falls away love will still be there, no matter what. In any time of war, love has always been there. In any time of peace love has always been there; always love has been the constant factor in life.

'These other situations are situations that arise because human beings have a tendency to want to master each other. They want to be on top, they want to be the ones who can control everybody on the Earth because the belief system starts out that you are living life from the outside in, that if you control the world outside of you that somehow you're going to be happy, somehow that's the way that you going to find peace in your life, that's where you're going to find power in your life and such. **But in truth, the real power, the real peace, the real light, the real love comes from the things that happen inside yourself.**

'Money comes and goes, and hierarchal structures are built up and they fall down because they simply don't work, the reality is you're all the same sort of being upon the Earth, you're all even, you're all equal in all ways because you are children of God, and you are created from God's heart, from God's love, and that is the core of who you really are.

'So, there is no need for hierarchy, there is no need for trying to be on top or trying to be the most powerful. If you would embrace the fact that you are a child of God and that you have love in your heart you would see how powerful you really are. You would find that creating your reality would become much more simple, because you would understand who you are, what it is you really want, rather than striving to think that you want to have certain things in your life because that's what the commercials are telling you, and that's what people around you, and your friends and family are telling you, you have to have in order to be happy.

'My goodness gracious, we can tell you there are more people upon the planet Earth who have listened to their family, friends, and others about what happiness is and followed their rules and regulations who are unhappy in their lives, because it doesn't work. It doesn't work because it can't happen from the outside in; it must happen from the inside out.

'You're here to learn about love. You're freeing yourself to be yourself; you are freeing yourself to be expressed truthfully and honestly, in integrity with who you really are. The true value of self is that you are made of love, bringing that to the surface is honouring of yourself, and honouring yourself is honouring of all creation.

'It's going to be necessary in this world to keep that going, so that you don't become encumbered by the energies of darkness that will be on the Earth; that will be at play; and some will be killed. And it's going to be a little scary for some people, no question about it.

'But it's also a time period where if you can see it as a collective upliftment of the planet Earth, a necessity, that people are growing in a wide variety of ways such as the very fact that there are going to be lots of people choosing to leave the planet Earth at this given time, because they don't want to go along with it; they don't want to be here, they want to go on to other things for a while, and get off this ship, so to speak, because it's getting a little too rocky for them. And that is okay, that's alright, but you have the courage to stick around and what does it take to have that courage? It takes a desire to see what's going to happen next. It take curiosity to allow for yourself to surrender into the day and say, "What a crazy mixed up world this is, let's see what it's got in store for us today", and watching it unfold, and praying for the world, sitting down and saying, "I love you so very much planet Earth, I love you so much my family of humanity, and I pray for your upliftment. I pray for your hearts to open up wide to receiving the light, love, inspiration, and truth that you are coming to understand, and being willing to express it in the world. I love you so very much, I pray that every single solitary person upon this school called planet Earth is at long last uplifted into the greater understanding of the love that they are, and be willing to release that into the world."

'It is by your very nature that you were created to grow; the universe was created to expand, that is the nature of the universe, that is what every single living being upon the planet Earth is doing, not just human beings.

'There are all sorts of different personalities within your nature, within the animals of the Earth and such, within the plants of the Earth and such, so much learning going on. These little blades of grass in your lawn looking to the sun, striving to figure out how to get around their neighbours to get a little bit more sunshine upon themselves; constantly in motion, you'd be surprised if you could hear the sounds of it. It is so beautiful and wondrous that you could fall in love with the life that you have upon this school called planet Earth, rather than fighting against it. Rather than letting all the negativity infiltrate your consciousness.

'This period of time upon the planet Earth you're all getting a lot of guidance, if you will, to go inside of yourself and get to know thyself. Be aware of who you are and don't be afraid to be that person. Just live your life accordingly and your life will begin to change radically. That doesn't mean it's all going to turn out the way that you think it's supposed to turn out, but you will find that there is going to be a certain level of peace inside of yourself. Understand that certain things just don't happen the way you think they're supposed to, because it's not going to bring you the greatest happiness, and the greatest peace. If you really release it all to God, it will happen if it is necessary for it to do so in order for you to grow.

'You are coming into a greater, greater frequency of love, and people are going to be starting to wriggle, because those who are not living their lives in integrity, are going to start to feel a little afraid of being exposed for who they really are; and that's really what's going to be happening; what happens when you shine a light into a room of cockroaches, the cockroaches panic and start to scatter.

'Well, that is what's going to be happening.

'The light is going to be shining brighter than ever, and people are really going to start to say, "Well my goodness gracious, I'm going to be exposed for who I really am and I'm scared of that. I don't want to be exposed. I thought I had it all figured out, I was trying to control the world around me. I was trying to control people through fear. I was trying to control people through a lot of sciences and other things and it's not working. How is it that it didn't work? I thought I could control life from the outside in."

'Well, that's been going on for centuries my dear friends, that's what Adolf Hitler tried to do, to control the world from the outside in, and to a certain measure he did, and a lot of people were hurt in that process, there's no question it. But the reality is it didn't work. It didn't last. Those sorts of things never last, it is always going to be love that wins, always.

'And you my dear friends, you're in a spiritual battle upon the planet Earth right now, inside of yourselves, mostly. Look inside of yourself and make a decision as to where you want to stand right now in life, and if you can, really stand in your truth, deeper truth, that you have inside of yourself, which is to stand in love.

'You are all very beautiful, very unique, very magical, all having the core of love underneath all that stuff that you are doing; that's the truth of who you are, remember it and embrace it. You might say, "Well, I don't think I'm so loving, Dr. Peebles," well perhaps you're not sharing it *with the world so much, perhaps you are not giving it to the world, maybe you don't want to right now and that's okay. But we're going to tell you this, you can do that for as long as you like but it's never going to change who you really are. You are birthed from the love of God; you are love at your core, as is every single solitary person upon the planet Earth.*

'If there's ever a time to really, really strive to understand the love that you are and the magnificent power that you have, in that knowing of that love inside of yourself, this is the time to do it.

'This is the time to really ride the current that is here, and that current, again, is the frequency of love being magnified, forgiving yourself first, forgiving others because it makes you feel good, letting go of anger and fear and other things that make you feel oppressed and frustrated and unhappy, and instead, choosing to play unabashedly, laugh loudly, and sing your song to the world. You will find peace and comfort in all of that; and that is what you're truly seeking, not the cars, not the houses, not the perfect employment or anything else, you're seeking peace and happiness. You're seeking the sense of love, inside and out, that really you can trust and there is where 'you live happily ever after'. There is where you know that there is no death; that is where you come to embrace and understand that you are an eternal soul; that is where you fall in love forevermore with the journey of expansion, the journey to the heart.

'Go your way in peace, love, and harmony, for life is indeed a joy. All you have to do is enjoy the journey to your own hearts, and certainly to your enlightenment. Simply lighten up just little bit more in those little tiny ways, find magnificent ways in which to share of yourself, your light, love, inspiration, and truth with the world, don't be afraid of you, you're a beautiful spirit my dear friends, you are made of love.

'God bless you indeed.'

The following spirit communication came through the medium Jacqui Rogers, author of books such as, *"Simply Spiritual: Small to Medium! The Life of a Psychic."* I was kindly given permission to share this message with readers. (See Links)

41. Simeon - 14th October 2021
Equilibrium

'I've been asked to explain the importance of balance through every area of the energy in your world and around you. It is important that you understand that I am not just referring to the physical layers of your world, everything you think and everything you do has an energetic effect on the signature of your life.

'You have heard that you are what you eat, and you also understand that you are what you think. And what you believe. For so very long this planet has been out of equilibrium within it, around it and on it, indeed within its place within the universe. There were some that were ready to just leave it and let it go and indeed it was almost decided that this planet would do just that, but somewhere there was a seed that was planted to bring round a miracle, the miracle of an old/new energy.

'Now every living being on this planet exists within the realms of energy, all realms, because there is more than one on your Earth, everything has an energetic signature and this signature is effected by everything else that is also around it and within it and within everyone, so think about the masses of energy that are included which has to be taken into consideration in Divine creation.

'It is certainly a complicated matrix, this matrix was constructed many years ago and before that there was another one another place, the original one. Well, the point of no return has been reached, and that is true for the planet, and regards the people. They have their own journeys, not all will be the same, there is not a lot you can do about that, as the individual always has choices, it is always up to them how they plead and what they do, it's called free will, a gift from the creator.

'The Equilibrium on the planet has been effected for a very long time, however, over the past few years the balance has been shifted, it is quite positive now because some of the major negative energy is no longer present, it has been sent to where it has been transmuted into the positive vibrations within the universe. Not all have yet left, not all have gone. We cannot tell you what is to come because that must be something that you experience, and it may leave apprehension for many if they knew, but you have to just walk through knowing that you are not alone and that everything will be just as it should be.

'You have been asked to keep your eyes to the skies, this will not be for much longer, and this will be understood. There maybe people who

may just vanish from your lives or from around you. There may be timelines that just disappear, you know somebody ... and no longer do. It is very sad from many perspectives that the world has to go through this, and that it's necessary, also for everyone on it and it is sad that so many are still sleeping, for their awakening will be nothing short of incredible for them.

'When people know it will trigger an energetic release that will certainly tip the Equilibrium of the Earth in a positive manner, but there will be many that will not survive in the physical state, but this is known and expected, and all that pass will indeed go to where they should be, all is understood, have no worry or doubt on this, you all know there is no death, there is only transmutation of energy. The Earth will never be the state it was, the Earth will never again have to go through this unbalanced state, it won't be possible; Never. The Earth will only grow stronger, the beings may change upon it, and they may be from other places in the cosmos living in peace, as you may be able to visit other places in peace.

'Within all of your lives there is the positive and the not so positive, and everyone of you is having this in your life, but do not hold on to that, for that is what will become the Earth's primary key. What you hold within your heart in the next few months will be your primary key on which you will eventually depend upon, so please ensure that you keep your energies up and smiling through love, laughter and all that keeps you smiling. Even though you may walk through the valley of the shadow death you remember, you fear no evil.

'Physically, daily situations will get more difficult, there will be more problems but you will find your solutions if you look. If you think ahead there will always be something put there for you, remember you are workers of the light and workers of God and you will be called at the most inappropriate times to stand up and be reminded of who you really are, all of you have indeed done that previously without question and worked with the infirm, the sick, and the needy.

'There will be many who will know not what to do, so you will have to guide, to calm. There will be many who no longer wish to be here on this earth and that is also okay, so do not worry about things that you do not know will happen, and start seeing what is in front of you all every day. Be thankful and grateful for what you have in your lives, and help others do the same.

'Equilibrium is equal light and equal dark and this planet has had so much of the dark within it for many millennia, much longer than you are told or know. The light is changing its vibration, not just inside but is changing on the outside to.

'Earth is spinning just as much through the cosmos as the rest of us within the worlds that we live in, and the places that we reside, but because we understand the energy of the physicality and non-physicality it is much easier for us to switch. You will also understand this in some point in the future, you will have access to the most amazing insights you never thought possible, and you will find that it will enhance your lives to the point of incredulousness.

'It is very important that you understand that God is with all of you, however you see that energy just know that it is always close and guiding you constantly. It is also important to understand that the equilibrium between yourselves, within your energy, you must remain equal, as that is all you can do, there is good and bad, and high and low, in everyone you know. It is important that you accept the shadows of who you were, and who you are, so you may walk into the light that is in front of your eyes.

'Do not reproach yourselves for what you think you have done or have been, it makes no difference, what matters is who you are now, and how you deal with the situations that are placed in front of you. No one ever said that life was easy on the planet; no one ever said that life was easy within a physical existence, but indeed you have chosen this path, so it's yours, all of it. So own and accept all you are without question, without a negative thought, because you are loved regardless.

'You do no harm, do no ill, you will have others that do that onto you, forgive them, because currently they do not understand what they are doing, they do not understand what they are saying or committing to, and they have not really done so. They have committed to the darker side of life that is a choice that they had to make within their lives, no matter how old they were, it was chosen.

'We are all responsible for our choices and understandings, and we must always be so, there can be no coercion or pushing from an external energy to get you to where you need to be, it must be from your free will and your choice. So choose, all of you in all you forms, in *all your ways, in all your lives, in all your colours, in all your people, in all your world, choose, all of you, all of the time, and all of the ways, in the light, in the dark, the up the down, choose, all of you, and smile, because you are as you are meant to be.*

'You have that Equilibrium; you walk the middle path, and you understand there are those who don't, who choose the darker side, and that's where they reside. They come into your lives and cause havoc, and upset, and sorrow, but you forgive them and walk away, because in feeding that energy you become that light yourself. So you let go and forgive, for that is the only thing that you can do, that is the only energy that matters, the energy of forgiveness, and God. So you see, the Equilibrium runs through everything and everywhere, the balance has to be.

'This planet has been out of equilibrium for so long, but it will soon be coming back to the light, into the balance, and you will see it; birth is a difficult process, it hurts, and you will see and feel that hurt, but you will know that the end result will be more wonderful for everyone than you can possibly imagine.

'We told you some years ago that there was a storm coming to and upon and inside this Earth, it has happened mainly within it, and now it is coming without it. It is coming to every single person in every single way and no one can escape the truth. There are many who have tried to place their head in the sand and indeed if that is what they will choose then that is what they will be, they will stay on in the existence of that time line and live that out, but there are others who look for an Earth of peace, love and beauty and hope, where everyone will reside within that created light. So will there be two Earths? Yes in a form, will there be two ways? Yes in a form ... although you may not realise it, you've already decided on which one you were going to be upon, and that will be completely understood by you all, it's all in your energy.

'I come to you now because it is close; tipping of the scales a little more everyday, where new information is being released to you and declassified. If you search you would be surprised, maybe shocked, at what is available for viewing, but it is alright, knowledge brings peace, it is promise, there is love, there is God, and there is hope. No matter who tries to move you off your equilibrium, no matter who tries to push you off your stool, or move you in a way into the darker agenda of negativity, and fear, do not go, do not allow yourself to be riled or upset,

keep calm, keep connected and keep to yourself and love all. You all know this information, but it is being returned to you now because there will be some situations that arise where you will need that calmness, that understanding, many have forgotten.

'There will be testing situations you will hear about that will inflame and upset you, but it is not because of you, it is in spite of you. You will feel angry for those before, you will feel angry for those who do not know, and for the innocence of the lives that have been wasted throughout the years. You will feel angry, want to vent that anger, and want to hit something, that's fine. But don't hurt your hands because you're going to need them. **There are still many secrets to be revealed upon this Earth, and 'thy will be done', not all by people of this Earth, can you imagine the look on the faces of the people when they realise that? How do you think they will cope when they see people coming from the sky? They will get their big guns out? It won't happen, because there are many who are in control and will have released it in a way where it will be acceptable, for some anyway, it will be up to you to know.**

'There is one completion that is being waited upon, when this is achieved and the moment is right, then all will start for un-awakened eyes, it has in some degrees already, but you will not hear about that part yet. **Please do not feel sorry or sorrow for those who have passed, or hear who have passed, for they will indeed be helped in the manner in which they need. It is all agreed, all chosen. Do not feel anger for them, for that is wasted energy and emotion. What you need to do is look for the future, and to help the people through the darkness that stems in front of them, because that is all they will see, they will not know that the light is there, because they cannot see it, so you have to show them, point it out to them, how bright and light and amazing things will be now, and how they are loved.**

'Yes there will be a lot of anger and upset, yes there will be a lot of sorrow about your parents and your families, all suffering, for needlessly suffering, when they need not have done. You must understand that everybody has an individual choice to do what they need to do, it is not our job to save everybody from their pathway, that is their choice, and their way; however, they will be at least shown the choice that they need to make. They will know one way or the other. We understand how important it is for your families to know, to have

that protection around them, we hear you and we comply as much as we can.

'The Energy is being brought around you all now, as information and Light; it is all in light codes, and going directly into your DNA, and some days you will feel so exhausted and tired, and other days you will feel so busy and you won't know what to do. Some days you will feel something strange is going on and it is, so pay attention to the way you feel, it's nothing personal, it's just the way you are accepting the information that is coming at you at that time.

'Whatever happens your physical self may not know, but your eternal self and your light self will, and it is one battling the other, but it is not a negative battle, it's a battle of positivity and light for the balance. Light codes are being activated within you, these codes have been suppressed for thousands of years and were deliberately co-engineered within your bodies to stop the development of your DNA, but within the energetic realms, within the power of all, that is, there has been work done to reverse a little of that engineering, so is why some of you may feel a little unsettled at times.

'There are many working on this side of life to work within the biological, the physiological, chemical and crystal, they are all working together to make something new and wonderful for all on Earth. There are thousands, thousands who have left and returned, left and returned who have gone round in that vein for many centuries, purely to get to this point in this time line, because it was known what was coming.

'We all give thanks for (sitters) sitting here tonight and listening to me talk on this subject. We hope that you gain a little peace and understanding and know that there is not any negative there that can hold you back now. Your Earth is secured.

'My name is Simeon, and I come to you now to tell you that you will all see what is your reality, and what is not.

'Thanks and Blessings to you all and may your Light shine around, always.'

Next are some selections from a recording of a Dr Peebles communication.

42. Dr Peebles - 27th October 2021
Trust in God

'It is a remarkable time to be upon this planet Earth. Rather than feeling that you are being punished in some sort of way by the universe, understand that you are being asked by God to do some hard work here at this given time; to not fall into fear. To realize that you have the ability as you band together as human beings to rise up against the sorts of things that are happening upon the planet Earth that are striving to control you, to manipulate you, to cut you down, to stop you from crossing your own borders, from seeing family members and friends and others.

'You have this opportunity to change this world, to get people to understand that you need each other.

'Human beings have come together in this lifetime, this particular time period, to create change and growth together, to magnify love upon the planet Earth. That is the point and purpose of you being here at this given time. There are always going to be people who are going to try to drag everybody down, try to control and manipulate everybody. There are going to be lots of these sorts of things happening for centuries to come, but there is a beautiful change that is happening here right now and that is that human beings are awakening to their hearts, and they are awakening to the awareness that they want to behave as one family rather than to hold each other at arm's length.

'This is a time period upon the planet where human beings are going to have to band together in order to make the changes happen because, otherwise, if you're going to continue to comply then you are going to find yourselves crying in the corner saying, "Why, why did it happen?" Because, my dear friends, the many rather than the few are letting the few rather than the many have charge.

'Walk by faith, not by sight, and trust that God is real. Reach to God, seek God. Surrender your doubts and fears and begin living your life through faith.

'God is not going to come pouncing on you and say, "I'm here!" and shake you. God is not going to move you around like a chess piece on a board either. God, is just loving you, that's it; God keeps saying, "I love you! I love you!" And waits and waits and waits on human beings to respond to and acknowledge that. God loves you right here and now,

not because of what you are doing, not because of how you think, not what belief you have.

'You don't have to seek God in a particular way. Just seek in your heart. Look for the love that is there within you. That is the God within you.

'Does God have a plan? Well, the plan is to love you, and God's following through on that every day.'

Below is again from Dr Peebles, this time from one of the transcripts that Summer Bacon kindly shared with me.

43. Dr Peebles - 3rd November 2021

*'Get a little bit of a sense of humour here about your world that is absolutely absurd in so very many ways with so many different ideologies that are coming to the surface, things that are being splattered all over your news channels and that sort of thing. **Trying to stir you up, stir up the masses into mass hysteria, mass fear and so on and so forth. Start to see that, stand back from it objectively and realise so much of this is part of a manipulation that is going on. Don't allow for it to take over your mind, do not allow for the mind control to happen to you. You have control and charge of your mind; remember this.***

'When you are watching the television, you make your decisions as to whether or not you're buying what they're selling, and you make a decision as to whether or not you're going to adopt certain philosophies into your life, certain spiritual perspectives, certain perspectives on whatever it might be. These are all choices that you make, that the world can't make for you, but can dish out an awful lot for you to consider. But remember, seek your heart first, before you start to buy into anything anybody's selling to you in the world.

'Seek your heart, trust and understand your intuition there. That is where you're going to step into your power, that is where you're going to understand why we can't do it for you, why we cannot just simply say, "This is the way it is, here's the who, where, what, when, and why of what is happening". We have no permission to do that because there are human beings upon the Earth who are in their own education, who are striving to control the masses right

now, who are striving, if you will, to change the world through vaccinations, all driven by financial gain and financial drive, in other words, driven by greed, that is what is occurring here.

'But these are individuals who are growing as well, and we're not out to point fingers and name names, and that sort of thing. Search your heart and you'll understand who, what, where, when, and why all of this is happening. And people will say, "I don't understand it, why would anybody want to take charge of the world, to control the world, to have that sort of power". Well, my dear friends, that is a false power that they believe they can have. It is very temporary at best, even if they were to be able to conquer the world the way they thought they should, to change everybody to comply with a certain way of living and such, it would be something that would be temporary because eventually every single one of you is going to drop the coat of the human form and come over here, and eventually these individuals shall come over here and they will be looking at their lives, and they will be re-living their lives, and they will be scratching their heads and saying, "Why, why, why would I do such a thing to anybody".

'So be aware that all over the world there's going to be a lot of skirmishes; there's going to be a lot more uprisings; a lot of things you're not even going to hear about. There's going to be a lot of people helping and assisting the masses. Right at this very moment, for example, there are children that are being freed-up and certainly they are being given the opportunity to, at long last, live a beautiful life upon the Earth. There are military forces that are at work, that are helping and assisting the many rather than the few but, in the background, and again, we cannot tell you the, who, what, where, when, and why of it, but it is happening my dear friends, so take heart.

'Good things are happening upon the Earth right now; so many things behind the scenes, that you're not even aware of because, frankly my dear friends, it's not going to make the television stations any money to share it. So instead, there is a need, a necessity, for these individuals in order to keep what they believe is the better reality alive, they have a need to manipulate and to control and to give to the world what they think the world needs to hear in order to maintain that control.

'So understand the same thing occurs within your politicians. Not all of them, we're never going to say that anybody here on the Earth is evil, *but you're simply in a place of great misunderstanding, and not all of your politicians are in any way shape or form trying to manipulate the masses, or do terrible things, so many of them go into politics with the awareness that they want very much to serve; they want very much to create good changes and such; but there is certainly a foundation into which they step, which has been carried on for many, many centuries and certainly this is something that is very hard to change.*

'But there are, again, take heart, individuals who are working on the inside of that, striving to change politics, the way they're being worked in a positive direction, getting back to basics, which means getting back to helping humanity rather than hindering humanity, getting back to helping the many rather than the few move forward.

'So certainly you will find that there will be some spectacular changes that will be for the positive, as a result of people coming together, expressing themselves loudly; sometimes shamelessly, and realizing that there are going to be moments where you're going to have to stop and really listen in order to make those changes happen in the world.

'So human beings are going to be cooperating more on different levels, and they're going to say, "Enough is enough", and, "We want to make ourselves heard". You're going to join together arm in arm, there will be situations wherein people will invade different political buildings in the world, not just in the United States of America but in other countries, saying, "Enough is enough, we're going to take it down, we don't want this anymore, we are not going to stand for it anymore". There will be uprisings with individuals who will say, "We are going to band together and we're not going to pay our taxes until things begin to change so that we can have our freedoms and securities once again", rather than having to comply in order to make this happen.

'There are lots of things that are happening in your world, the addition of the vaccination passports is going to be something that will be causing a lot of skirmish's because individuals do not want this. Most individuals are saying "No", the numbers and such that you are hearing in your news networks and everything else, take a moment, close your eyes, relax, release, surrender, search your heart and see if those are real or not, because often times numbers are very easy to manipulate. Statistics really aren't necessarily counting what is going on in your heart for example.

'So remember, take it all with a bit of a grain of salt here, and search your heart. Trust your intuition; trust yourself, your instincts as well. Trust your instincts and really, when they are heightened realise that that is telling you something, pay attention there. If you have a feeling that you must do something, for example to stock up on food or what have you, perhaps gather together blankets to give to children who are in need, by all means move with that rhythm inside of yourself, that is God speaking to your heart, pressing on your heart saying, "It's time now to take some action in a particular area".

'This is a time, on this school called planet Earth, that is very, very, if you will, again, going to feel like insanity. It is going to be a little crazy making, and you're going to say, "When is it going to stop?", and it's not going to stop until you, humanity, stops being so crazy here and realises that you've got to embrace each other and say, "We are sorry, will you forgive me, we need to stand together, we need to band together, we need to work together".

'It's going to happen, perhaps one person at a time, two people at a time; hundreds of thousands of people banding together, eventually, and creating beautiful massive change on the planet Earth.

'We want you to know there are so many who are in concern about what they would call "Great evils" that are happening upon the Earth. Lots of people who are saying, "Well this place is more evil than not and so on and so forth". In truth, it is not more evil, it is more loving.

'**Human beings are moving consciously into a greater, deeper understanding of love, in the 5th dimension of understanding of love; that is beyond compare. It is where people will begin to awaken to themselves as the spiritual beings that they are, which means that you will have more sightings of UFO's, Extra Terrestrials, of that you would call ghosts, that are really your spirit guides and such, of angels and angelic intervention, and that sort of thing. It's going to become something that is going to be talked about more and more by those who are indeed awakening, by staying in a place of love in their hearts.**

'Is it difficult? Of course it is sometimes, but once you do it you'll get the hang of it, because it feels good once again. You'll say, "It really does feel better to relax, release, and surrender in a given moment when everything seems to be going haywire". The insanity is working to change you into understanding that insanity is doing the same thing over and over and over again, the same way through wars and disagreement and arguing and pummelling of one another, trying to force feed each other your opinions and perspectives. It doesn't work, never has, never will.

'The only things that will work on the Earth are respect and love, gratitude, a willingness to operate from peace, a willingness to be gentle and kind with nature, a willingness to make some changes in your life, even though it might be painful. Changing the structuring of your life, not living your life centred round stuff, but rather centred round the things that you are going to take with you; the things that are within your heart. This is what you are being asked to do, and if you stay in the other place of centring and focusing around the things you have, this that you acquire, money in the bank, etc., etc., if those are the places that you are looking all the time for your happiness to be, you will never ever be happy.*

'It is time now to understand the focus must be retained on those things that have true value rather than those things that do not.

'Yes, money in the bank, we understand that's necessary for some things, you can buy your food and have shelter and have clothing and that sort of thing, but it's when you start to obsess about those things, when you feel that that is more important than anything, when counting the money in your bank account takes precedence over sitting for twenty minutes with God every day, that is where it's out of balance my dear friends. It's time to regain your balance; it is time to take charge of your spirit; it's time for you to focus upon those things that really do matter; those things that are within your heart. Seek God without failing, seek constantly, without ceasing, and you will find that you will feel better, more and more.*

'It is a time period where it's very divisive, but this is necessary, the soil must be tilled, there is no going backward, there is only going forward. There is a new world that is being created now, not the new world order that some speak of, and are fearful of, that is not what's going to reign.

'There is a new world that is going to reorganize itself in a way that is going to be beautiful, because it's going to be helping the planet Earth too, at long last, clean-up and clean-out the dark* *areas of the heart, and bring to the surface more and more love. But again, it's not going to happen without certain tensions.'*

Next, a contribution kindly sent to me by my friend, Ray Edwards, who is well known for his spiritual poetry. Ray channelled the following message, via trance mediumship, from *"The Philosopher"*, with poetic phrase included for us to enjoy.

44. The Philosopher - 12th November 2021
Truth and Trust

'We wish to speak this evening about truth and trust and these have already been touched on by some of the other speakers. Truth and trust – two words so close that only one letter separates them. They are like the opposite sides of the same coin – and the bond that keeps those two sides together is love.

'For who can you trust if there is no love? If there is no trust how are you to perceive the truth? Where do you experience your truth? When your mind tells you something is true – is it because another has spoken the words and told you this? Or is it because you have experienced this yourself, you have worked it out for yourself.

'Do you trust yourself? For it is important - and this has been spoken of before – for you to be honest with yourself; for you to be open-minded, open-hearted; and to allow your truth to shine clearly through your thoughts, your words, your actions, your intentions. Yet in your world as you cast your eyes around – you can see many good and well-meaning people whose truths are not the same. Does this make them untruthful? Or merely that their experience and their beliefs are somewhat different?

'This medium, as he writes his poetry – he has a verse which he has called, "Your Truth".....

'Your truth,
May not be my truth,
Which in truth
May not be right;
But if your truth,
Allows for my truth,

144

There's no need

For us to fight...'

'What matters is the feeling of the vibration, the frequency of the loving energy that flows through you, with you and around you. When you find the truth you feel it in your heart, in your gut – for this is what resonates with your own vibration. You know that everything is energy, and energy fluctuates and moves, and it massages, it connects. When there is a truth spoken you feel it deeply in your heart – this is because it is travelling along the Web of Energy, the Web of Love. Its essence cannot be anything except truthful. It is important every one of you to sit and connect, to find your own truth.*

'Truth is not in the words of another. Truth is in your connection with the Divine, with the Source of All, with God – whatever label you wish to attribute to it. When you are connected, when you are in harmony with the energy of the Source – there you will find your truth. As you cast around your world today – and I have to say that sometimes we view with great sadness the behaviour of some in your world at this time – as you cast your eyes around, who do you feel you can trust?

'As you look in the eyes of a politician – can you believe - can you have trust? Do you believe they speak the truth? For these are people who have trained themselves to be able to avoid the truth; to manipulate the truth; to make situations occur in the way that suits their personal political ends. Many are in these positions because they seek the power, the wealth, and the influence. Many find themselves in these situations being influenced by others who are also within the domain of power and influence and strength.

'It is a hard road for you to walk in these days where you must pick your way between the boulders of inaccuracies, of lack of honesty, of untruthfulness. Unfortunately in your world at this time it is the financial wealth and power which seems to exert the greatest influence. The Great Sage spoke of this when he said.....

'I have seen

That those who seek to take the world

And shape it to their will,

Never, I notice, succeed;

For the Earth is a vessel so sacred

That at the mere approach of the profane
It is marred;
As they reach out their fingers for it
It is gone;
For a time in the world
Some force their way ahead,
And some are left behind;
Yet the world,
In its goodness,
Is always to honesty inclined.'

Clearly "The Philosopher", like all the spirit guides, is awake to current world events. If anyone would like to find more of Ray Edwards poetry he can be found on Facebook. (See Links)

The following, is once again taken from a transcript of a communication from Dr Peebles.

45. Dr Peebles - 17th November 2021

'Because you're great creators, and your technologies are expanding, you're going to find that your sciences are going to eventually prove the existence of that energy that comes and radiates off of your hands; and how it is used; and how it is directed through your thoughts; through your willingness to allow for the love to flow through you into another person to help to heal.

'What an incredibly joyful, amazing place that you live upon. Create with joy in your heart and know that there is always, always going to be a possibility of a better world. There are always going to be people who are going to try to break it down, tear it down, try to destroy, and try to control, but eventually human beings will come to know that it is much more fun to create and spread the light, love, inspiration, and truth that you are, than to try to tear things down.

'Essentially you will understand that what happens upon the planet Earth through your wars, deceptions, corruptions within your

governments and other things, it's not helping anybody, not even those who are doing it. It is crushing the planet Earth on very many levels and eventually human beings will come to understand this.

'You will find that there are fantastic creators upon your Earth who are going to start to realise that there are animals who need assistance, and some of these animals cannot be returned to nature, and there are, of course, many places where human beings are helping animals in distress, but there's going to other ways in which you are going to create an even better environment for these animals to live in.

'You're going to find even a deeper level of compassion in helping and assisting the animals to live wonderful lives until the very end. (And many of these animals are going to be human beings). A much deeper compassionate world that will be willing to take care of the elders, to learn from the elders, to help and to assist the elders, not just thrust them into a bed and leave them there to rot, but to help and to assist, to find ways to help them to continue to create and to continue to enjoy life, even if it's on a lesser scale than it was before, it will still be on a magnificent scale because it will come from love.

'Right now there are many things happening within your governments around the world. There are many governments who are striving to create totalitarian societies. There are the few trying to control the many, trying to create a reality that they can then feel they are on top of the world, they think it's their power, but it's going to work against them ultimately because they're not going to find peace there.

'They are going to say, "Well, then I even need more power", through greediness and such they will never satiate their appetite for power, it will never be enough.

'The only thing that they will ultimately find is that love is enough; because love doesn't stop, love is continuously growing. It is not an end point, it is the alpha and the omega all at one time, the beginning and the ending, always and forever more, and that, my dear friend, is God, the expansion of the God light within you.

'It's going to be magnificent, as you explore more and more within your sciences the things that will come to the surface, that no longer can be hidden.

'That which is hidden shall be revealed.

147

'Right now, from your eyes is hidden perhaps the movement of spirits, your guides around you, family members on the other side, and that sort of thing. Your sciences are going to bump right into them as you learn more about different frequencies, and how they work, as you learn to fine tune that, and you will find that there will be communication and contact with spirits in other dimensions.

'It's going to happen before you're going to know it, people involved in the projects will know it, and not talk about it for quite a while, but eventually technology is going to catch up a little bit more, not entirely, with all the vibrational frequencies that there are in the universe.

'There are more and more still, as you dig deeper and deeper into more and more dimensions you will find that there is even more to study, and to explore; that's the beauty and wonder of existence; creativity and expansion of yourself, always.

'So take heart, your world is not going to hell in a hand basket, goodness gracious no, your world is in a state of upliftment. Oh, yes, yes, yes, it's not easy; it's like taking a table and moving it across the room with a bunch of stuff on it and trying to move it carefully so that nothing falls off.

'It's not an easy time, some things come tumbling down, and they're going to be replaced by other things that are better than what were there before, even more beautiful, ever more wondrous, even more magnificent. Oh my dear friends, don't give up, certainly don't give up.

'There will be spiritual and political leaders who will be coming to the surface; great men and women of great faith in God, who will come to the surface, and will help and to assist the world. Nothing is ever, ever stagnant, it is always growing.

'There are many things happening behind the scenes that you are unaware of, we are helping and assisting always; nurturing that little baby right now who's going to come to the surface and become a great spiritual teacher in the next twenty-five years. We are working with these souls, we are working with these beings, we are working with each and every one of you, and we care deeply about the light that you carry within, it is your greatest gift.

'Human beings are going to turn more and more and more away from the medical system, and more and more to natural healing, natural modalities, energetics, as the energetics become more and

more understood upon the planet Earth, the energetics of light, love, inspiration, and truth.

'There will be more laying on of hands, there will be more in terms of human beings helping and assisting, not only in the physical, but also to help people in the mental state as well. To help people clear more and more of garbage that they have carried for centuries, a sudden dissolution of old past life paradigms that no longer serve them.

'There will be people who will help and assist with this, already are people like that, but it's going to be even more magnificent, can you fathom how remarkable it will be once the sciences understand that you can see the light projecting from ones hands and by knowing that it is there and seeing it you can start to through, for example, seeing that on a computer screen, start to learn how to fine tune it and how to focus as a beam of light, as a laser of sorts that goes directly to a tumour and destroys it with love? Love it to death, what a wonderful way to create fantastic healing for the many rather than the few.

'It's a remarkable time upon this school called planet Earth, fantastic things coming to the surface. Always there will be wars, for the time being you will see that, and you'll say, "Not again", yes my dear friends, again, because human beings still don't understand that what they are creating is destroying, and what they can do is create to create even more to uplift, to rebuild, that is the direction you are going in.

'But, in the meantime, certain things are going to happen and they have to happen. Stirring up of energies, like a light storm coming to the Earth, tingling everybody from head to toe where they at long last are awakened and say, "There's got to be something more than what meets the eye".

'Eventually the lion and the lamb will lay down together, partners in peace, and they'll have a little chat together. You the lion, me the lamb, "Look at that, aren't we quite different, isn't that glorious? My goodness gracious, what can we do together that will create more peace and love in the world? Let us take a bit of you and a bit of me, your power, my gentleness, and let us go forth and be the great creators we are individually, and put ourselves together, and find what we can create when we unite".

'You are beautiful spirits, we love you so, so, very much my dear friends. You can only change the world by making God first, the God *light within you, bringing that to the surface and shining it brightly forever more. God bless you indeed.'*

It was lovely to read in the above communication from Dr Peebles that, *'many of these animals are going to be human beings'*, personally, I have known of this path of soul evolution for some years now. I even wrote a short book on the subject titled: *"The Evolvement of the Soul: The Origins and Development of Life".*

Next, is another communication from Jonathan, via the medium, Elaine Thorpe.

46. Jonathan - November 2021
Earth Changes

'I know that at the current time there is a lot going on in your physical world, and I would say to you be strong in your physical world, try to come together and love one another and unite. People are uniting all over the world, coming together, fighting for their freedom, like never before.

'I don't think there has been anything quite like it in your world. Many people gather, in different countries, to try to unite together. That is wonderful, considering that many of you may have never seen each other before, yet you gather together for the same subject, the same cause.

'Well it is happening everywhere, and it is bringing quite a surge of energy, and of course what they are doing is connecting their minds to the universe, without they realise it.

'So the universe is going to act upon it. Thought is energy; and energy is travelling at a great speed. It has no limitations, so what you think has a cause and an effect, so try to think in a positive manner, and it will have a positive outcome.

'So I will bring that subject to another subject, that in your world, things are going to change, mountains will move, water will raise, Earth will shake. It doesn't mean to say that you've all got to run and be frightened.

'The Earth changes much like you do, it is always going to progress, as it has done for millions and millions of years. It is now decided to make

great change; a lot of you think that the world is going to come to an end just because the Earth is shifting. But for many years land has shifted, and volcanoes have erupted to create new land. Or land has parted, and in between that land comes sea. It creates a new island, perhaps, so you need to look at it from that point of view and stop fearing. Because the world is always going to shift itself and progress, it always has done and always will do; there is no doubt about it.

'If you look back through historical times you will see from the start that it was a barren place, before the humans came to it. Parts of it were beautiful, parts of it were barren, yet it managed to grow things, it managed to progress itself, to make it habitable for humans to thrive upon. It is really the only planet that surrounds you, with its cousins and brothers and sisters, I will call them, that is habitable; the rest are inhabitable. So I will say to you appreciate the Earth that you are in, appreciate each other, no matter how much you may annoy each other sometimes. Have love for one another, and do not be afraid of the Earth changes.

'We send our fondest of love to you, and remember, we are never going to leave you, or desert you, in any way. If you need us, we are here for you. Talk to your guides, talk to your loved ones, you are not going mad, we truly exist. In fact, it is practically proven that the consciousness lives on after physical death; there are so many near-death experiences that you cannot deny it. Listen to them, listen to their experiences, you may learn something from them.'

Next is more transcript dialogue from Dr Peebles via Summer Bacon.

47. Dr Peebles - 2nd December 2021

'There will be changes on your Earth; there will be discussions about extraterrestrials and such coming to the planet Earth. There will be more wide-open conversations about the possibilities in terms of the existence of spirits, and the existence of spirituality, and the existence of love as an energy field that is real, and alive, that is absolutely the greatest force in the universe, that holds everything together.

'Human beings sometimes seems like they're not getting much smarter, but you are, you're learning, you're growing, your sciences are expanding and touching different places in the universe, finding out that there are new frequencies there.

'There will be communications and such, down the road apiece, it's not going be for a while yet, but there will be communications from the heavens to the Earth, we don't mean from heaven to the Earth necessarily, that's happening in your hearts all the time, but we mean through your technologies bumping into the technologies of extraterrestrials, those who are not of the Earth, and having communications there.

'You might even, yourself, if you are highly sensitized to it, in several years, find yourself suddenly standing somewhere and hearing tones coming to you, and you will hear these tones and you will say, "What is that coming from, is that a clock, is that something on the television somewhere?"

'But you'll realise there's nothing near you and yet, you'll be hearing these sounds. Well that will mean that you have really heightened yourself, your senses, your awareness's, your vibrational frequency, wherein you are dipping in to other dimensions, other frequency bands, where you are hearing the sounds and tones. Perhaps even the sounds of the Celestial Choir, and the music that is there, that is so exquisite and beautiful and stirring of the heart.

'So there are plenty of things that are going to be happening, and we certainly do agree it is time to wake up. It's time to attune yourself to the mystic that you are, because that is where you're going to find your salvation. That is where you're going to find your greatest growth, adhering to yourself, understanding that the stirrings within you have value.

'When you feel something is wrong, perhaps you simply say, "Ah ha, I felt that so strongly, I'm going to trust that". When you feel something is really right for you then you say, "Ah ha, I'm really going to trust that and I'm going to operate as if that is truly right for me".

'Try to get in touch with what is happening inside of you. These so called feelings really are vibrational frequencies that you're sensing, and if you awaken to them you can really start to read the bandwidths of the universe; read the bandwidths of human life around you; read the various things that are happening upon your planet Earth; the actions or inactions of governments and such.

'Go into that, and say, "Well, I wonder what that's all about, why are they not taking action in a particular way at a particular time, what is that about? Are they hiding something, is there something else I need to know?" Go inside of yourself, look for it, feel it, and perhaps you will see an entire story unfolding inside of you that is very real, because you can feel it, and you'll sense the realness of it.

'There are so many things happening in your world right now that we understand. There are lots of negotiations going on between countries. There are human beings planning a course of action that is going to hurt lots of people, and that sort of thing. Well, those things are indeed going on, are you going to sit and fret about it, or are you going to pray about it? You just simply send love and prayers and say, "I would like to simply ask that more love goes into this equation, I'm shining my light brightly upon this dark surface and asking that these human beings wake up to the love that they are, that they come to understand themselves, that they come to understand that the control does not come from trying to control everything from the outside in, but from the inside out, through greater and greater love."

'Watch as your world starts to turn in a different direction. Watch as governments come to the surface and say, "You know something, we're simply not going to play this game anymore, and we're going to get back to our lives, and we're going to make it even better, and so on and so forth." And they're going to do this through lots of communication within the government, through speaking to members of their communities and such, and it will turn things around in a very beautiful way, with less fear, and more love, which will eventually become a slogan on your Earth, 'less fear, more love'. That is the point and purpose of this period of time upon this school called planet Earth, as you are raised into the 5th dimension of understanding of love, God bless you indeed.'

Next, is an encouraging communication from the spirit guide, Monty, via the mediumship of Warren James.

48. Monty – 14th December 2021
The Great Awakening

'Your consciousness, which many of you are starting to truly hear and feel, others are yet to understand it, but they will. What you are experiencing is the impermanence of life. What you can change are other people's actions.

'What you cannot change is the natural cause.

'What you need to understand is natural cause, for it to become more active in your way of living. And that is happening naturally, not just for you, but for all.

'The people who run your world, I'm sorry if people disagree, there are people who run your world, and they don't want that to happen. They know it is coming, and they know it is going to happen, and they are trying to fight nature, and they can't change it.

'They may be able to stem its flow for a short time. They may be able to influence it a little, but they can't change it.

'Now you may have thought I was going to tell you that there is nothing you can change. That you can't change what is taking place in your world; but you can.

'It is them, those people, who consider themselves far grander, far wiser and higher; it is they who will fail here my friends.

'They rely on you doing as you are told but consciousness is rising everywhere; and they can't stop it.

'The greatest thing you can do right now, is to learn to raise your consciousness to the highest possible degree. The way to do this, my friends, is to not try to raise your consciousness, but allow nature to take you where you need to go.

'Many other people's consciousnesses are also trying right now to rise. And it will happen, my friends, it has to happen for it is nature. Those who are trying to prevent it cannot prevent that nature from taking place.

'Consciousness all over the world is rising and rising. As one of your great philosophers once said in your world, "The truth vibrations are coming", and they are; and all around the world, this is happening for many more people my friends.

'Whilst I know it feels dark for you right now. You must know that the true failing will be those who try, desperately, to prevent nature taking its course, and nature must take its course.

'Consciousnesses of this world you occupy and its frequency must rise and become more profound upon how humanity lives. And those changes are happening; that is why, others wish to oppress you.

'**But if your consciousness is rising and strong, if you are connected with it, if you are aware of it, you will know no fear, you will not accept any form of oppression and you will not do as you are told if your consciousness says it is wrong.**

'**Consciousness is rising all over your planet, not just the people, animal kind, plant life, even insects, will be affected, by the rise of the consciousness of you all.**

'**So, rather than spending time getting annoyed about people whose consciousness seems to be ever so oppressed, spend more time focusing on yours. Because the quicker your consciousness rises, the quicker other people around you, their consciousness will rise; and then they will influence others, and each other, and your oppressors will have no choice but to crumble.'**

The following and final communication I have included from 2021 came through the medium Al Fike.

ET's, angels, archangels, along with spirit guides truly do exist, and all play a role in this wondrous universe.

49. Archangel Michael – 17th December 2021
Declaration of the Beginning of the Transformation of Our World

'I am who many have called the Archangel Michael. I am known by many names. I say to you that even we who are involved with the workings of the universe will come to assist you in this crucial time of transformation. We do not concern ourselves with the daily affairs of men but indeed, all resources are called into action and engagement with this time that is fast approaching.

'You will be able to rely upon our services and our efforts to uplift humanity for it is not that we are immune to feel love for you, for we do love you as we love all of God's creation, and all of the universe. It is *that we have our place and our roles to fulfil, and know that in the case of these conditions and situations that are forthcoming, that we will walk with man and bring the powers vested within our beings for the upliftment and awakening of humanity and this world.*

'All are being called, beloved souls. All are being called. The clarion call of God is heard by all and there will be a response like none other. You will see and witness many miracles and blessings upon your world. Many of you will be instrumental in bringing these blessings forward. Be assured, my beloved and beautiful friends, children of God, that all that is required, and necessary in the coming times to assure the awakening and survival of humanity, will be given. God has decreed it so, and so it shall be given without restriction, and so it shall be given in great abundance.

'God has involved all the powers of the universe to ensure that His plan will be successful and that the world will be transformed. Be assured, beloved souls. Be assured that this shall be the case, that you may trust in the Will of God and the actions of God, your Creator, our Creator for all that is forthcoming shall indeed be.

'I proclaim this to your world; that the world shall be healed and awakened and that life shall be awakened in ways that have not been awakened in the past, that light shall be present in ways that have not been present in the past, that all shall come in the glory of God, the Most High and Wondrous Creator.

'God bless you, beloved souls. I am Archangel Michael. I have not spoken through this instrument before but I come with this message. I urge you to bring this message into your hearts and your souls and your minds so that you may truly believe. God bless you. God bless you all.'

The following, just part of a longer message, also came through the medium Al Fike; and to remind readers, all of the messages via Al Fike can be found in full at the divine love sanctuary website. (See Links)

50. Orion – 12th February 2022
Escalating Earth Changes are Coming

'Changes are upon you now, my beloved friends. Great change will continue to unfold as God's plan unfolds for the destiny of humanity. But I must say that the expression and unfolding of this plan will not be one of ease and comfort and reassurance, but one where many things that you have come to rely upon, and ways of life that have brought great comfort and security to you, will be no more.

'Thus, you, along with all of your brothers and sisters upon this planet, must make great adjustments and assume that the world as it is will not be sustained, nor will the world that is coming have much similarity to what has been and is at this moment.

'This is why we are preparing you. We are continuing to voice our perceptions and concerns to all who will listen. With great change, all those things that man has constructed in his own image, that which is not in harmony with God's laws and plan, must capitulate. In the ashes, the phoenix will rise and a new world will be born, a world that is different indeed, but is in much greater harmony with God. Your lives will be simplified. Your ways of interacting will be somewhat limited. Although, as the challenge of a new situation emerges, the gifts and capacities that you have to communicate with one another will be expedited and emerge in powerful ways, surprising ways for each of you.

'You will not feel a sense of isolation and disconnection from your brothers and sisters around the world. Rather, that sense will be augmented and intensified by your abilities and gifts to communicate mind to mind, soul to soul. In all of this chaos, in all of this recalibration of how humanity lives upon the Earth plane, the many spirits, angels, and those of us who are your brothers and sisters will converge upon your planet and assist you in the uplifting and reshaping of your world, as God's Hand is upon all that is to be, all that will happen.

'So, there will be harmony rather than great pain and distress and difficulty. Although, if you ascribe to this response and reaction to what has taken place, then indeed you will experience this as will many upon your Earth plane, a great distress and fear, confusion. But as you have been told and taught, it is for you to be the rock, the steadiness that will bring truth to humanity and assure humanity that what has taken place

is necessary for the consequences of what humanity has created, and would continue to create would be far harsher than what will happen at this time. For humanity, given its own devices, desires, and intentions, would have created deeper darkness and greater destruction. This cannot be, for God cannot allow His precious Earth to be destroyed, to be abused, and to be downtrodden in darkness; though there is much, of these conditions in the world.

'What you are experiencing today is both light and dark, but what could come in the future has no light and greater darkness. So, the resetting and recalibration of life upon the Earth is now in process and will intensify in many ways. I urge you to be in prayer, to seek guidance; to walk in this world in such a way that you will come to accept what is coming.

'As your earthly time marches on, there will be events that will be dramatic and difficult to comprehend. The world will feel as if it has been turned upside down. You must find your equilibrium, beloved friends, in such a chaotic world. You are used to the luxuries, the pleasantness, the comforts, and the abundance of the material life. Many things you take for granted, and many things you have come to rely upon, and see as necessities.

'I do not wish to engender fear within you, my friends, but to tell you, that your greatest comfort, and your greatest necessity, is your relationship with God, the Creator of All.

'For in building this relationship ever stronger and wider, expansive in its scope, you will be guided in such a way, provided for in such a way, that the deprivation of those things that will fall away from you will not be felt. Rather, you will adjust to a new way of being in the world, come to understand that the world must be this way in order for God's plan to be fulfilled.

'Many of you do not see yourselves as leaders nor as great channels of light and expressions of truth. But I say to you, within your soul is a great light and that light must come to the fore, liberated from the restrictions of your mind, restrictions that have been well in place for all of your life. Now is the time to loosen those restrictions, to be free of your fears, your cautions, and awaken to that part of you that is far beyond the limited capacity of your minds, and will be able not only to cope with the changes that are coming, but to thrive within it.

'This is God's intention for you and for all of His children. But because He will not thwart free will, it will be up to each individual to choose. As the choice becomes obvious and intense, so humanity will not be able to turn its face away from the choice given, and the conditions present. There is a desire within every individual to survive and to thrive. This will be the primary motivation of many. But the way of survival in the new world will be nothing like that which has been a part of the old world. So, you must come to the realization that you cannot take with you those accoutrements of a material life that are contrary to the Laws of God's Creation.

'**It is not that you will be laid bare and naked and without any shelter or ability to be safe from the intransigence of the material world. But rather, your view of these things and the way in which you utilize your life expressed will be dramatically different. You will not see that these necessities, as you call them of today, as important or required for tomorrow. A great detachment will come into your consciousness and a great faith will emerge, as you walk in the world as a precious soul of God's creation, rather than one that is hobbled by the error and great human condition that continues to thrive in your world.'**

'All that is coming is designed to break the great hold humanity has on these earthly conditions and to bring about liberation, truth, and light, to bring about the new world, a world where love may manifest freely. Those who are a part of your world, this world, will seek to build something beautiful and in greater alignment with God. It is a wondrous time to be alive, my friends. Many, many events, opportunities, and things of remarkable nature will come to be in your personal lives and in your service and instrumentality.'

'We are with you and will never leave. In fact, we will be closer and closer, your true friends, as will your angel friends and many more, even those upon the Earth plane who are a part of this great beginning. Your lives will open up in ways that you cannot fathom at this time. But indeed, these openings will bring great joy and relief and affirmation and all that which you need in order to step forward in confidence and strength.

'May God bless you with His Love, my beloved friends, for it is the power of this Love that awakens all, that opens up all that which I have spoken of that is a part of you, and your destiny. May God bless you, *my friends; I am Orion. I am happy to be with you today, this beautiful day of a new beginning. God bless you.'*

In regard to the above message, it is difficult to estimate when some of the predicted future times will unfold; as I'm sure they will, and to degree are already happening. This is why I included the earlier communication from Copernicus, *"The Measure of Time on Earth is Very Different Than in the Celestial Heavens"* (see number 11 in this chapter).

Next is part of a "Zac chat" conversation between Hazel Newton with Zac speaking through the medium Janet Treloar.

51. Zac - February 2022
Schumann Resonance & Harmonising with the Cosmos

'Imagine you're on a satellite you are looking at the Earth, and the Earth has of course its magnetic waves, but it also has this fundamental heart signature, this energy which is known as the Schumann resonance, as it gets higher and higher and higher, it is now very much in accordance with the solar energies coming in.

'It will always have worked together in certain ways, but it is incredibly powerful now, so the influxes, and particularly this year, we are seeing is the harmonization between the solar cosmic rays with the Earth's own higher vibrational resonance.

'Now before you think what is all this jargon, what it means is, as the cosmos and Earth finally come into a far more higher vibrational frequency and harmony, naturally, everything of the Earth will do so as well. But it is going through it at the moment, to get to that. So we are expecting there to be a softening, to be a harmonizing, to be a far more comfortable interaction within, between the cosmic and the Earth, but to get there, we are experiencing what the Earth and the cosmos are experiencing.

'Therefore, at this particular time, the electromagnetic waves, the movement of the poles, all of these things, all are being felt within individuals so much more because of this influx with the solar. When we started speaking, maybe last year, regarding the light and the photons coming in, this increased and helped the Earth to get to this

point, but initially that is what was being felt, rather than what was going on, now we have this balance between the two, but that means double whammy, does it not, in the body, feeling both. It will get more harmonized.

'It is a journey to go through, for that deep harmonizing on a higher level, it cannot happen unless the Earth is at the higher level, because the cosmos has been downplaying for a long time to reach the energies of the Earth for hundreds, thousands, years of time. Now, we're at a point where it is reaching up to match you.'

The following is part of a message that came through the medium Al Fike.

52. Nikola Tesla - 15th May 2022
Discourse on Spirit and Power of Love

'The universe is such a vast place, my friends. The knowledge of humanity is small indeed in comparison to what is the universe.'

'I made great strides in my day upon this Earth plane of yours but I did not do it alone. I had those helpers around me who assisted me to some degree. But most importantly, I had spirit helpers as well, and guidance. Not that I would sit as you do and ask. Rather, I would contemplate. I would consider various problems and solutions to those problems. Solutions would come; it was like something that would come out of nowhere. Of course, in my mind I thought this was the genius within the genius.

'But indeed, now that I live in this place, this part of reality, I understand the mechanism much better. Indeed, for each of you in your lives, depending upon your pursuits and interests and abilities, you too are being impressed and inspired. This has been so for the entire journey of humanity; that much has been given to the world in ways that many men, who are stuck within their mindful ideas, would not acknowledge; their egos insist that all comes from their minds and their minds alone.'

'Now I work in the spirit world, I am working on many projects. I am working with many scientists in your world, many of whom do not know that I am there, by their side. Indeed, by my side are many others. This is the way the universe works, my friends, that there is bountiful, generous, and purposeful support that comes

from those in the higher spheres of life to those in the lower spheres, and those upon the Earth plane.

'There is much that can come in this way. We are working with many who are coming to understand the physics of the universe. Some have an interest in the quantum physics. That, at this time, is not well-understood, but will be understood in time, and other dimensions of reality which will be understood as well.

'There is much yet to be revealed to humanity. Indeed, there is a deep caution that comes with our work, for humanity has an inclination to use the power of a truth, of an understanding that in ways are destructive rather than constructive. The moral nature of man is not well-developed. So, there is an inclination to utilize what is given in ways and means to make profit, to engender power, to control, to make war. This is not what is meant. Humanity must progress beyond these inclinations, and can certainly do so. But first, each individual must examine their own hearts, their own motivations, their own fears and that which they desire, for the world is rife with those who are filled with fear, anxiety, scepticism, a need to control the world, and to have that control at their fingertips.

'Yet, God has created an open-ended universe. So, control cannot truly be established. Instead, those who are curious, those who are scientists, those who are travellers upon the spiritual path, those who seek to serve humanity in many ways, must realize that knowledge, truth, service, creativity and invention, all are upon a continuum that flows in one direction, toward great progress. Not the progress that you have been told is progress, not the building up and the building up until all collapses under its own weight.

'True progress is in utilizing the Laws of the Universe for the benefit of all, not the control of all, not the ways in which control is gained through wealth and manipulation and politics and all of those things that humanity has empowered in order to ensure that there is control. Rather, true control comes from the individual who has opened themselves to the wonderment of the universe. At once, realizing how very small and how very wondrous is their being in God's creation. This engenders a deep humility, a deep respect for what life is. With this, no one can turn against their fellow man and express the need for great power and control. Rather, one sees that these things are false, that they are an illusion.

'Humanity must awaken to their own potentials, to who they are and what is truly a part of them. Humanity must come to see that it is important to prioritize their thoughts and actions in such a way that there is greater harmony. This leads to the power of perception, of understanding truth and seeing the world in a way that is in harmony with all that exists.

'Putting aside the illusion, that which you have been taught to believe in, the structures, and edicts of those in power, to manipulate and to control the majority. To be an independent thinker is a great thing. To be a soul who has a desire to be in light and harmony with all that is, is the highest aspiration. You can go far with these simple pieces of advice. You can in an instant come to see the world and the universe for what it is, given the right inclination and effort to do so.

'Yes, there is much waiting for humanity to discover, but the power of discovery put in the wrong hands can be a disaster. These discoveries must come slowly, drop by drop, into the consciousness of man so that they may adjust. Indeed, as the world changes and as life continues to evolve in the direction that is divinely inspired, then the strength and wisdom needed in order to incorporate greater discoveries and understanding of the universe is done in such a way that these dark inclinations are not given their range of expression.

'So, I see you are together in this light-filled place (the Monet Chapel) and you seek spiritual enlightenment and awakening. This is a powerful key to man's future, for this is the thing that is needed to truly be awakened within, in order to access the wisdom and love that is within each individual. That part of you that is the soul needs your attention, needs to be seen for what it is, that eternal part that is the greatest gift that God has given to humanity. All other things pale in comparison. All inventions and ideas and concepts which are primarily of the mind, and the wonderful invention of the mind, pale in comparison to the capacities of the soul to understand truly the reality of the universe, and to understand truly how this understanding may be utilized for the betterment of humanity.'

'There is much waiting to come to humanity, to help change the world and reform the world. May you all be a part of this, for there is a great plan afoot, my friends. We are all working toward the healing and transformation of your world, for it must be sustained; it must be *enlivened. It must come back to balance and harmony. Each of you may play your part in this; given you have the wisdom and the heart for it.*

'May God bless you in love; may you come to know love like you have never known love; may you come to see the world like you have never seen the world. May you come to love yourself, and all those around you, in a profound and deep way, that your entire life will reflect something beautiful and magnificent.

'I am Nikola Tesla. I do indeed come to Earth to assist others. I assist many, as many assist me. So, the chain of truth and light is sustained for all eternity. Thank you. Thank you, my friends.'

Next are some transcribed extracts from a communication with the spirit guide Zac. Firstly, he describes us as currently living and experiencing in a particular "cuboid" or "quadrant" of the universe where time and space are seen as linear. (While in his 26th dimension he operates outside of time and space).

However, with the coming Great Awakening and inflow of universal energies, it seems that more and more of us will begin to experience life from a higher, more timeless, perspective. (And I'm sure far more than I might presently imagine).

53. Zac - May 2022
This Cuboid of the Universe

'The cuboid does not have a wall around it; it is not like your physical world; however energetically there is a vibrational space, that allows the dimension that sits within this part of the cuboid that allows the physicality of the reality of the three, four, five, six, seven, D (dimension) and so forth, all to be in placement in a harmonic nature which sound can penetrate throughout.

'Now it does not mean to say that everything changes here (Earth), and then on another part of the universe it is completely separate. It is more that it (Earth) is moving into an area where it would start to then be able to vibrate with parts of the universe that are already vibrating at what you would consider now a higher resonance, a higher sound frequency. There are sound frequencies which are energetically grounding and keeping the cuboid as it is while you evalate (evolve). In a way it's a bit

like in a laboratory, if you are setting a particular experiment you may do it behind a certain partition, you understand, you may create it separate from the rest of the laboratory. This is the same here with the universe, when I talk about the cuboid, everything within the cuboid is connected, everything one end of the universe to the other. So as you evalate, everything changes; it is not just your dimension, it is all dimensions that are evalating.

'Even what you would like to think of as the gods and the goddesses, everything is evalating, even the realms of the Angels, the Archangels, it is not all of us you know just looking at little old Earth and saying, "I wonder what that human being is doing, if they are evalating", this is why I urge you to remember that what you do influences the universe, and what the universe does influences you.

'It is a constant shift and change, so that everything, everything, evalates here together, and then the union will happen of your cuboid of the universe into the multi-verse, universes, and Galactic areas that you could only just imagine.

'Nothing is stagnant, nothing is dead space, even the transits that you have, the movements that you have, not in just your solar system, but all the other Galactic solar systems as well, and beyond, and beyond, and beyond'. Everything, if you could look from, as you would call it, the Eagles perch, so high above, the light that is emitted, the source of creation, this is about the most complex choreographed dance that you could ever imagine.

'Why do you think in certain tribal societies certain dances, certain movements, especially ones that depict and mimic the movement of stars, may send people into trance, may send people into higher states of consciousness, or even, let us not use the word higher states, connected consciousness. The universe is within you, the whole cuboid of the universe is there within you, within your heart, within yourself, and you are part of this whole universe.

'Let change to change you, because the universe knows, the universe knows what to do, just play your part to the best of your ability, and you can claim your badge of honour after this lifetime.'

54. Zac - May 2022
Truth and Empathy

'There needs to be a change in mentality, there is already a big change we are seeing in the heart, we have seen this through truth more than anything else. Not just a desire for truth, I am not talking about when people want to know the truth so that they can share blame, so that they can have righteous anger, all the things that we have spoken of before. Simply the need for truth, so that they can have their own standing, they can be their own counsellor, they can be their own truth seeker, deep in their heart. Because when you know the truth yourself, and truth can be fluid, but the truth that you need to know in that moment, you can make decisions and choices and you can feel a certain way, without being pulled along by the tide, one direction or another, like the polarization we have thought of.

'When you have that, and you have more and more people doing that, which also acknowledge the blame and the retribution and all these other things are old paradigm, when we can simply evalate ourselves above the need for those types of things, we can be in a space when we do not actually need a victor or a victim. Those that "change" and I've used this word so much, it is a new word I would prefer, rather than "win".

'We have gone off the back of a paradigm that lasted thousands of years, where through force, there was a winner and a loser, a victor and a victim; and then, as we know, over time so often the victim would rise up and through righteous anger and blame, and all sorts, become a victor, but then the cycle will continue, because it is never balanced.

'It is always one feeling beaten down, and now they're feeling satisfaction for a short time and then feeling like they have to keep up the force, this is a way of the world that even though you are still seeing it on the surface, is changing deep within, because in people's hearts they are not drawn to just go, "Isn't that victor so strong", and want to be like them, or, "Isn't the victim so weak, I don't want to be them". We all have victors and victims within us, because everybody living here has had so many different lives, whether on this planet or others, that have experienced this, and as the empathy grows, remember, the emotional intelligence of people at this time, and going forward, is absolutely essential for evalation.

'To feel empathy, do not desire for there to be a victor or a victim, to help them both in their heart, and wish and desire for there to be a future of harmony, a future of harmony where yes, even if you think to yourself, "Well, they did wrong", that rather than vilify, you accept that they also wish to change. And for those, who in the past would have become victim, because again of sharing of love, of lifting them up, of sharing, physically sharing as well, they are no longer victims, because again they gain by the sharing of all.

'I know at the moment you think I am living in a Utopia land, and we do not have. What I see is the potentials, what I see is everybody's hearts changing, everybody's energy is changing, those who are the empathic being off the scale empathy, something that sometimes they have to deal with and can be quite difficult, but for those who were not empathetic to be confused by their feelings, and actually the desire to help those that in the past would have been called victims, the desire to not vilify any more, but let bygones be bygones, if the person is willing to change.'

55. Zac - May 2022
DNA Optimisation

'In the first original existence of you in the Incarnation as you are now, when it is formed in the cellular nature as you go through the foetus, embryo, and so forth, and your DNA follows you, it cannot just be the map, it cannot just be the blueprint, if that was the case evalation could not happen. All you could do would be follow a pattern, that has been followed time and time and time again. However, what actually happens within the DNA is a constant flow of consciousness.

'**Not just your consciousness, not just your thoughts, your dreams, with your heart's desires, not just your soul's consciousness that has far greater awareness than your personality could ever know, but the consciousness of the universe.**

'This is why your DNA is so interlinked with your evalation, and the evalation of all within this cuboid of universe and beyond. The reason being, is so that the consciousness can do its work; there are so many facets to your change, to your growth, to your ability to become more than you were yesterday. It is not just to your emotional presence, what your actions are, how you choose to live your life, the level of your vibration, however, the higher your vibration, the clearer the consciousness of the universe, beyond your personality, can flow through your DNA.

'So imagine this, if you should live a life where your vibration maintains quite a dense low level, for whatever reason, but it remains quite dense and low, it is like thick treacle, it is very hard for that consciousness to flow. Therefore only the personality and the soul consciousness, and it takes more time, the lighter your vibration, the easier the flow, the more it actually encourages a flow from those lighter vibrations to flood through the DNA, to be in a position to change from your blueprint, from within.

'For this, you must be able, even if it is just on a philosophical level, rather than a literal level, to think that there is no time. If you think of things in terms of time, then you would say, "Well there is time enough, or how long does time take for an evalation to happen, how long does it take for the DNA to change?" Or you may have been schooled to believe that your DNA does not change throughout your lifetime.

'But if you just, put a pin in it, if you think of this idea, instead of time as just something that is apparent, but you do not have to follow what you are told the laws of time, then, in any moment with the raising of your own vibration, with the desire of your heart, you can flood with more and more universe consciousness.

'What we know of the universe, it is ahead of time, producing the solutions that are needed on your planet and other places of course too, ahead, so that once the issue appears, there is already a solution in place. And as you are becoming more of a collective species, a more collective in terms of consciousness, the more that your consciousness benefits others, and vice versa, in lightening, shifting, changing, and evalating the DNA, in response to your changing world, for betterment, for yourself, and for all.

'For many, many years, adepts and others have been focusing on how to shift and change and improve DNA, all of that, all very good, all of that still stands, however, you are moving through space and time in the cosmos in a way where you are open to the photonic light that I have spoken of in a way that has not been present upon your planet for thousands upon thousands of years. Now, we can activate; it is like looking at it from a different perspective, rather than going in, rather than saying, "This needs *to change, this needs to change", it is saying, "Let me become the light that is part of me, let me become master, or mistress of my energy, let me be part of the universal solution, and in so doing optimize everything about myself"; and this is what is encoded, and more, and more, and more, and more.*

'But it is only now we need you to go through certain conjunctions, we needed to go through certain situations of planetary alignments, we needed to go through certain belts. But rather than going into this, the detail of why this needs to happen, just know this is an optimum time now to take advantage, and that is the thing to amplify. This will happen to all people. But it can be slow progress, it can be difficult, and as I say with density, it takes time to get through the treacle.

'So as you start to do this, as you start to allow yourself, I would encourage anybody to use this meditation (at website). This is not one of the meditations you say, "If you need this", everybody can benefit, and by taking the act into your own hands, by saying, "This is what I want to do, and if I do so myself, in a very enjoyable way, by using the beautiful, beautiful, beautiful music, sound encoding within, as well, it is like putting the cherry on top, is it not".

'And there we have it, you know, you can toil in your gardens, you can toil at work, you can toil in lots of things that you do to make strides and improvement, here, you do not need to toil. Here you need to allow and believe in yourself, that is the one thing that I asked, when you listen to the meditation. Do not think this is just for other people, this is for you, believe in yourself and everything that I say is possible for you, and then you can start to improve, and when we desire in our heart that the improvement is not just for us, we do not limit it. When we desire in our heart that the improvement is for all, boom, as they say; (it is) explosive in the fundamental nature of betterment that inspires your universe, and my universe too.

'When you have a consciousness flowing, it adapts to environment, it adapts to what is needed. When you're looking in a scientific laboratory, and you are looking at the physiology of a body, what you are looking at is what you expect to happen due to damage. That is what is looked at from the day someone is born. There is often a thought that what is happening in biology is repair and regeneration, but ultimately degradation.

'But actually, what we'll be seeing, and this we expect to not be limited by somebody's age, this is not about the age and degradation, that is expected, and what it can do at certain periods of a lifespan, and we are back to time here as well, due to the presence of the consciousness coming through, adapting instead to the environment. To the environment, yes, the toxins', but also to the good things, adapting to someone who may have not have felt kindness and compassion to them for many years and then is feeling it. To somebody else who is finding a group of like-minded people, and feeling inspired by them. The situation where you could say the environment you are creating yourself is an artistic one, maybe you have never been creative in your life, and you are desiring to harness the creative flow within you.

'So as well as what we are so often talking about, toxins, environmental damage, all of these things, drugs and tribulations that they're affecting, we are also seeing the positive, and so this is why we may see many academic scientists, let's put it this way, ones that are looking at historical fact, scratching their heads, thinking the DNA is not reacting in the way that it used to, and it is changing far more in this lifetime than it ever did before.'

I come next to a communication from White Feather, from a recording, later titled, *"Stand in Your Light"*. I divided the recording into some short videos, and what follows is some of what was said. Robert Goodwin, the medium through whom White Feather communicates, later said of the sitting that:

"The communication turned out to be one of the most forthright and direct received from the sage - in terms of his responses to questions relating directly to the current global situation, and the threat to humanity, and the agenda of those behind it."

56. White Feather- 7th June 2022
Stand in Your Light - Introduction Talk

'You may wonder at times what on Earth you're doing here on the Earth at this moment, with all that is going on, with all to which you are subjected. You may say to yourself, "why did I sign up for this".

'Well, sign up you did, it was your soul, your higher aspect that made that decision; that made that choice.

'Not under duress, you were not forced, you were not coerced, that decision came from within yourself, the only place that it could ever come from. It originated from your soul, and you decided to come here at this time, having been here many times before, each of you, because of the challenges that mankind is facing, that affect everything and everyone upon this planet.

'You did so using the knowledge that you had in my world, and the courage to make that decision, because you knew that it was the right decision, so your soul placed a facet of itself, never the totality, but a facet, of the diamond of itself, into this body, in this form, and this personality, in this environment, this you call, "You".

'It is only when you leave this body that you can see things more clearly, particularly at this time, where conditioning, where indoctrination, and where the dictates of comparatively few in your world, who have an agenda of their own, are so prevalent.

'**You have to learn to stand free from the conditioning, and see things clearly. The mind takes it on board and absorbs it and largely obeys it, as if it were a command, without question. The awakened soul, however, does not do this. It sees through it, because it has disrobed itself of this conditioning, and it stands clearly, freely alone, and can observe what it sees around it; and this largely is the difference between those who have an insight and an understanding into the nature of life, the nature of your world, and those who have yet to reach this point of awareness.**

'Now you may say, "We can help them; we can change them; we can guide them; we can inform them". But a mind can only be informed if it is ready to receive that information, and so many minds are closed down. You cannot enter a closed mind, the mind has to, in a sense, invite that entry, invite that connection. If it is not prepared to do that, then your words will fall like seeds on barren ground, they will not take root, and your energies will be wasted in that sense.

'**So you may say, "Yes, we are facing difficulties, we are facing a difficult time upon the Earth"; and if you look with the eyes and the vision of the soul, you will see precisely where those who are manipulating your experience plan to take you. Then you can resist, then you do not have to follow, then your true courage** *must come to the fore, and the real reasons why you came here at this time can be expressed in your thinking, in your actions individually and collectively, but always you have to be able to notice your own programming, notice your own belief systems, and to be able to transcend them, to work through them, not necessarily to totally disregard them, but to see them clearly, and it can be quite an eye-opener because, when you see your own conditioning for the first time, you may be astounded. As you look back on the decisions that you have made, the way that you have been led, and coerced, and directed, and you may say, "How on Earth could I have allowed that to happen. How on Earth could I have fallen for that?"*

'Perhaps a classic example, an ideal example I could give you, are those of you who have been educated into religious beliefs. Certain religions seem to have a monopoly in your world, as though they were accepted as the absolute truth, not to be questioned, to be blindly followed, and yet, how many of you reached a point perhaps at a very young age when you rejected this. You began to think this is nonsense, this is not right, this is not true, what I'm being told here by my superiors, my elders, which I should follow and respect; their knowledge and wisdom is not right. So you begin to explore other avenues, and you reject one thing, and perhaps then, you embrace another, and you find that even that is lacking.

'So it goes on, and the same processes deeply embedded in the unconscious mind of the child follow through into adulthood, and you look for those in authority, you look for monarchs or politicians or presidents, or even religious leaders, to guide you, to tell you what is happening in the world and what you need to do. And how you should respond, and because of your conditioning, you still follow this.

'Yet the rebellious nature of the soul will come to the surface, and I'm willing to suggest to you that for a long time you have all sensed that there is something deeply wrong with this world. Even before this latest round of events and occurrences that have resulted in so much turmoil and even deaths of the physical body.

'So many you would have known or sensed there was something wrong, but you didn't quite know what it was, couldn't quite put your finger on it, and even now there's a part of you that doesn't want to go there, doesn't want to look at it, for fear of it as it were, upsetting the apple cart, and challenging your very core beliefs.

But that you have to do, only if you are prepared to face what is, will the greater picture emerge.

'You cannot choose simply to look at light and joy and happiness and freedom, without seeing darkness and ignorance and evil and captivity, and fear and all of the negative things you see. You cannot, because they are parts of the same whole. So never be afraid to challenge yourself, to challenge others, your peers, and most importantly see what this great myth of authority is. What is authority? There is only one authority, and that is the Great Spirit, or God, or the Creator, that is the only authority I recognize.

'No one has authority over another, they may say that they do, they may appear that they do through their presentation, their clothing, their persona, the laws that they quote, the way that they speak to you, the assumption that they have authority over you, but they do not. No one, no individual, no body, no government, no country, no creed, no religion, has authority over you.

'Yes, you must have laws, you have to follow certain protocol in order for society to function, I understand that. The race that I was part of when last upon your Earth had its own laws that were obeyed, they were not written, as yours are, but they were known, and they were appreciated. Your laws seem to come from a mythical authority, from an authority figure or authority organization, and that is a danger to freedom. Freedom is your birthright, you are free, because you are of the spirit, it doesn't mean that you can act recklessly, that you can upturn everything that is necessary for society to function; you know that.

'You have to act in accordance with your soul, with your wisdom, with your understanding, and any knowledgeable advanced evolved soul will do that automatically.

'Those of a lower mind, a lower intelligence, or should I say ignorance, tend to be the ones who are disruptive, and in that sense they have to be restricted, that is understood. But it is when authority gets out of hand, and when those who think they have a divine right to control the lives of others revel in their own self-importance, and think that they can dictate to you, that's when it has to be challenged, and it is as important for the aware soul to challenge ignorance at every turn without fear, it is as important to

***do that, as it is to try and live a spiritual life; you cannot have one
without the other.***

*'So understanding that yes, you agreed to be here, your soul agreed to
be here, understand what the responsibility that that places on your
shoulders, we do not ask the impossible, we only ask that you see
yourself clearly, free of conditioning. That you see the obstacles, and
the difficulties, that have been placed there to control the flow of
information, and the path of humanity, to their design, see it clearly, and
then make your decisions from that point of knowing. You will always
find the answer lies within yourself if you are aligned to yourself, and to
the truth within. You will not go far wrong, you may be challenged, you
may at times find yourself in difficult situations, but remain true to that
higher knowledge and you will not go far wrong.*

*'So I hope that will give you further food for thought, try to understand
and remember that you are the Great Spirit itself, you are not separate,
there is no external deity, there is no God that has to be appeased or
feared, you are that, you are that, that is how powerful you are, there is
no power higher than this.'*

Continuing, from the same White Feather communication, next the
guide was replying to a question as to whether someone who received
two jabs or so-called vaccines (or experimental injections) should be
concerned about long-term side effects and whether fear is justified.
The reply contains informative confirmation that not all jabs are the
same, not only do they have different manufacturers, but also different
batches that do not necessarily contain the same in each. There is also
some excellent advice given for those who have been given any of the
experimental injections.

57. White Feather – 7th June 2022
Q&A on Jabs

*'I don't know whether fear is ever justified, because fear itself is a
negative energy that creates great disturbance at all levels of the being.
So I wouldn't recommend one should be fearful under any
circumstances.*

*'But once the vaccine has been taken, and I know it is a vaccine that
isn't a vaccine, it is a substance. And it operates in a way upon the*

physical level in a way that no vaccine has ever done, in that it directly modifies human DNA. So once it has been imbibed that cannot be reversed.

'However, there are different types of this substance; they are not all the same. Some have an effect on one that does not apply to another. Some have an effect on a particular age group, and not on another. Some are placebos, they have no effect at all; and who can say which one has been given to whom.

'What I would say is if you have been unfortunate enough to have taken this vaccine do not dwell on it, do not worry, do not be fearful, what has happened has happened. Keep yourself positive, try to live in accordance with your higher self, and realise that if any change can come about, it will do so from the higher not from the lower.

'What has happened on the Earth vibration has happened, but if you raise your heart and your mind and your soul to the highest state of being, realise that ultimately that has control over your whole being.

'That can overcome most things, indeed all things, in accordance with your alignment to it. The more that you are aligned with the higher self, the greater influence it can have on all levels of being. That is what their equation has not taken into account.

'Don't give it control over you, don't surrender to it, surrender only to the higher knowledge, to the higher state; allow your higher state to influence every facet of your life. If you can do that, you will be transformed; do not give that substance, which is within your physical body, the power that it doesn't deserve. It's there, you can't extract it, but you can transcend it, by the knowledge and understanding of your true nature.

'Remember this, let me sum it up in one phrase, spirit is master, matter is servant, spirit is master, matter is servant.'

White Feather said, *"Don't surrender to it"*, while Zac (see number 32 in this chapter) said, *"You have the ability within you to transmute it"*, (whatever you take in). Scientists such as Bruce Lipton and others also tell us that consciousness (how we think) can change DNA, so even the scientific community is awakening to our true soul capabilities.

More than one spirit guide has warned of the potential pitfalls of switching to a digital cashless society. If this comes about, it will not be brought about with the pure intent that it will be 'good of everyone'. It will be a further way in which those with a dark agenda will, potentially at very least, seek to gain ever greater control and domination over the lives of the people.

The following is what White Feather said on this subject when he was asked whether we were heading for a global financial collapse; and if we might be moving towards a cashless system, and whether this could be better in terms of global equality.

58. White Feather – 7th June 2022
Q&A on Cash Banking

'That is what is planned, in terms of a financial collapse, without a doubt, that is part of their scenario; as is, the removal of cash; and the implementation of a digital monetary system.

'As to whether that is beneficial, I would say not; because when one can respond by removing one's right to buy and sell and trade, and indeed do anything if one has not conformed to the dictates of those who control the system, then one is heading for trouble.

'One should always have the ability to earn, the right to buy and sell and trade, and put a roof over one's head.

'In my time upon the Earth there was no money, there was no monetary system, no cash, but we traded by serving others. We traded goods, we traded experiences, and we traded services. It was a natural quality to help one's brother if one could do something that they could not.

'That of course was changed with the introduction of money and the banking system, but the banking system has become corrupt, it has become corrupt, and the removal of banks, the removal of cash, the implementation of a digital system, will only further transfer power to those who are controlling it. So that is another red flag I'm afraid, that you have to be aware of.'

The spirit guide "Monty" has also spoken of the dark agenda plan to remove cash, and to expect this plan to be pushed forward during 2024. This is a warning. He advises that, without violence, we fight this plan, we resist, we collectively say "No". Remember, we the people, are the majority, we are sovereign human beings and hold far greater power than may be realised. Recognise this, where and whenever possible insist on the rights of the people to be heard and met; and, never comply with any agenda that places us 'under the thumb' or 'under the jackboot' of the would-be dictators of this world. Be courageous, never fearful, always remembering that we are free immortal spirit beings.

Next, the final part I am sharing from the same White Feather communication, and in this he is replying to a question about the planned 'end game' of those with a dark agenda. And, believe me it is a very, very dark agenda. Which is why people need to stand in their light, to stand up for what is fair, for justice based on spiritual principles, and not impositions 'decreed' by those obeying the orders of the 'puppet masters' with their darkest of dark agendas. This, echoing what Rudolf Steiner had forewarned us of back in 1917.

59. White Feather – 7th June 2022

Q&A - On the Planned End Game

'It is through the use of technology, the forceful imposition of technology, that a few in your world, I won't call them elite, because they are not, but let us say that they have a lot of material wealth and influence and control, 'the end game' is for the technological subversion of humanity, that will result in a technological device implanted within all at birth.

'So that the soul, the spirit, the natural inclinations of the mind, can be subjugated, and also controlled in an artificial sense. So the world into which one incarnates will be a false narrative, a false world, an illusionary world. It is already that to an extent, because the world that you see, the world that you manifest in your consciousness, is nothing like the reality that it should be. It is a false world that you live in, and it is becoming more false by the day.

'But when this falsehood is fully controlled, artificially through technology, it is planned, that you will be connected to a computer, a super intelligent computer, that will not involve any emotional decisions, any empathy, any compassion, but merely to work as a slave to serve the system of the chosen few. Then, they will have reached their ideology; they will have completed their 'coup de grace', of humanity. That is what you are faced with.

'Some have described this as the end times, of the battle between good and evil, between God and the Devil, or whatever they conceive that to be, and in some ways I can see the analogy. I can see the inference there. It certainly is a challenge to the soul, to the freedom, to the natural state of being, that should be your divine right, is your divine right.

'So this is why you have to stand up, and expose this; it is through the exposing of it, that many will awaken, and that is already underway, by the way many are awakening, but it has to increase, it has to quicken.

'The good news is that this awakening, this expansion, is exponential. If you think of a balloon, when you blow a balloon up, it expands in all directions. With each expansion, that is exponential, it increases, and that is what's happening.

'Much of it is what you would call, 'below the surface', of consciousness. So you can't see it; particularly in the world which is controlled through the media. Which feeds you your narrative; you have to withdraw from that, step back from it, and find the inner narrative of the soul; and you'll see that awakening is taking place on an enormous scale. They know that, those who would manipulate you know that, which is why they are quickening their own agenda.

'But let me just finish with this, that light is greater than darkness, truth is greater than ignorance; and if you place a light into a darkened room, that darkness has no defence against it. It is powerless.

'People speak of darkness as though it were a substance, as though it was something very, very, powerful. That had to be feared. Let me tell you this, darkness 'per se' does not exist. It is not a thing, it is not the opposite of light; **it is the absence of light.**

'Light is a power, light is energy; darkness is only the absence of that; so you tell me where the power lies.

'Light will always succeed, because it has to, and it will do so, it may not be in this physical lifetime that you're experiencing, but think ahead, think of your children, and your grandchildren, and their grandchildren.'

The spirit guide I mentioned earlier, "Monty", who is channelled by Warren James, like White Feather, has spoken out about the dark agenda and the plans that these would-be tyrants are working towards. In a June 2022 recording Monty speaks of part of their desires and plan. Below is some of what he said.

60. Monty - June 2022
They Want Your Homes, They Want It All

'I must point out to you and remind you what I said in March of this year, they are coming for your money, to drain your money; they want your money.

'Then they will come for your homes, and they will come for your belongings, remember this, I told you the fight is not over and it is not lost. You must stand your ground, you must be courageous, you must remember that you are you, and you do not bend because they make you.

'You do what you must do to fight back, you understand me, you don't take any of this lying down, you are in charge, and you encourage others to do the same. I told you they are coming for your money, and indeed they are; they are coming for your wealth, they are coming for your savings, they are coming for your belongings; they will extract what they can.

'For them, they must take back, and, for want of a word, drag in the net. That's what they are doing, for in order to change the system, in order to destroy the current Financial System of your World, you must first of all bring in the net. So that you can totally remove it; and replace it with the new one.

'In the same manner that you must bring countries down, in order to move borders; and that is what is taking place now. The calling in of the net, taking back everything that you owe them, including the money that they gave you all, because it's not your money you understand it's theirs, and they want it back now. In order to replace it, you've got to take it out of circulation, to replace it with the new.

'So remember this, it is not over, you must continue on, this is your job. This is your job, and the more successful you are as individuals, the more success people will see, the more you will inspire, you will

emanate, as I've told you in the past, that wonderful glow that will inspire others.

'So remember this, ignore the new illnesses, ignore all the distraction and the excitement and the dramatization of everything that they show you, ignore it, ignore it, it is nonsense.

'Stand your ground; if something is not right that is being done to you then you stand your ground, because you know it's not right. When things are not right, you do not go along with it, you live true to yourself, you understand.

'They will offer you money to rescue you, from the problem they created. They want your homes, they want your property, they want your land, they want it for them; they want to control it. They want it all, and they are working towards it, so, stand your ground, the game is not over. You're still only on the first round, the plans ahead are "Monumental", so my friends, stay strong. Ignore the new 'illnesses', they don't exist, ignore the new 'medicines', they are not medicines.

'They're coming for your property, your wealth, do not bend.'

Question: How, could they take your home?

'Because when you can no longer afford it, they can offer to take it, take on the responsibility of your home, they will come to save you, allegedly. "We will give you what you need, but we will own your home, your home will be ours, but you will be okay, but you must do as we say". They want your Gardens, they want your Pathways, they want your roof above your head; they want to own it all. They won't stop until they achieve it. But they won't, they must not.

'They're coming for your money; they're coming for all of it, all of it. Do not look out your window and see something that you believe to be yours, when you see that, recognize they're coming for that as well. These people have a plan, they want to own the world, it is the sure way that they can nudge you, and make you do what they want you to do, what they want you to do.

'So be clearly aware of this, don't let them take from you, do not give them an inch, when it comes to them taking money from you tell them they're not having it. You must all be strong, otherwise you'll just be blown down, you'll passively sit down and take it, and it's not right. Stand tall, do not let them take your money off you, no, don't give them what they want without at least a fight.'

Question: Will recent awakenings change this?

'People forget in a very short time, people have already forgotten the last two years of your lives. That, as I told you, so long ago, that you were incarcerated in your own homes. It is as though that's been forgotten, the misery that was inflicted, its forgotten. They've forgiven, that is what happens; it's called "Stockholm syndrome". When you become sympathetic to your captors and you go around in circles, and circles.

'Before too long you will be invited to vote for Team A or Team B like everybody else around the world does in their own countries. The same trick; Team A or Team B, no other option on the cards, just A or B.

'Ignore them, ignore them all, don't play their games anymore, don't cooperate with what they want you to do, just make sure you stand your ground, if you do that you fight your own corner at all times, just remember, it's your money. Don't let them take you down without a fight.

'Try and ignore them, don't 'air-off' too much, otherwise you're punishing yourself. You don't deserve to punish yourself. That's all anger is, self-punishment, you've somehow got to do this without anger. Otherwise you're only hurting yourself, I know, I know, the joys of Earth. You wouldn't put me back there again not in a million years, no, but you do have a duty, to leave it in a better condition. By that I mean, these things matter, these issues that I talk of are more pressing than other issues that people may wish you to think are far more important. These are truly important my friend, so be aware, be aware.

'I want you to take what I've said as a positive signal, to go out into your world, stand your ground, and keep standing your ground. You've made your links with many people through your gatherings, and your comings together with like-minded people, you've achieved this, with your groups that you've created, use those groups, come together and stand your ground against these idiotic decisions, which are simply the people who create the wealth pulling the net back in with you all getting dragged in with it.

'If you're aware of that, then you know your next ambition to achieve, you know your next course, to chart your journey to, that is your next part of your course. If you can use that to your advantage continue to do so my friends. Cheerio, stay happy my friends, and keep smiling.'

The following is from another recording of Dr Peebles, speaking through Summer Bacon.

61. Dr Peebles - 29th July 2022

'Your politicians and others - you are wondering what they're going to do. How they're going to create a new reality here upon the planet Earth. Is it going to be a change that is going to be dramatic in terms of financial relationships and such? Is it going to be a disruption of the food chain that is going to destroy the planet Earth or make people live life in fear and such, and comply with the government etc, etc?

'All these things are possible, yes, these are things that are in the works that people are trying to create, not only the politicians, but those who fear them, because they are saying, "Well, if it happens, I'll just comply because I'm terrified, I don't want to be killed for my perspective on things. I'll just do what the government says I should do", etc.

'But there will be many others who will say, "You know something, it's all fine and dandy what they are trying to do but we still have the love within our hearts. We still can go out and care for each other. We can still help and nurture each other; we can offer food to those who need it. We can also find ways to plant our own fields of food, so that we don't have to find this great dependency upon the government to provide for us the bare minimum of what we need here".

'Your politicians are just doing what they are doing, they're striving to fit everybody into a box, they're trying to make everybody comply, they want everybody to be treated equally 100 percent all around, **except for themselves often times, this is as old as time.**

'And it will continue on for a while, perhaps another 20 years or so, but people will start to get sick and tired of it; and people will really start to see how truly you need each other, and how truly that can only happen by being of service to the heart of God and bringing that to the surface through you, by looking inside of self, and realising that everything that happens in your life happens inside first, and it is then expressed in the world.

'So know that your world is in turmoil, and, is also growing and expanding in beautiful ways. More people aware of each other than ever before; and some of the muck is coming up to the surface, to be cleared out. Not because it's going to take over; it's

going to be cleared out by the human heart, by the love of God within you.

'So when it seems like disaster is on the horizon, and everything's falling into decay, please know my dear friends, the only thing that's falling into decay is the old way of doing things, things that no longer serve you upon the Earth. And that new experiences of self, and of others, a desire to cooperate and communicate with each other in a wide variety of ways, celebrating the diversity and the unity therein, is the direction your world is going in.

'Take heart my dear friends you're all going to end up living happily ever after, all are going to have a happy ending, all are going to return to the greater awareness that you are birthed from the heart of God, and all of you will eventually come to understand how much God loves you, and that that has never stopped because it is the one greatest force in the universe that permeates all of life.

'We love you so very much my dear friends, we are constantly reaching out to you, accept our embrace, know that we love you, and go your way in peace, love and harmony. For life is indeed a joy, and all you have to do is you enjoy the journey to your own hearts and, suddenly, to your enlightenment. Simply lighten up just a little bit more, God bless you indeed.'

As I have said before, it all depends upon from which perspective one approaches the 'story' of current world events, and I feel that we do need to consider both sides of what is unfolding, the earthly and the spiritual. Although I would suggest that while observing and being aware of the earthly corruption, we make sure to never allow it to in any way dominate our thinking. I believe it is far more important to remember, and to never forget, that we are spirit beings and that life is eternal. We will, sooner or later, 'go home' (to spirit life). This is not something to dread or worry about; although, at the same time, if we possibly can, we should endeavour to leave this world in as good a state as we possibly can for future generations to experience.

A spirit guide, known as "Sanaya", representing a highly evolved spirit group communicates through the (trance) mediumship of Suzanne Giesemann. In part of a June 2022 video Sanaya replied as follows in response to a question.

62. Sanaya - June 2022
Major Shift in Evolution

Question: 'We've heard so much about a big shift Sanaya, is humanity nearing a major shift in evolution right now?

'There is no nearing about it. You are in that shift, and this is like a snowball, and when one rolls around in the snowball there is that tumbling, is there not.

'Some of you can feel the shakeup, but not only is it a shakeup, it is a wakeup, and so the wakeup call is yours for the taking. Will you resist it, or will you roll with that, and roll with the changes.

'It is not only your virus which is causing this shift in awareness. It is so many people saying, "We are tired of the way of doing things; we are looking for fairness and equality". That is the human's birthright, and we wish you to understand that humans are doing their very best.

'But when you find yourselves clashing please understand that that is because you are stuck in your human viewpoint. The greatest favour you can do for each other to increase this change in consciousness is to shift your viewpoint.

'See from each other's eyes and find the common ground, the middle ground, this will help to accelerate this shift in consciousness. It is the human way to not appreciate change, but growth only happens through change.

'So be patience with each other, be compassionate with each other, have understanding that you are all tumbling about right now. But what happens when a snowball rolls, it becomes larger and larger and your consciousness is rising in kind.'

Next is more from Jonathan via Elaine Thorpe.

63. Jonathan - July 2022
The Light and the Awakening

'I think that the Earth is having very much of an awakening. Looking at it from the human side of things, many truths are going to come to your Earth like never before. They are already happening at present, but there are more, more of them to come.

'And because the world is having a spiritual awakening that means that the whole world is going to experience some sort of an awakening.

'It doesn't mean to say that everyone is going to become spiritual overnight. Because they may have a religion of sorts or they may have other beliefs, or they may not believe, but I know that they're all going to feel something.

'Because time is already changing in your world; a lot of people have said that it is moving a little quicker, which it is, time has changed. It is not to say that it is going to go extra fast and you cannot have any time to do anything, but it has made a change.

'So the energy of the Earth and the people of the Earth are going to change along with it. And when you have an individual spiritual awakening, you will experience many things surfacing in the way of truth.

'Sometimes there may be fears within you that you have not let go of, or emotions that you have not come to terms with. But I would say that once you start healing yourself with that you will start experiencing more joy in your life, and you will become more empathic and forgiving and understanding of people's way of life. But there are also your own emotions to go through, to let go of, and learning how to love yourself and to connect with our world should we wish to. It is not forced upon one to do so. But it is fine to love yourself; it is fine to want to love you.

'**And to become spiritual is the bonus isn't it, to connect with heaven is wonderful. To connect with an angel is wonderful. And to connect with God, to connect with your guides is wonderful. So when you are awakening, let go of things that don't any longer serve you.**

'And the sooner you do that, the better and stronger in life and more determined you shall become. You will be faced with these fears, but see them as things that don't any longer serve you, and see them as emotions that can be let go should you wish to. And it is good to let go of them. So when we talk about putting the light over the Earth, it is not that we are going to come there out of the skies. What it is, is to let you find love in your hearts, let you find light within you.

'**The God-like being is within you, the soul is within you, the light is within you. It is already present, but it is just you taking notice of it. That is what it is. It's you taking notice of it and seeing it within you. Because when I say that to you, you are a soul within,** *it is the truth. So when you leave your physical body, you become a light being. You become a soul that is pure of light and love and truth.*

'But at the moment, in this physical world, this realm that you are in, you are made up of physical flesh. But you have a soul within still that is there. Take note of that soul. It is your intuitiveness. Take note of it when it tries to show you things. Take note of it when it is showing you the truth, and love your soul, within yourself. When you love yourself, you are being true to yourself.'

Next are three more contributions from the spirit guide "Zac", who speaks through the medium, Janet Treloar.

64. Zac - July 2022
Universal Integrity

'Everything has come very, very, much more into focus. Everything is much more in your living room with you, and not only because of this, but this is a helpful part of the process of bringing into light the paradigms that we do and we do not want to live in anymore. And therefore, what we are seeing, as well at the time most of you I'm sure who are listening to this, have been feeling a collapse around you, the dismantling of the old, let us put it this way, rather than a complete falling down, for the new to appear.

'And this is just another way it is manifesting in the world, the time has come, certainly for people in their homes to demand to have a life around them of that which comes into their home to be more aligned into how they wish to be. One of the main words I would use is "integrity".

'Integrity is ageless, now this is not about anything specific, because we do not get into the detail, but what I can tell you, is integrity was here before humanity. Sounds a bit strange I know, universe is based on integrity. Otherwise you would have, like your superheroes you know, you would have planets being popped out of existence, because the gods and goddesses and all sorts of things. But that actually doesn't happen, you know. We have, of course, the nature and the universal laws. However, everything is bound together, and you could call it by, integrity.

'Therefore, in the day and age that you are living in now, when you get a fall down as well of integrity, for the principles of the future, so not integrity by what you or they or whoever think, but the integrity of actually the Earth, and the goodness of the Earth, and the more harmonic and holistic living of everything together, something has to fall down. **Because ultimately the integrity is saying if you cannot go forward with integrity that actually supports the way of life for the planet, then it must go.**

'This is why we are beyond a tipping point, you'll be very pleased to hear, we are in the process of manifestation now, we are in the process of the manifestation, so even if what you see, and of course it is like an interior designer looking and says, "This wallpaper may work" or "These curtains may work" or "This settee may work" and then they say, "No", and have a little change around, and a little change around, so you may see things that change, it is not necessarily one goes and then suddenly, wham bam, this is the pinnacle and this happens. **It is a process to get there, but it is an upward process, every change, knowing what you don't want, is almost as useful as knowing what you do want, is it not.**

'So there we are now, in the manifestation process, of the universe having its integrity for life to live on Earth in a harmonious way, because I've always said, that is the direction, that is the clear goal, should we say.'

From the same original July 2022 recording included below, is Zac, in conversation with Hazel Newton, who always interacts so well with the spirit guide.

65. Zac - July 2022
DNA Change Makers

Hazel: I think it's great to touch on this, because for those that are leaving the planet at the moment, and those of us that are staying behind observing that, it's great for us to be reminded that their energy continues, their soul is continuing back home. For many people, that's quite a new consideration. But it's so helpful, and there are huge numbers of people around the world who believe, and have believed through their cultures in reincarnation, and I hope that this is something that will bring great solace to many.

'It will not be too long before it will be received as information that is fact. There is scientific discoveries that are happening in laboratory conditions will actually verify this now, so it does not have to be belief anymore. But everything that I'm saying, I do not want anyone to feel there is a disregard to the pain and suffering that comes before, and for all those who miss, naturally, the physical presence of their loved ones.

'We should not be shooting off, you know, saying, goodbye, good riddance planet Earth, because it is such a special energy to be here. However, for those that do, simply to say the life that comes after is, better than the one that went before.'

Hazel: I'd love to ask you a question that's come through about DNA. Rudolph Steiner wrote about viruses being excreted from our DNA, rather than being caught, as we evalate as a species, and as there's quite a big focus on DNA and changes to it on the planet at the moment, I wonder if you could expand upon the nature of viruses for us?

'Timely is it not, it is actually both, the reason why I say this is, ancestrally speaking, from a long, long, time ago, the viruses lay dormant within the body and they may not ever even be triggered, depends on the environment, depends on toxicity, toxicity is one of the major things that activates a virus running rampant in the body.

'So this is gone on for generation, after generation, after generation, after generation, the toxicity levels of the Earth had not got to a stage, until around the time of Industrial Revolution starting it, for there to be many variants of virus that did not only correspond with what was in an energetic format within the body. However, as everything changes and nature evolves, and blah, blah, blah, and all of these things, and the environment changes things as well, the environment not just to do with toxicity, but how it adapts to that toxicity, means that other things develop.

'Now we will not get into too much conversation here because this is not so relevant for this part, regarding the hand that people have to then, also, activating for the viruses, but simply to say some are within and some come from the outside.

'Now, when a new one comes in from the outside, of course the body needs to adapt, to accommodate, and to find a place, you could say, for it within everything else, it needs to learn about it.

'It is a bit like a teacher with a classroom of students, all a bit hurly burly, all with their own minds and just knows how everyone sits. Then, a new student comes in, who brings out different attributes of people's personalities. Suddenly they're sitting next to someone in the class who is normally meek and mild, but due to their own presence brings out another side of them.

'So you see, when a new virus comes in it is not just that virus, but it is how it is interacting and affecting the other viruses that are in the body, and then of course the immunity system is a bit like the teacher, it has to work out how to take charge, how to not just tell a thing to go away, but how to manage it.

'Now something that is very useful, because you think why has the body developed and not got rid of them, is they are change makers, remember I have said so many times, let change to change you. This is because a fact of life on the Earth, whether you're human, whether you're a polar bear, whether you're fly, whether you're a beetle, blah, blah, blah, whether you're fish, dolphin, whatever, you are constantly changing at the cellular level.

'You do not get born and change the same, you grow, you develop yourself, replenish self, all of these things, it has to change and because the environment is constantly changing, you know nature has to up its game, it has to have more and more ways to be able to implement a change within the body. One of the ways of doing this is with viruses, because they are like, you know, the bowling ball that goes flying through that takes something, it can be very dramatic, however, it can spark changes that then learn from the inside about new environmental situations, and then what the immunity can do, can then create, what is needed.

'Remember I told you many, many times, regarding the evolution we are here with the light, with the movement through the evolution into a light being within your physical form, one of these ways of doing this is with viruses. This is why I say this very difficult to pinpoint something and say, that is a bad thing or a good thing, because everything has both, does it not. It depends how it reacts with you, it is not the case that you are always fully in charge, I'm afraid. I would love to be able to tell you, but if you know this you can do this, this, and this, because they're very strong, and it is dependent of course on how body reacts and all of these things.

'But the fact remains, these are big change makers in evolution, understand, I do not want to cast them in a light as the great saviour, because they cause so much difficulty, I simply want to tell you that they are part of life on Earth. They are within everything that is living, it is part of the design, that it is one of the ways, and remember this, is only one of the ways, for change to happen, to adapt to a new environment, or get ready for an environment that is coming.'

66. Zac – August 2022
Rocket Fuelled Inspiration

'If you look into the future no technology (for healing) will be needed, because, this is the whole thing about this time, your bodies are changing into all the technology that you need. In terms of healing devices and others, there are many that are coming through that are wonderful for this particular time.

'However, there's nothing quite so effective in the belief of your own power, because when you believe fully in your own power, you can amplify everything you do. Why do you think for the last year or so we have been building, building, particularly with the meditations, to help you all engage, to really get the most out of your energy system, as it is adapting and changing to the world as it is now.

'We are coming into the place where from imbalance you can come into balance, from being out of harmony, you can come into harmony. Don't always look to the outside, allow yourself to change from within, because then you'll be able to really take charge of these new abilities.'

Robert Goodwin via Facebook kindly shared with us a couple of further White Feather communications; as follows.

67. White Feather – 1st September 2022
Seeds in the Wind

'As people awaken to the true reality of the lies and deceit that is being foisted upon them, they will do so exponentially.

'When a seed head releases its seeds, the wind does not carry them in a single direction, but far and wide in all directions, allowing them to fall where they will.

'Some never germinate, for the soil is unsuitable; but countless do and no one is aware of this, until the seedling emerges, and the flower is revealed.

'This is happening now in your world.'

68. White Feather – 30th September 2022
The Love Revolution

'When humanity truly begins to awaken to the full realisation of its divine inheritance, its momentum will be unstoppable; ignorance will fall powerless before truth; darkness will be vanquished by the light of knowing and those blinded by their prior servitude to falsity, tyranny and corruption will see clearly the error of their ways and thus be set free.

You are at the start of a revolution; not one created through hatred; not one fought with weapons; not one designed to take life; but one born out of pure love and the recognition of the divine Self within all.'

The Great Awakening is certainly gathering pace as each week, month and year come and go, and earthly corruption is, absolutely without doubt, reaching the awareness of greater and greater numbers of people.

Another trance medium I have had the pleasure of communicating with, and seeing her demonstrate, *Catherine Stegner Cowan*, channelled the following message from one of our Native American friends, *Chief Joseph*.

Like all the other mediums I have been able to ask, Catherine kindly gave me permission to use what the Chief said in this book. I think this in itself speaks volumes for each of the mediums; they are all working for the light and the right reasons, being willing to freely share so much of themselves and what comes through them.

69. Chief Joseph – October 2022
Mother Earth

'I come here today with the greatest joy and pleasure. I come with my fortitude, my steadfastness, my focus, and my desire.

'We come together with a purpose in mind, we want to make a difference in the world today, a world that is downtrodden, a world

191

that has gone astray under the greed, and self-serving personalities, attitudes, and hearts of some of the leaders in the world today.

'They think nothing of Mother Earth, they think Mother Earth is something to be used; to be exploited, and above all, that Mother Earth does not need or warrant their protection because she is all there for them.

'It brings us all such great sadness when we think back across history to the times when we were on the Earth, before the Europeans came. When they saw this land, our lives, our practices, our beliefs, our way of living with Mother Earth in a synchronistic way, meaning, we synchronized ourselves to her rhythms. She gave freely to us, knowing that we blessed her; we revered her; and we knew that our very existence depended upon her. That everything that the Great Spirit created was in a circle; some with more consciousness than others, but everything with a consciousness; from the rocks that were underneath our feet, to the grasses, to the beautiful flowers, to the herbs that were there for our use, not our exploitation, but our use. We learned, slowly, over time, how they could help our people, and we ensured that they could thrive well; we never took more than was needed, we never dug up the Earth, to bring out her resources, for no reason.

'Everything has its purpose, everything has its place within the beautiful creation, and we understood that fully, so all our ceremony, all our way of living, all our dances, honoured this deep knowledge within us, this deep and abiding love that we had, and continue to have, within us, for Mother Earth.

'Sadly, it has been overshadowed by the grief, and the corruption, of many of the leaders today. We knew well in advance, from the many experiences we had, with the Europeans who did not value us in any way, who made every effort to wipe out our civilization, and instil in us the European ways of living. Many, many, tears have been shed over this, not so much for ourselves, although we'd have felt that deeply, but for Mother Earth herself, because a lot of her vibrancy has been lost over the centuries.

'Mother Earth is hurting; you all know this to be the case. We all know it in our hearts, in our souls, and we come now en masse, to the people that are willing to work with us, we're finding every soul that we possibly can, that has a fragment of their soul here, that

came at this time because they knew this time was so very special, and the time is dire, and they held in their hearts the desire to make a difference, and many of them especially the foreseers, the prophets, the mediums, came to connect with us, a part of a team that was established well before birth, that would work together, time after time.

'*Without respect, without honour, we are nothing, maybe this sounds a little extreme, but it is truly our higher-selves that is speaking here, to say that these are characteristic, qualities, of what it means to be in service, to dedicate ourselves to something so much higher than ourselves.*'

At this point it may be worth mentioning that "Mother Earth", or "Gaia", or "Pachamama", as Sanaya calls her, is a living being. So abuse to her, just as abuse to a person, will inevitably bring consequences. We also affect her through the energies of our collective consciousness. When we are collectively in a rage, for instance, the weather patterns may reflect this. When we allow toxic poisons via chemical fertilizers, sprays to kill the creatures of the Earth, oil spillages and other such toxic wastes to enter the waters of our planet, together with an endless amount of largely unnecessary plastics, a response, sooner or later, is inevitable. So those, like Chief Joseph, who respected and caused no harm to the planet, are naturally concerned and from spirit life return to say so, and to help when and where and in any way they are able.

Next, is a little more to enjoy from Zac, communicating through the medium, Janet Treloar.

70. Zac - October 2022
In conversation with Pam Gregory - Astrologer

'*There's a lot of 'Doom and Gloom' as Janet would say. There's a lot of doom and gloom, but ultimately, this is just the shadows that we are moving through into the realm of light. What I really mean by that is light for everyone, light that does not have to be taken from another.*

'**Light that is permanently within you, giving you the answers, giving you the abilities, the skills, giving you these things, and it is** *not because it is bestowing it when I say giving, it is because it is your innate, new light wisdom, that will be coming through.*

'Everything, when I look to the future on so many different potential timelines for humanity, becomes easier, everything becomes easier you have all been locked into such a situation of, you know sort of, swimming against the current. But soon you'll be on the other side, and this is what we're seeing, but you need to keep feeding those potential lines with your choices, with your heart, with your desire to live upon this beautiful planet in a way that is leaving it better than when you got to it. You know, that could be so helpful, not just for yourself, but for everybody.'

Question asked about DNA, and reply below:

'The main thing to remember is there is an added wisdom within your DNA, it is not only ancestral, it is very much linked to not only who you are now, but who you are in every moment. Therefore, it lends to the theory that it must be in a permanent state of flux, a permanent state of change, if we are not looking at our own DNA the whole time, because how good we, you know we have lives to live here on this planet, then what you are getting is influences, and there is much influence of light codes and other that are coming in, again, available to everybody, to naturally evalate within the DNA system.

'The DNA of course is communicating throughout all the trillions of cells and into the tiniest areas and across the board of the whole energy body system, but it also is directly linked to the soul, and to the whole lineage. Therefore if it is getting this added help, it enables the person as well to be able to adapt into what their heart is desiring for the future, what the energy is connecting with, within the environment, emotional as well as physical, and other environment, and so really something that is so important, is to ensure that you do not think of your DNA as a something that is set in stone, think of it just like how you can change your thoughts in a moment, things can shift and change which will be representing your needs of life.

'It is not just lay back then let it all happen, be the creator of your destiny, what you are really desiring in your heart, you have universal help to make manifest, and that is what is so important, yes, these things from the past, the toxicity, is coming up for many different reasons, but do not be defined by this, see it as

something you are letting go of, if you want to define yourself at all, define yourself as an ever-changing, evalating sentient being that is here to enjoy life, and to make things better for self, for others, for collectively, live life in kindness and grace and love, and how then could anything go wrong.'

The Zac message above again confirms that our consciousness, how we think, can change our DNA; just as White Feather effectively said earlier. (See number 57 in this chapter).

Next I include a couple of short passages shared by Suzanne Giesemann, these are two of her Sanaya 'Daily Way Messages'.

71. Sanaya – 13th October 2022
Growing

'Your world is changing; that is what it does. Just as the Earth upon which you rest never rests, life evolves. You are part of this evolution. Your personal growth results from the changes around you, and you change the world from the changes within. You are part of an ecosystem. Systems are interconnected parts that form a whole. You can choose to see yourself as the part, the whole, or both. Either way, round and round you go. To resist change is to fight Nature. You are so very loved.'

72. Sanaya – 31st October 2022
The Tools

'You do not have to heal the world all at once. You cannot. It is a work in progress, and progress is a process, a flow, a dynamic movement onward and upward. Yes, you will have quantum leaps, and yes, some slippage, but ever onward, ever upward is the trajectory. Do not lose hope. Hope is part of the process. It is the by-product of Love which fuels the process and ensures the progress.

'You are babes in the grand scheme of things, yet being endowed with the attributes of the Creator you have the intellect and awareness to know when things are not in alignment with Love and when they can improve.

'Use your God-given gifts to bring more Love into the world with patience, compassion, kindness, and understanding. These are the tools of evolution.

'You are so very loved.'

This planet and us too are growing and evolving ever onwards and upwards in vibration and spiritual understanding, even the 'dark side' are really part of the light currently dimmed down by their own misconceptions of what it means to be human, not realising or remembering that they, as we, are all spirit beings temporarily experiencing upon the planet Earth. If they don't 'wake up' while here they will do so when they 'go home' (pass) to spirit life. If it is when they have left this Earth, they will, rather quickly, perhaps, have regrets concerning their behaviour and eventually feel the need to make amends in one way or another. What they need to know, and what spirit communications tell us, is that doing so on Earth is the most fruitful and desirable place to at least start making amends.

Next are some more insightful and inspiring words that came from the spirit guide, White Feather; these were shared by Robert Goodwin, his medium, via Facebook.

73. White Feather – 6th November 2022
It is Always Darkest Just Before the Dawn

'The nature of creation is energetic, comprising dimensional realities based upon frequency. All is light and all is consciousness - pure potential manifesting as actuality. Just as there are ascending planes of greater magnitude, light and beauty, so there are correspondingly descending levels of diminishing light, ignorance and ugliness. Souls exist upon all planes in accordance with their essential inner nature.

'The work of more highly evolved beings is therefore directed towards uplifting the lower planes and their inhabitants by increasing their frequency to the point where a shift in awareness occurs that effectively elevates their energy and light to a superior state - a natural state of being.

'However, the Earth, whilst essentially at a mid-point between the higher and lower states, is currently descending in its vibrational energy

due to the gross ignorance and subsequent behaviour of certain elements that are seeking to destroy any vestiges of light and goodness that remain.

'Yet, paradoxically a shift in human consciousness is also underway; one that is acting as a counter force to the increasingly darker influence amongst it. You are not here by accident - there are no accidents or chance happenings. All unfolds as it is meant to. You are then, here to address the imbalance and restore the harmony that is being eroded. This you will do ultimately through love, but directly through non cooperation, the challenging of ignorance at each and every turn and the setting by example of the ways of truth, justice and honour to your fellow man and all of creation. You will not fail if you are steadfast in your knowledge and your assertion of the divine principles of natural law. Do unto others that which you would have them do unto you.

'Remember this - it is always darkest just before the dawn. The light awaits you.'

Next are three final short extracts from the good doctor.

74. Dr Peebles - 5th December 2022

'There is a plan for your existence. Fall in line with that and you will finally realize that life does not have to be a struggle.

'Do you have the courage to be your beautiful unique self upon this school called planet Earth? Because that is what everybody is being called to do at this time, to awaken to your own heart, to your own truth, to your own beauty.

'It might be simple, it might be complex. You might enjoy dancing in the rain naked, you might enjoy just sleeping in late. Find out who you are and honour this. Can you do it for at least a day, perhaps two, and then perhaps three? Goodness gracious, if you do you might find it becomes a habit to be you all the time without hiding yourself away, giving yourself to the world automatically, realizing this will change your life in remarkable ways.

'You might find that you change your job, you might change relationships, or you might find that your work becomes more pleasant, and that your relationships become more satisfying, because you are

more satisfied with yourself and you're not struggling against who you really are, as everything starts to fall into place with simplicity and ease.

'It is a comforting way to live your life, to be authentic and not hide yourself away, to give of the magic of yourself to the world.

'When you are awakened to your true self, to your true heart, you are not out to hurt anybody, you're not out to take advantage of anybody, you're not out to manipulate anybody. What you are doing is just simply living authentically, the loving being that you are, expressing yourself in the world without striving to change anyone around you, but instead, living your life as a demonstration to others as to what is possible by being authentic, by being true to yourself and letting others just simply observe you.

'Not everybody has to like you, because not everybody understands you. You, my dear friends, are unique. You are extraordinary unto yourself. Find your heart, all of the God light within you.'

75. Dr Peebles – 30th December 2022
Surrender to God

'You'll find my dear friends that manners will start to resurface, it will start slowly, but it will emerge almost as if it is a trend that is happening upon the Earth. Human beings will be sick and tired of being sick and tired, and they will say, "You know something; I just want to put my faith and trust in God, I'd rather have one good day of life than 60 years of worry about death".

'And suddenly my dear friends, human beings will surrender into the journey, and there will be spiritual teachers who will come to the surface, and will be teaching humanity about how to do this, how to surrender and trust in God. To be at peace with that, the more you do so you will all find that you will have less illness, you will feel better in yourself. It will have nothing to do with what you are eating, what you are wearing, what weight you are; all these conditions that society is putting upon you for your happiness.

'You will suddenly find this peace that surpasses understanding, the aches and pains in your body will melt away, you will start to feel absolutely comfortable in your body, large or small, tall or short, more *so than ever before, because you will know that everything in the world is in right order.*

'Now that may sound, my dear friends, a little optimistic for some of you, but in the reality of your world, and the reality and truth of God within you, that is really the way that it is, my dear friends. And suddenly we'll find that so many pains will disappear, when you start to realize that everything is in right order.

'You will find faith and trust becomes a necessity, because you can't put your faith and trust in the world around you necessarily, because there are so many opinions, so many other things that people want to change, about you, perhaps, the only place you can find true faith and trust is within yourself. What happens in this, when you trust those things that you feel inside, when you are coming truly from love, when you are truly in touch with the God light within you, when you find and touch the face of God within, all of a sudden a whole new world opens up to you.

'You're here upon the planet Earth, but now you have the insights and the awareness that there is something more than what meets the eye, and you will suddenly find, my dear friends, that you are never ever alone, and you will have an awareness and a sense of the beautiful guidance from your spirit guides, who are around you.

'You will have the awareness of God as a voice within you. You will have the awareness, my dear friends, of energy, and how it works, and how you are an energetic being, and how you can transform your reality when you are in touch with the magnificent strength and power of that light and energy within you.

'You will discover my dear friends that you can project your thoughts to another, and they will hear you, and you can hear their thoughts as well, so you can develop your telepathy, and you will begin to understand my dear friends that your dearly departed loved ones are not departed at all, but they are right there with you, right there within you, and you can hear them, and feel them, and you can consult with them when you need help. There are so many things that will open up, it's a magical year, with an awareness of self, as the mystics that you are.

'Not everybody will find this within self, because there are some students upon this Earth who are quite new to the planet, and they will still be, if you will, wanting to find their joy and their satisfaction in

striving to get as much money as they possibly can. Greed has been around for centuries, and that's not just simply going to disappear; but there is an awakening that is happening upon the Earth, in the hearts of the many, rather than the few.

'This is an extraordinary time upon the Earth, where it will be known that the many, rather than the few, are beginning to become much wiser, and realizing that there is more than meets the eye, it's not about all the stuff in your world, it's about the stuff inside of yourself that really counts, the things that you take with you in terms of your development and your awareness of the love that you are.'

76. Dr Peebles – 30th December 2022
Time to Live Our Truth

'There are going to be magnificent changes on your Earth within technology, human beings will be starting to take charge, and saying what they really do want to see in terms of external growth, in terms of technology, and how it's used, and how it's played with, and such in your world.

'There will be a deeper awareness and understanding of individuals who are not being so honest, and those people will be fingered out, and they will be shown to the world, and the world will say, "Ah, well, we don't want this anymore it's time to become more honest with each other, it's time to live our truth and speak our truth, and be, if you will, genuine in the world, and come from love, not from greed, not from a manipulative standpoint trying to manipulate people into compliance etc."

'You will find my dear friends that there will be lots of discussions about money, how it ought to be structured, how it ought to be used, how it ought to be played with, how it ought to be given to the many, rather than the few. So that everybody can live, not equitably necessarily, but can be comfortable in their lives. Human beings are coming to a deeper awareness, money has been a great controller of humanity, and now you will find that human beings will say, "You know something, money isn't working for me", and there will be lots and lots of people on the planet Earth who say, "I don't want to work with money, let's do this through trade, that's one thing that people can't manipulate about me, I *can say I want to give you my services, and you can say I will give you this service, in return."*

'It's a beautiful time to be alive, my dear friends, despite the circumstances, it is perhaps one of the most difficult times upon your planet Earth because of the grand awareness that you have of each other. It's not as if you are just living in a small town, and that's all you can see, and that's all you are dealing with. Now you've got these broader perspectives that everybody's in this together, you are one, you are one family, no matter what the society you are living in, no matter what country, no matter whose rule you are under in terms of political rule, you're beginning to understand that you're all made of the same stuff, you all bleed, you all love, you all want to know more, you all want to learn, you want to grow, and you want to feel that peace that surpasses understanding.

'You all want to be acknowledged and seen and heard and felt by the world. But most of all you want to be seen and felt and heard and acknowledged by you; you to self, and then my dear friends you will find that it doesn't really matter what anybody thinks of you, no matter what, you will know who you are, you will not doubt who you are, you will find my dear friends that your relationship with God is very, very, real and tangible. And you will not have to, if you will, prove anything to anybody, because you will know, that you know, who you are, and God knows who you are, and that is truly, truly, all that matters.

'You my dear friends are a beautiful spirit, a student of the Divine, go your way in peace love and harmony as you enter into the year of 2023, relax, release, surrender, and remember to breathe deeply, and know that you are love. God bless you indeed.'

There is plenty of 'food for thought' in this chapter; the good news and the dark to overcome with the power of the light and love within. The next chapter, I'd suggest, is even more exciting; and points to a time when people are more truly awake to their true nature, and can harness and work with this awareness to create a wonderful enlightened future world; a new Earth.

3. Spirit Guides Speak of the Unfolding Age of Aquarius

It was in the "The Spirit's Book" by Allan Kardec published in 1857 that the final answer to a question effectively spoke of the times to come that are now unfolding upon Earth.

The fact that more than one-hundred and fifty years have passed since this spirit communication shows us that the transformation of planet Earth was never going to be some overnight affair.

So the process of transforming this Earth into a more enlightened and peaceful planet is a slow ongoing process of evolution. Although I do believe the potential for speeding-up this process is (and always has been) in our own hands. It will happen; this fact is certainly promised by a number of guides. But, as effectively mentioned, we can help to make it a more speedy transformation.

The question asked in the Spirit's Book and the reply was as follows.

Question:
Will the reign of goodness ever be established upon the Earth?

'Goodness will reign upon the Earth when, among the spirits who come to dwell in it, the good shall be more numerous than the bad; for they will then bring in the reign of love and justice, which are the source of good and of happiness.

'It is through moral progress and practical conformity with the laws of God, that men will attract to the Earth good spirits, who will keep bad ones away from it; but the latter will not definitively quit the Earth until its people shall be completely purified from pride and selfishness.

'The transformation of the human race has been predicted from the most ancient times, and you are now approaching the period when it is destined to take place.

'All those among you who are labouring to advance the progress of mankind are helping to hasten this transformation, which will be effected through the incarnation, in your Earth, of spirits of higher degree, who will constitute a new population, of greater moral advancement than the human races they will gradually have replaced.

'The spirits of the wicked people will be excluded from the Earth, and compelled to incarnate themselves elsewhere; for they would be out of place among those nobler races of human beings, whose felicity (happiness) would be impaired by their presence among them. They will be sent into worlds less advanced than the Earth, which will furnish them with the means of advancing, while contributing also to the advancement of their brethren of those younger worlds.'

The above immediately tells us much. Because it suggests that even in, or prior to 1857, a transformation of the people of planet Earth was not only promised, but it was 'predicted from the most ancient times'.

This promise, or prediction, I know dates back at least two-thousand plus years, to the time of the highly evolved soul known to us as Jesus.

It was also known by the two spirit guides I mention next, Red Cloud and White Eagle.

Red Cloud

In a collation of Red Cloud teachings from the 1930's, now published by *Brandon J. Kim* as, *Red Cloud's Inner Teachings*, the guide at times spoke of the Age of Aquarius as already taking some effect from perhaps as far back as the 1850's.

He also said that some of the teachings of Jesus alluded to what was then an Age to follow the Age in which Jesus, or the "Nazarene", as Red Cloud mostly called him, was on Earth.

Red Cloud also spoke of an Age lasting around 2000 years; and that the Astrology is significant or, at least, a reflection of changing times and energies coming to planet Earth and all life upon her.

On 13th October 1933 Red Cloud said this about Jesus.

'He also taught you many things that were about to come to pass, and one of them was that at the end of 2000 years a revelation should come to pass. That was the new Aquarian Age which ye (you) entered somewhere about fifty to eighty years ago.'

Red Cloud also said that a new Master or Great Teacher will be born about 200 years from the time he was speaking, this should therefore be sometime around the year 2133. And that the people by then will be prepared, through their own evolution, to accept such a soul entering the physical world. Interestingly he said:

'...the second coming that you talk about will not be of the Nazarene, but of one on even a higher plane of evolution...'

The Great Awakening is unfolding now, in this 21st century as I write, and Red Cloud was sharing information that confirms that many things currently being spoken of in this 21st century, and promised by communicating spirit teachers, he spoke of ninety years ago. (Where Red Cloud said "Man" this encompasses all of Humanity, men and women).

Such as the following (still on 13th October 1933):

'Ye (you) who are children of the light, are leaving behind you in the sands of time an immortal record which will cleanse matter, and when that Master enters into matter and teaches this world after its travail there WILL be a new heaven and a new Earth, and slowly through the evolution of earthly matter there will be the vibrations of spirit entering so clearly, so perfect will be the vibrations of man in matter that man shall be conscious that he walketh daily with spirits, that he shall be hand in hand with angels.

'Slowly, as the evolution of man continues so will man bring about that condition he calls and prays for, Heaven will be brought upon Earth, and man WILL be able to walk side by side with those spirit messengers, and man will be able to see his fellow men as they are, for the record of a man's life shall be implanted upon his spirit, and his spirit shall be seen by his fellow man, and as thou art so shall thy record be.

'And in those days that are to come to pass man, in walking side by side with angels shall slowly realise that his endurance in matter is but to accomplish the power of discernment that which is his God. And as he discerns in matter that which is his God so will he discern himself the spirit, for he is part of the law and part of the Godhead.

'When this realisation of the consciousness of himself enters man then the kingdom of heaven will enter into matter. It is already here, but the heaviness of matter obliterates the possibilities at the moment.

'In two to three hundred years yet, a greater revelation shall be given to man, and he will become master of the elements; at the moment the elements are master of man. Once man becomes master of the elements, then he is at-oneness with his God and the kingdom of heaven.'

On 10th November 1933 Red Cloud spoke about Atlantis and the fact that some in that period were awake in the sense of spiritual consciousness, while some amongst them were not.

Just as today, with increased "Light" or "Cosmic Light" presently reaching this planet, we find that there are those people 'awake' or 'awakening' and responding to these incoming energies, that bring a higher level of consciousness and vibration, and those people who remain ignorant of them. With the latter in particular remaining just as materialistic in their approach to life as ever they were.

Consequently, they fail not only to realise that life is eternal, but also that they are so often being misled and 'encouraged' or manipulated by those whose agenda is far removed from the vibration of love and light. Of those 'asleep' to the greater realities of spirit life, Red Cloud said:

'These are the children today in the darkened spaces and places of matter who in the extinguished state of their soul evolution brought about, north, south, east and west of your world planet, the conditions of suffering and war.

'They are those who walk in darkness, in blindness, outside the laws of consciousness. They have come through matter on to this planet without the fuller realisation of their own consciousness, and in their disorganised state are running rampant in the world of matter, they are bringing about wars, suffering degradation, shame, bankruptcy, and all the things appertaining to matter, which are but illusions to spiritual consciousness. And I want you to realise that you have the light of consciousness today, you must not be led blindfolded by those who are endeavouring to lead you by the law of materialism.'

So even ninety years ago, back in 1933, we were being warned, or advised, 'not be led blindfolded' by those advancing a materialistic (or globalist) agenda.

We are on this planet for what is but a short visit, be it one or one-hundred years. In eternity, in relation to the multiple lifetimes most souls on Earth have undertaken, it is but a moment in time. A moment that principally ought to be spent advancing our own soul, in one of countless ways.

Chasing earthly riches, ever-greater wealth and possessions, power and control of others, and the like, purely for one's own gratification with no desire to use whatever wealth is obtained to help anyone else, save perhaps the odd family member or friend, I would suggest is not an ideal use of a lifetime. (Far from it, I feel).

On the 23rd November 1934 Red Cloud also said:

'When I speak of the kingdoms of the world I am not speaking of the kingdom of crowns, but the kingdoms raised by men. The kingdom of selfishness, hate and power in abuse, those attributes which are not of the world of God, those are the kingdoms which are being overthrown. The greatest kingdom which we shall have to overthrow is the kingdom of ignorance.

'What did the Nazarene tell you? I am going to tell you ere (before) I depart, "The kingdom of truth shall come amongst men because the truth shall set you free." Free from the persecutions of your world, free to think for yourselves, free to worship your own way. Free to love your own way, that is what we have come to teach you, free to breathe and to live in the happiness of God and the beauty of the world in which you exist.

'Those are the kingdoms we have come to establish. I speak not of the kingdoms of crowns, for automatically they will fall according to cause and effect and evolution.'

On 4th January 1935 Red Cloud effectively, in the following few words, said something that to me still echoes all too true with so many propagating and promoting agendas that through their investments add greater and greater wealth to their already bulging bank accounts and assets that in financial terms total billions of pounds or dollars or any currency they choose. While those materialistically least secure, 'living on the breadline' as it used to be termed, find themselves increasingly less able to financially manage:

'Social Reform! It is a mockery. You raise great buildings to the glory of man instead of to the glory of God. In your great buildings you place men who do not think of the betterment of humanity but of themselves.'

However, remaining positive in the certain knowledge that new Earth, and one of fairness, kindness, honestly, sharing, love and abundance for all will and already is beginning to unfold around us, this is something that Red Cloud said 21st June 1935:

'There shall come upon your Earth plane, through the travail of birth, a new born soul in consciousness and man shall have revealed to him the powers of healing through the mental states of his own conscious mind; man shall heal, for many diverse plans shall be brought about, and Man shall realise through the effect of the many senses which are in him of the power, of the possibility, of the rays which shall come from space, which are held in man's keeping.

'He shall work side by side with Angels, not just a few mediums here and there, but every man shall know his kingdom, for man shall know when he passes from the limitations of matter into the Spirit; he shall know how to readjust the law for those in their lowly state of evolution. There will be no need for the physical doctors; I don't mean this unkindly, I am just prophesying for the future generation. For the effect upon man's body he will get down to the cause in his mind, himself, which is perfection already. He will find that the wondrous teaching is true which the Nazarene taught, "Be still and know that I am God."

'Where now he suffers from his own mental distraction and confusion at the moment, he will be able to readjust, reveal and recharge the physical at his own bidding.

'There will come about in the consciousness a new man; the law of the elements will be adjusted, the physical idea in its crudity, in

its suffering will pass, and man shall know he is as he is known, a perfect being.'

When Red Cloud quotes, *"Be still and know that I am God."* He means that each person at some time in the future will realise that they are God, or an aspect of God, and that all is One, that everything in creation, in all universes, is God.

In regard to healing, interestingly, the spirit guide-teacher "Zac" during an August 2022 video chat, shared on the Hazel Grace Newton YouTube channel (see Links), more or less said the same thing. That doctors and even new technology that may, and likely will, come about as an interim aid to public health will in 'the future' be unnecessary as we, humanity at that point in time, will know that the power is within each of us to heal. While he also said that we can have social gatherings with friends and assist in healing each other. (See number 66 in chapter two for some of what Zac said).

White Eagle

Grace Cook was a medium (from as early as 1913) and most noted as the channel through whom White Eagle spoke and delivered a vast array of informative and enlightening communications. She passed to spirit life (went home) in 1979 age 87.

When I contacted them to ask for permission to use some extracts from their books, the White Eagle Lodge UK kindly gave me a little more background information. Informing me that White Eagle started speaking through Grace Cooke in the 1920's, although the early messages were not recorded. It is known, that White Eagle spoke to a closed Spiritualist circle around 1930. While the earliest public addresses were from 1933. The very earliest White Eagle book was simply titled, *A Little Book of Prayers*, and appeared in February 1937; and the first book of teaching was called, *Illumination*, and that was published in July 1937.

What especially interested me while reading a couple of the White Eagle books was his mention of the Aquarian Age and the changes that will take place with people in future generations, and with life on Earth itself.

One of the White Eagle books I wish to mention is: *The Light Bringer – The Ray of John and the Age of Intuition.*

What follows are some passages from the above mentioned book that I feel will be of interest to readers, and relevant (similar or the same) to what is being revealed to us today by some of the present spirit communicators I include quotes from in this book. In, *The Light Bringer*, White Eagle answered the following question.

Q. What will the Aquarian Age be like?

'Many beautiful qualities in human nature are going to be brought forth in this new age. Men and women are already beginning to extend their term of life in the physical body, and there will come a further prolongation. Life will become longer, because as each person evolves he or she will touch divine wisdom; though at first no one will recognize having done so.

'Science, when wielded by the mind of the heart, will become a power for the blessing of humankind. Wonderful things are in store for the world when this blending, this balancing of the scientific mind with the spiritual mind, has been established. We can see into the future to a time when each man and woman has attained son-daughtership, by a process of self-master. We see a world made beautiful. We see cities built not only with material substance, but beautified by the light of the spirit, and this spiritual power harnessed to physical and material needs. We see graceful and spacious buildings, with light radiating from the walls of the room, from the ceilings, although there seems to be no one particular point from which the light shines. This light will give warmth when necessary, but we also see that there will be a change in the climate.

'Souls preparing for incarnation are now being so strengthened - by your help, if you are working for the light - that incoming personalities to your world, the newborn, will bring with them a memory of the beauty of the spirit worlds.'

White Eagle went on to say more about the Aquarian Age; and the following examples are collated from a range of different pages of *"The Light Bringer"*. I do recommend reading the whole book, available at the White Eagle website. (See Links)

'Extremes of heat and cold will no longer exist, for the climate will be adjusted according to the needs of the people. This may sound to you like a fairy story, but if you will develop your inner vision you will begin to realise the possibilities for humankind as the spiritual power manifests more definitely. When spirit becomes dominant in matter you will see the results in all forms of life, in all the arts and the sciences and in the lives of people themselves.

'With the Aquarian Age you will see a revolution in education, in religion, in science. Instead of education being a process of intensive mental study, so that the mind becomes blocked and stuffy, the new influences will penetrate the spirit; and the intuition of the children will be unfolded and stimulated by vibrations of beauty, of colour, and art and form.

'On the etheric plane are grand libraries in which the soul can search. It will be possible for you to do this in the Aquarian Age. Instead of a process of cramming, education will be so applied that it will strike into the very innermost part of the soul and will open out and bring forth knowledge which is within. Make no mistake, knowledge and wisdom come primarily from within, and with the right process, with the correct motive and aspiration, the soul can unfold the fruits of all knowledge and wisdom.

'May we tell you, also, of the part music and speech are going to play in the future? Even now the stimulation in people of the love of music has begun. The power of music is going to increase. Beauty itself is going to increase. More beautiful music will stimulate the mental qualities and will gently open the heart centre. That music is coming, and will raise the vibrations of the Earth. It will have a great effect upon the soul-development of the race, and those beautiful buildings that are suitable and have the right acoustics will be used, and the music will be sent forth from such places into human life. Music is a tool, an avenue, a channel through which these great spiritual forces will flow to humankind, stimulating again, in turn, the sleeping powers latent in every human being.

'Music is beautiful architecture. Music is beautiful art, for music produces colours more exquisite than you have ever seen. The use of the throat centre, the use of speech, is of great importance. Beautiful language has a part to play in the new age in the building-up of constructive good.'

'Works of art will become living creations, and the vibrations of nature will be so heightened, so quickened, and the gardeners will be so trained by the human creative spirit, that the gardens will be beauty enshrined. You raise the question: 'Can we improve on nature? With pure spirit functioning through the mind of God's highest creation on Earth - the human - beauty will be expressed in the arrangement and control of nature. We speak with knowledge; we know of that which we have seen in the higher worlds. We know that nature, as you see it on Earth, is not yet perfect; but with men and women working harmoniously with nature, there will come further unfoldment. We see indeed a beautiful Earth!'

Revolution or Evolution?

'There will be many unexpected happenings in the new age. Miracles, my children, the world will call them. From many quarters a flash of light will come to illumine the darkness of the Earth. The effect will be like a revolution, but not of the kind you think - a revolution of thought and ideas, which are going to flood in before very long.

'The truth of the Brotherhood of the ancient wisdom and of the White Light, established long ago, will be re-established on your Earth. Groups will be formed all over the world, and even the governments of the nations will be formed of men and women initiated into the ancient brotherhood of the light of the Son-Daughter of God. The wisdom from the East will be established in the West, to work on the outer planes, on governments, and in the commercial world. It sounds impossible for the spirit of the Son of God to be established in the commercial world, but it will be so. Instead of competition there will be cooperation and brotherhood, and the goodwill which is to come in the Age of Aquarius.'

'Even the form of governments to which humanity has clung for centuries will die out, and it will be government for all - and not for protecting the rights of a few - by a government under direction from the council chamber of the cosmic hierarchies. This method of guiding and inspiring the leaders of all the nations with the ideal of goodwill, with the ideal of the good in the whole of humanity, is in course of preparation and Will lead to a universal brotherhood of individuals and of nations.

'Great changes come. Keep calm, simple and humble, and give from your hearts the truest brotherhood you understand and you will assist not in revolution, but in steady, progressive evolution.

'What comes before this? Will the Uranian influence of Aquarius cause floods and Earthquakes, and the sweeping away of that which is unwanted in the new age? Or will that which appears useless be woven into its fabric? So much depends upon the response of those who are now living on Earth and who understand. What a responsibility is yours! You are builders - master masons - and your Master, the Grand Architect, has issued his orders, not through the lips of any human being, but through the heart. Within the heart, through the sufferings and restrictions brought by the influence of Saturn, the password is sounded which flings wide the gateway into the Age of Aquarius.

'There must come cataclysms, not necessarily of a physical nature, but perhaps through the soul of things changing - a revolution which will not necessarily cause bloodshed, but a revolution of thought. The human spirit will rise up and say: 'We cannot slay our brother-sister.' The whole being will rebel against war. Already we see the influence of the new age creeping into the hearts of people, demanding that there shall be peace, equality, brotherhood, the right to express the spirit and to live harmoniously, freely, to worship God in their own true way. Slowly into people's hearts is creeping the spirit which says: 'There are other worlds beyond the material world; there are other ideals to live for beyond the accumulation of material wealth and power - which fades in time and leaves behind only dust and ashes.'

'THE SPECIAL outpouring of power from the spiritual Sun, of which we speak, comes at the close of a spiritual cycle. At the end of each two thousand years a happening occurs cosmically, and there is a conjunction between the earthly sun and that spiritual sphere of light which is animating the sun, and all life on Earth. The power which is poured out was known to the ancients as the solar force.'

'This mystery teaching which we are imparting in a minor degree has existed over aeons of time. Great temples in remote parts of the world are mysteries to your investigators today, and they will remain mysteries until men and women learn the inner secret. When they become possessed of spiritual secrets, then they will understand the purpose of the temples of Egypt, Tibet, China, the Andes, Mexico, Atlantis. They will understand the purpose of the *temples in Britain where the priests of the sun, the priests who had the wisdom of the solar force, worshipped and worked to control and direct the elements; and worshipped and worked to direct the great masses of beings belonging to those elements for the creation and the projection of a rich and beautiful life in a beautiful world. This is God's gift to humanity - God's plan for humanity - not the present state of greed and selfishness which exists. Can you not see that the only way for the true reform, for evolution to come, is not the way of rebellion and revolution amongst the masses and the nations, but the way of spiritual evolution? Then there will come true and lasting peace, and the golden age will be ushered in.'*

'In the same degree as the individuals progress, so the whole race approaches this point of brotherhood and awareness. You may feel that many centuries may elapse before the world can respond. Nevertheless, we assure you that during the coming fifty years, you will be astonished at the soul-progress of the world, because within this time unbelievable changes will come.'

Fifty years plus may have elapsed since the above was said, and readers may feel that the world is still in a mess. But much has changed, mentally at least, as nowadays more people than ever know that we are all immortal spirit beings, souls who choose to incarnate in human form on Earth. The dark agenda is also now being exposed and recognised for what it is, and can no longer be hidden from view. And, of course, in the process of more and more people awakening, and understanding that it is not simply a fantasised conspiracy but a real one. This still growing awareness, and with the consequent reactions and actions of many, many good people, the dark corners of secrets are and will further be revealed, along with those involved; and the agenda will be dismantled, and a new Earth, that is now in the process of creation, will replace it.

Continuing next with some extracts from the same White Eagle book, *The Light Bringer*, and I notice that some of these are affirming what I have said above.

'The difficult part is for a soul to live, day by day, in a dark world, absorbing the lessons which the outer life is intended to teach.

Above all, we would ask you to cast out all fear. If you persevere with this one small lesson for even just a few weeks, at the end of that time you will realise what a great step forward you have taken. Be without fear; Surrender to God. You will be filled with love and light; you will help the world forward towards peace and will help all those who are in darkness because they are full of fear - even your so-called enemies.'

'In this new age into which you are advancing, there will be great stimulation of both the materiality and the spirituality of the human race. There are already a large number of souls in incarnation who, consciously or unconsciously, knowing or unknowing, have come to be pioneers for this new age. We would have you realise that however simple, however obscure your own life; you have a very special charge. You have come back to Earth for a special purpose; you have come not only to develop your divine consciousness but also to pioneer the pathway which will become the path for all who will follow. You cannot help but develop your own character and divinity if you are truly serving others. At the same time, do not concern yourself too much with your own growth and development, so long as you have a true outlook. All you have to do is to obey spiritual law, and then you will find yourself on a path.

'This path is the path of all pioneers of the spirit. Those in incarnation today are having a hard time, for they are preparing for the coming at a later period in the Aquarian Age of many brothers and sisters of the Great White Lodge. Angel beings, too, will draw near. Men and women will walk and talk with angels, but remember that it takes an angel to recognize an angel, a god to recognize a god, so until men and women have developed the necessary qualities within themselves, they remain unconscious of the presence of angels or of gods. A perfect law is working through life and no one can escape either reward or suffering, either joy or pain. You are a magnet and you attract to yourself that which you are yourself. The vibrations you create within yourself are very powerful. They draw to you similar vibrations.'

'Now the destructive power of evil is necessary on the Earth, for there is a great deal to be cleared away - outworn ideas, and outworn methods in many different departments of life. To this end the powers are working to clean up - or, shall we say, destroy - because when a condition has served its purpose it must be

absorbed, it must go, and this is the value of the destructive element in life. We would give you a true perspective of the value of destruction - of the clearing away of old methods and old ideas, and of making ready for the coming of the good, the true and the beautiful. This is what we mean when we say that the balance must be maintained.

'Before the new age of Aquarius can fully be ushered in, there has to be a breaking-down of old conditions. We witness this breaking down everywhere; but those hurt in the process need healing. Indeed, they must be healed in order to bring forth the new, beautiful age of the spirit.'

Next, continuing with White Eagle, the following collated extracts come from various pages of the book, *Group Consciousness – Realising Brotherhood on Earth*. Again, to find much more the book can be read.

'We have told you many times that the positive good thought of one individual is more powerful than the nebulous negative thought of ten thousand. And so we say, cast out fear. There is nothing for you to fear. Fear in the minds of men and women is a very bad thing my children, because fear is a weakness, and it is like a chink in the armour of God. If you fear anything you are making way for the enemies, the adversaries of God. Therefore when you find yourselves fearing, either about yourself, your health, your conditions or anything that comes into your life, you are weakening yourself.'

'If you would be happy, my brothers and my sisters, and give happiness to all you contact, seek the quiet places of the spirit, and discriminate between the unreal, which is of the world, and the reality, which is of the spirit. Watch quietly, in confidence; never let your confidence be shaken, but watch confidently the gradual breaking through of this light in the affairs of the world. The dawn of this glorious brotherhood is now appearing.'

'Love; love much. Love each other, love all nature; love your brethren of the animal kingdom. Reach out through the dark veil of illusion, the dark veil of matter, into that higher mental world, to the brotherhood of the nature spirits, the brotherhood of angels and the brotherhood of the great solar universe. You are in it.'

'THE WORLD is advancing. In the world each one of you is needed; each one is a spoke in the wheel, and we bless you, all brethren, for we work together to bring light, knowledge, wisdom, love, into the hearts of all peoples. When these groups of White Brethren are formed all over the world, as they will be, the light will perform spiritual miracles in physical matter and the governments will all unite in service.

'The time is not distant when the White Brotherhood will be the established religion of all peoples. Materialism will die, through the spirit rising like a fire in the heart of man and woman. This is the way of evolution. The pure white light is like a white fire which cannot be extinguished. People may try to smother it, as they do at the present time, but the flames of truth will burst forth. We only need to let the divine fire burn brightly upon our own altar, the one within the temple of our own soul, and we shall set free many another soul.

'So, my brethren, in the words used in the ancient days of Atlantis, we say: "Let the light shine! Let the divine fires burn upon the sacred altar".

'Your work means continually remembering the spiritual state of life from which your spirit has come and to which it will return. It means continually making an effort to live with the spiritual values ever in your heart and mind, to live refusing to be entangled or held down by wrong values; and when you see the right, keep to the right and do not be influenced by material conditions. The spiritual law is such that it will never lead you astray. If you follow the truly spiritual law you cannot go wrong, but you will have to have the courage to hold fast to a decision in favour of spiritual law.'

'What is regarded as evil has its work to do in bringing forth light out of its own darkness.

'Be at peace, then, for your mission is to be peace; and your mission is to be constructive in your thought, not destructive. We reiterate that the world is moving forward towards one great brotherhood of life. Let us all remember once again that we are one with all life, that there is the one lifestream running through every form of life on many planes of consciousness.'

'Listen, for you are in the company, on the inner planes, not only of those dear ones whom you have known all through your history

and even in your present incarnation, but with those beings who peopled the Earth millions of years ago. Moreover, you are not only in contact with ageless souls who were once human beings, but you are also in the company of beings who dwell on other planets. This is important for you to know, and all that we tell you is important for you to know and for you to believe and to realise, because progress is now rapid on your Earth plane and humans have to become much more spiritualized to enable them to attract and to converse with beings from other planets.

'The plan, the ideal, was given to men and women of ages and ages past. Through human beings it came, beings whom your very clever people once used to call savages! It is well to remember that a body which appears to be savage is the remnant of a great being. We are referring particularly to an ancient race that we will call an Indian race, an Indian of the West not the East. You have no conception at all of the age of our Indian brotherhood.'

'Humanity is quite unaware as yet of the immensity of the unfoldment which will take place within every human being.

'We want you to learn to draw aside the veil between physical matter and the astral plane and the mental plane and the celestial plane so that in your own way, by your own freewill, you can rise and live on these other invisible planes of life. The salvation of this Earth depends on the power of love to transform the life of pain and suffering to a life of harmony and brotherhood, beauty and wisdom. When the balance between the heart and the head in humankind is achieved, the way will be opened for the visitation not only of angels, but of friends from outer space. If only we could persuade you that by living the life of the spirit, by devoting your prayers and service to the spirit, you can raise the whole world from darkness to light!'

'It is now coming slowly before your notice, but in this new age not only will the mental body be stimulated but also the soul power, and instead of having a few so-called mediums or psychics you will find that all people will have soul development, the quickening of the throat and the heart centre. All will accept what is now a mystery and what is ignorantly denied by the world. They will accept the truth of these invisible forces that are working through matter to raise it to a higher rate of vibration.'

As readers may observe, there is much corroboration of what White Eagle said with what so many spirit guides are presently saying.

Next, in a book called, *"Divine Healing of Mind & Body"* can be found a series of 14 talks delivered in 1948 by the spirit we know as Jesus, through the trance mediumship of Murdo MacDonald-Bayne. A few passages of which I quote, first, speaking of the 'vision of Daniel' (as featured in the Bible Book of Daniel), in Talk 11, he said:

'It is the vision of the things to come, the vision and purpose of the great Architect of the Universe, who created all planets and suns in the Universe and everything that exists therein and thereon.

'Each planet is controlled and directed by a spirit. Just as the Christ (spirit) controls this world, so does the great Ether Spirit control the various ether planets in this Universe. These Spirits are known to us; we understand them; we commune with them, because there is no space, no time, no distance.

'Each planet has its various degrees of influence upon the Earth, all ordained by the great Architect of the Universe.

'Daniel's vision is an understanding of the wavelengths of the expression of these Solar Angels, Solar Angels working for the unfoldment and upliftment of this Earth and all that dwells thereon. The end shall be Peace and Love. This message I bring to you, Truly I tell you that God has ordained that the end shall be peace, Love and Goodwill between all souls.'

In the above 'the end' I feel refers to the end of one Age and the time that we are unfolding more and more into as each day passes, the Age of Aquarius. It will eventually be a time when undoubtedly peace, love and goodwill between all souls shall become a reality.

Next, from Talk 12:

'I am one with humanity – in the Garden of Humanity one of the first blooms; and I shall be with you all days, even unto the end of the world.

'Many, who have lived on Earth in ignorance, misunderstanding their power, used it wrongly, because they did not understand the Infinite Love of God. But now they are growing and unfolding into freedom, through understanding of love.'

Even though the above words were delivered decades ago, it takes a long while for many if not most souls to grow and evolve, to become more enlightened. Collectively upon this planet there are now, I believe, far more souls who have grown and have reached the stage where they can recognise injustice, and stand peacefully against this. Also, that great numbers amongst these souls understand that life is eternal, and therefore there is never anything that need be feared. My guess is that the shift into a more spiritual and loving and love orientated attitude developed, or was certainly further propagated, out of the 'free-love', hippy, peace loving, revolutionary music loving generations of the 1960's. In fact, it was a 'movement' that has never really 'died'.

I include the next passages for two reasons, first to highlight the fact that we all have it within us to reach a spirit status akin to that of Jesus. In fact, it is a certainty that, one day, we will do so. Secondly, to show that the term "Christ" is not one reserved for one person, or spirit being. It, basically, represents an elevated degree of consciousness; one that we all possess, if somewhat passively at present. But, nonetheless it is there, ready for us to awaken to our potential, and thus reach this level of consciousness.

The following is from Talk 13:

'In your minds you have pictured the experience of seeing loved ones again, and know them face to face; this I truly tell you is real. Even those who injured you and those you also injured through ignorance will rejoice at meeting you again.

'This is the eternal law of the Spirit, the unfoldment of the Christ. As the consciousness becomes aware of this inner life, a change takes place in the consciousness, and all these hatreds disappear. Then it is wise for you to understand this while on Earth.

'Some born in ignorance die in ignorance. Now this shall not be your fate. The mist dissolves away, and there remains the beauty of the Christ of God.

'When I talk of the Christ of God I know that you are beginning to understand what the Christ means. It is the great Divine Man of God. Christ is the Divine man on Earth which includes all human souls. As cells exist in the one body, so does each one of you exist in the Christ of God. The seed of God is in you and it is sure to grow to maturity.

'No greater joy can ever be experienced than when that which you vaguely thought true becomes a Reality. You find that you have lost nothing but all is gained with a new understanding.

'You will be overwhelmed by the unlimited sense that takes hold of you, while all the false beliefs will drop from you.

'You will be the same living soul, no matter in which way you leave your body. You are still you; and in all those you loved, you will find a greater love and a greater attraction, a greater understanding, for nothing in love is lost.'

Another spirit guide or teacher whom I have already included some contributions from in this book is Zac.

There is a book I can certainly recommend, titled, *Layered Reality* by Valo Ray published August 2020 which features questions and answers between the author and Zac during private consultations. This contains plenty of what I would consider highly advanced information and explanations. In places it is also relevant to what is currently happening on Earth and to the new age that is unfolding. From this book I have 'borrowed' some passages and put these together in this chapter as pointers to better, interesting times to come. (Book page numbers are shown in brackets).

'It is not the future birth of children who are given this evolved brain. We are seeing this in the current lifetime now.' (p. 56)

'The shift that some people talk about is moving to a phase on Earth which gives rise to an opening that allows an expansion of the mind. The mind is a vehicle here on Earth which is one of the reasons why souls choose so many of the experiences on Earth. There is the physicality around it, which is the brain that allows the optimal level of evolution that can happen through the gathering and the understanding of data. Unlike a computer, which only takes the data and makes calculations from it, a human mind does much more than just calculations but allows the expansion to the next level.' (p. 61)

'By the gathering of experience, which the Source does not already know, we expand our consciousness. The way to do it is not through old wisdom and knowledge, but through experience. Experience that comes from emotions and thoughts. This idea is quite central

throughout this part of the universe. This little planet that seems to be hurting itself, killing itself, and, at the same time, a huge amount of love and good happen. What we would see, and why we help so much, is that it can be a pretty difficult place to be. The knowledge, the data, that come after this are quite immense, which allows for a vast progression to be happening on many layers. Humans, or shall we say the souls in human form, affect everything else. Imagine the collective consciousness of the universe. If one has an experience, everyone benefits from it.' (p. 62-3)

'People always talk about the Garden of Eden, and there is where the Earth is going. I do not want to I press the bubble, because it is not. It is moving more towards survival and more of a place of comfort. What I mean by this is that we are moving out of competitiveness into coherence, togetherness with one another. It is not going to take a week, a month, a year. It is going to take a few lifetimes.' (p. 107)

'However, the psychology of humanity has changed. They do not listen to one man or one woman anymore. So we need to work differently. One of the ways is via direct communications, just like what I am having with you. Another way is to increase the frequency of the Earth. We are shifting the energy within your cosmos in order to allow more influences - energetic cosmic influences - to come into the Earth. This is why so many people are channelling these things from other star systems and so on. What it is doing is harnessing the energy into the Earth so the Earth itself can be inspiring, and thereby lifting people's energies, and then we wait. It is a bit like putting a pot of water onto a stove, putting the heat on, and watch what happens. What we are doing is that we are influencing energy systems, awaking your energy system, so that you can be more aware of the love, the guidance that is coming from the 'nucleus' of the soul - more closely connected. We are putting the fire underneath.

'The idea behind it is that people will take note because their souls are also in charge, and so they will start making changes. Now, what happens is that it would always start with a minority of people first and move to the majority. It is true that there are people on this planet who not only have nothing, they have minus nothing. These are the souls. We know that with the energy impression, that this is a bit like a fallout, what is happening to the Earth, regarding the weather patterns and so forth. But we are holding on tightly, let us say, a ship in a storm. We

hold on tightly to anoint the knowledge of what humanity is capable of.' (p. 110-111)

'Unfortunately, it will not be immediately. This has actually started, to give you a date, around 1870s in very subtle ways. It came into human consciousness far more in the '30s, '40s, '50s, etc., all the way into the '60s and '70s. It is becoming on people's lips to talk of. But we actually know that the needle is turning towards annihilation in the 1870s. Particularly in the awareness of the increase in the industries, and what was happening, and we could see what would be happening to the environment and the greed that would come from it.

'Truly, the war that is happening on Earth is between the heart and the head. Do we listen to our head or do we listen to our heart? This is what it all boils down to. The more that we listen to our heart than our head, the more we will move towards peace and coherence on this Earth. Head has its place, but it is not the place to make big decisions because the heart is connected to everything else. It will be sending signals, even if they are not conscious signals, of the best for the whole rather than for the one. The mind makes the decision for what is right for the one, not for the whole.' (p. 112-113)

'What we have done is that we have people who are being born relatively recently, about 20 to 40 years ago, whose jobs, let us say, are not so much on an individual path, but are to infiltrate the darkest places. So we have those in the large industrial corporations that, should we say, do everything with their head. We have them in all of these. We have them in politics. We have them in all sorts of places. During the past two to five years, we realise that we need to move quicker. There are some of those who are from the 26th dimension who have actually manifested and have roles - roles that are not as the president of a company or a country, as we do not want to take it out of the hands of humanity. However, they are influential. They are more the people who stand behind - the secretary, the head of the finances, etc. We are not ignoring those parts which we think are the darkest. They are the ones we are trying to put most light into.' (p. 114)

'Remember that the DNA is changing at this time because we are wanting to be able to give people more freedom within their body. So after 1982, that was the first large influx with bodies being born with 'updated', let us call it, DNA, and we are seeing more of these in certain parts of China. And there are places like the Scandinavia

and others, where there are more of these - 'upgrades', let's call it - in the '90s. There is a revolution in the spirituality side of things that is happening in humanity. There is a level of conditioning of the physical self that is aligned with the vibration of the Earth at this time as well to allow more fluidity, more change.' (p. 131-132)

'One thing I would like to tell you is that in the events of pandemics or natural disasters which take a lot of lives, people may be tempted to think that they are ways for us to rebalance the book. This is not the case. I just want to tell you. It is not that there are too many people living on Earth, and so we need to wipe out some in order to rebalance the population. It is not at all true. We do not do that. When I talk about 'we', I mean we as souls. Each individual who dies under these circumstances is part of their own exit plan.' (p. 136-137)

'Now, for you and for those who are living at this particular time on Earth, there is a vast difference in vibration on the Earth (compared to those living in the past on Earth). Through these differences in vibration, it is allowing greater streaming of consciousness to be delivered directly from the higher selves. So, for the future - we are talking about the energies from the Earth's point of view - you have more choices because you are constantly accessing your souls, far more so than the lives that you have lived before in the linear time. It is not so much about the development of the soul, but, of course, it does happen. It is more about the principle of energetic evolution.

'The period that you are living in now is part of a cycle where there is an advancement of the evolution of the future. This allows a far higher vibration to be through. Thus, those who are incarnating in this period of the (linear) time are also part of this higher vibration as well. Even if you want to remain closed, like keeping the sun from entering the room using a curtain, the light would still slip through. The period of time that you are living now, particularly in about 2035 to 2037, everybody would have shifted.' (p. 163-164)

'Now, of course, there has been a collective consciousness with the desire to change, and this is where all of this is coming from. Also, this change is due to the change in the energy consciousness that is connected to your cuboid of the universe.

'Note that this energetic change does not happen overnight, and certainly does not come easily. As we know, the dense energy that *corresponds to the history of humanity would not be easily let go. People are still holding on to the past dense energy. Whatever nature does, people would suppress it with their dense energies. Do you know in the garden, where people are using the old-fashioned sieve to filter out small pieces of soil from the larger pieces of stones? The heavier and denser materials will stay on the top, and the finer particles go through. There is a lot of shaking and sieving that need to be done, and this is similar to what is going on at the moment. This period of energetic shift would be met with a lot of resistance due to the presence of old and outdated values, and this sieving can be quite a violent action. This is what humanity is experiencing for some time, and will continue to happen. The difficulty is the conflict involves vast differences in poverty and wealth, power and the lack of power, etc. However, in a way, it is necessary.' (p. 165)*

'There are other times, particularly in the future, when people are not so bothered, and the population would go down to five billion or so. More comfortable for the Earth, more comfortable, but there will be more tranquil times. So, from the human's perspective, that is the time you want to be living in, not the chaos - but souls are interesting beings, ha ha. They always want to learn more, discover more. Yes, yes, yes. So they all want to go for difficult times.' (p. 209-210)

'An intention can travel beyond the space-time, and so it is not constrained by the restriction of space-time as matter is. It goes to the 'void', where it has access to everything else. Thus, it can travel from one end of the universe to another end with a blink of an eye. This, in essence, starts to affect time. It is easier to travel through space than it is through time. Time, we have to bend a little in your cuboid of the universe. But due to a recent change that happens upon your Earth, like that which happens in March (2019), people can harness the power to move through time. With time, it is like speeding up - a bit like putting heat, some kind of catalyst, under the kettle. With time, it is about speeding up the molecular structure, say, of a person. When you shift through dimension, speed is important. Because everything is moving, rotating, spinning, the quicker you go, the more you can move into that dimension.

'Our thoughts and intentions can have the power to not just muse on something, think and dream about something. They can do much more. The way this is done is at the quantum level, where the space-time restriction no longer applies.' (p. 246)

'We do want people to be aware of the invisible world, we do want people to be aware of their soul. There will always be people who are not interested in this, and that is fine. This knowledge is not prescriptive. It is not for everyone. But what we want to see is the tipping point. What we want is enough people at the tipping point that this goes from myth to a commonly accepted fact, and through that, people would then take more responsibility to their lives.' (p. 299)

As I said about this book, it does contain what I consider highly advanced information; but information that I feel gives us a little more understanding of where this world, and humanity, is heading.

4. The Dark Agenda – Part Two

Power   Money   Control

The above, Power, Money and Control are absolutely, one-hundred percent what certain people in this world want. They do not care about public health, nor do they care about the climate, pollution, the rainforests or anything else – unless it impacts on their personal lives.

They do not care if their policies hurt the average person in any way, physically, emotionally, or mentally. Nor do they care if their policies cause the premature departure from Earth of the average person. No matter whether such people die from hypothermia, starvation, obesity, suicide, disease, or the side effects of drugs, whether prescription or recreational, or the effects of a genuine or so-called vaccine. Then, of course, there are those who 'die' because of some conflict or war they have caused. And those they have murdered for having the affront to discover a cure for some disease; or find some alternative, more or less, free source of energy. How dare such people expect not to be murdered for trying to help the average person; when those of the dark agenda are raking in billions and billions of pounds or dollars from their current (recommended, by them!) medical treatments and energy sales.

It is obvious that not everyone who is 'playing along' for personal gain with the policies and recommendations of the dark agenda is evil or desires the power to totally dominate and control society. Most of the 'foot soldiers' are such as corporation executives, politicians, and others who help to direct political and corporate decisions. No doubt most, or at least many of them, feel secure and that what is planned to unfold will not affect them. That they are 'doing alright' (financially) so will be above and beyond all harm; physically or material. Then there are those who are concerned, deeply concerned in some cases, about what is unfolding. For instance some of the doctors and nurses who are on the front line of potential abuse and blame; having been so often left with the choice of two evils. To either go-along with what they were instructed to do, or to resign or be sacked if they didn't, or if they spoke out about their concerns. It is of course easy for some of us to say that those with concerns about giving jabs or the medical protocols they were told to follow, should have spoken out even when it was sure to cost them their jobs. Ideally they should have. But can anyone blame some younger person who perhaps has a mortgage and a young family that would suffer as a result? When, so many of their colleagues were saying nothing, remaining silent; and those in management giving 'orders that must be obeyed', remained in the shadows. Whose orders were they obeying?

I will not be attempting to comment on all that is, and could be, on the agenda of those who are often referred to as "Globalists" or the "Elite" – in the materialistic sense. Those behind the big "Corporations" who, effectively at least, run most and probably ALL of the world institutions and organisations that on the surface may seem to work for the betterment of humanity when, in fact, one delves into the structure and nature of such institutions and organisations, they find that they work for the 'elite' globalists who are 'hell bent' on controlling every facet of human life.

Basically, these people are following a fascist agenda with, as I have said, no more care for the 'average person' than the Nazi regime had for those they chose to persecute and kill; the Jewish, Gypsies, and basically any ethnic minority they took a dislike to, which was probably all ethnic minorities, along with anyone who did not 'measure up' to their 'Aryan race' ideal or 'obey orders'. This included any courageous German citizen who spoke against the Nazi regime, propaganda and agenda. These German people were also censored, silenced, or arrested and eventually, in some cases, murdered. Does this remind anyone of recent times? It should do. Oh, and let us not forget that the Nazis controlled the German media at that time; and it was through the media, newspapers, and cinema newsreels etc., that the population were effectively brainwashed by the repetitive bombardment of propaganda that convinced so many to hate, and in this case it was mostly those of the Jewish faith, who were the selected target.

Who controls the media these days? It is the globalists; they own most newspapers, so 'the free press', in the main, no longer exist. They are not free to publish or say anything that goes against or undermines the dark agenda.

In February or March 2021 I did a list of questions, printed it, and distributed it through the doors of neighbours. Below is an extended updated version with the questions now statements.

Statements of Fact

1. In the February 2021 BBC Panorama documentary titled: "Vaccines the Disinformation War", and championing the jabs, the programme featured Professor Liam Smeeth of the "London School of Hygiene and Tropical Medicine". This is a "school" that has received grants totalling over $250 million from the Bill and Melinda Gates Foundation; as have the University of Oxford, where the AstraZeneca vaccine was developed. BBC Media Action also received over $55 million in grants from the foundation. Bill Gates, previously, in a public interview, said that vaccines were the best financial investment he ever made.

These grants, some may say, *inducements,* seem like fortunes to most of us, which they are; but in terms of profits derived from vaccine sales, which run into trillions of pounds or dollars, they represent just a small percent, a fraction of this income being invested to ensure the continuation and smooth running of their industry.

This, I would suggest, is why the likes of Bill Gates, and many other people who were (and still are) pushing what I call the dark agenda, are happy to run foundations or organisations that outwardly portray themselves as caring for humanity, the planet and its environment, when, in reality, they represent and are attempting to usher-in a dark agenda of totalitarian authority. One that would deny the average person the God given rights of freedom to live as they see fit, to travel where they wish, and to say no to medical procedures, as is their right guaranteed in charters such as the Magna Carta and Nuremberg code.

The Magna Carta being a royal charter of rights agreed to by King John of England at Runnymede, near Windsor, on 15th June 1215. It put into writing the principle that the king and his government was not above the law. The law being the common law rights of the people. Not any totalitarian dictates that a fascist government may decree and say is law.

The Nuremberg code, in regard to permissible medical experiments states that: **"The voluntary consent of the human subject is absolutely essential".** *This means that the person involved should have legal capacity to give consent; should be so situated as to be able to exercise free power of choice, without the intervention of any element of force, fraud, deceit, duress, over-reaching, or other ulterior form of constraint or coercion; and should have sufficient knowledge and comprehension of the elements of the subject matter involved as to* *enable him or her to make an understanding and enlightened decision. This latter element requires that before the acceptance of an affirmative decision by the experimental subject there should be made known to him the nature, duration, and purpose of the experiment; the method and means by which it is to be conducted; all inconveniences and hazards reasonably to be expected; and the effects upon his health or person which may possibly come from his participation in the experiment.*

Bear the above in mind with number two.

2. The vaccines used from the latter part of 2020 for what is called "Covid 19" or "Coronavirus" were part of a two-year experimental trial. One must ask whether it was ever ethical or right to be told that these (so-called) vaccines were "Safe and effective" while the trial was still ongoing; and when some people were, and with the ongoing jabs, still are, having severe adverse reactions, and others have passed-on (died).

The leading adverse reactions, in addition to the deaths, include: strokes, heart attacks, miscarriages, Bell's palsy, sepsis, paralysis, psychiatric disorders, blindness, deafness, shingles, menstrual problems, and alopecia, and many having these reactions are now classified as permanently disabled.

3. The "Covid jabs" are a new type of so-called vaccine. They are "Messenger RNA (mRNA) Vaccines". How many people were told that all previous Coronavirus vaccine experiments, some initially appearing safe, resulted in the deaths of the test subjects (innocent animals) once they were re-exposed to the same virus? It certainly was not in the literature I was sent, which was trying to encourage me to go get jabbed; encouragement I ignored.

4. Many people do not realise that the vaccine manufacturers have financial indemnity for any permanent harm and deaths caused by their vaccines. In other words, they cannot be sued for damages. If someone is permanently harmed and unable to earn a living and do not qualify for a pension, they have to rely totally on what the government decide to give them in state benefits.

5. Many people do not realise that many doctors agree that face coverings (masks) protect neither the wearer nor anyone else. Fungi and bacteria can develop under a mask that the wearer will breathe-in, which can lead to disease, especially respiratory disease; while wearing a mask for too long can lead to neurological damage. They are especially bad for those already with health issues and for children.

6. Literally thousands of medical practitioners, doctors, nurses and other scientific researchers are being denied their right to free speech and have been censored, sacked, and had their videos removed and themselves blocked by such as YouTube, Facebook and other media platforms to prevent them from easily sharing their expert opinions. Opinions they give with no financial incentive, and often at personal cost to their careers. *(See more on free speech after number 10).*

7. Many people do not realise that up until now the media (BBC etc.) have refused to allow open debate with these medical experts.

8. Many people do not know that many of the sacked doctors were administering readily available safe and highly effective (low priced) drugs such as Ivermectin and Hydroxychloroquine to their 'covid patients' who responded extremely well.

9. Many people are unaware that Nobel Prize winner Kary Mullis (passed-on 2019) the inventor of the Polymerase chain reaction technique (PCR tests) said that the test should not be used for diagnosis. It can deliver false results, false positive results, and it cannot identify a live virus from a dead strain. This being why people testing positive often have no symptoms of flu or anything else; in other words, they are not ill and put no one else at risk of catching anything from them.

Studies have been carried out confirming the 'false positive' results and been reported in "The Light" (paper) as far back as September 2020. *(All editions of The Light in PDF format can be downloaded free online).*

10. Many people might be shocked to learn that prizes, one of 225,000 Euros, (I think another I saw was for even more) was offered to anyone who could present a publication that scientifically proved the process of isolation of SARS-CoV-2 (covid 19 virus) and its genetic substance. To the best of my knowledge no one was ever able to provide any such evidence. Added to which Dr Sam Bailey, I believe, said that no virus, ever, has been truly isolated. That the procedure that claims to do so is scientifically flawed and not fit for purpose.

Number six above mentions doctors and free speech. The fact that the UK General Medical Council (GMC) unlawfully banned doctors from posting on social media may be one reason why so many never did. An article by Louize Small featured in The Light of January 2022 (page 4) about one such doctor who challenged the GMC in court and won his case. A little is included below from the article titled:

Doctor wins massive victory for free speech

'The victory is a triumph for free speech and sets a precedent for other cases. Responding to the news on Twitter, Dr Teck Khong commented that, "Freedom to challenge and criticise flawed covid policies is now assured."

'The High Court ruled that the GMC gag violated human rights laws and could not stand. It was said that guidelines relied on by the GMC tribunal made no reference to the human rights of doctors registered with them.'

Something else I feel is well worth our consideration, as number three above mentions, what is called 'Big Pharma', in other words the pharmaceutical industry, carry out experiments on animals; and this inflicts suffering to countless numbers of innocent animals. This is not some one-off situation; it is an ongoing process of experiments for many, and perhaps with every product they produce. So those people who 'get the jab' are, effectively condoning these hideous, often painful, then deadly procedures; and what for? Is it to perhaps add a little extra time to their personal lifespan on Earth? Leaving aside the fact that it may add nothing and take away quality, what makes people think that their lives are more valuable than that of a chimpanzee, for instance? I for one want no jab, medicine or anything else that has somewhere along the line involved vivisection and the torture of animals. It is often said that we in the UK are a nation of animal lovers; but how can we be when so many are happy to eat them and have them harmed, supposedly for our benefit, in tortuous experiments?

Whether anyone chooses to be vaccinated or continue to take 'boosters' is their own choice. But I think when people look back with hindsight they feel that they should have been privy to all the facts before they accepted the so-called Covid jab. Indeed they should be fully informed before any medical procedure, and especially an experimental one.

Those who would like to know more about what is in an mRNA so-called vaccine can read an article by Frances Leader on these that was featured in The Light of April 2021 (page 2), and of course find info many other places online. Personally I have seen a number of videos of doctors and scientists who are not on the payroll of the 'elite' and by what they, and the spirit guides say, I feel it is wise to stay well clear of them.

In the next chapter are some of what other people, the 'truth tellers on Earth' as I call them, have been saying. In this chapter I include a number of snippets and even some fuller examples of articles featured in The Light. I recommend taking a look at all editions of this excellent publication for its quality, and because within its pages can be found a number of links to informative websites and individuals who are helping to expose the truth.

If one feels particularly drawn to doing so, actual print copies can be purchased including bulk orders so that one can distribute to friends, family, groups, neighbours, and the general public even.

When I looked early March 2023 they were priced: £10 for 25 copies, £20 for 100 copies, £25 for 200 copies, and further options. (See Links)

5. Truth Tellers on Earth

Where I repeat certain things in this chapter that I have mention previously do forgive me, and consider this simply as a reminder.

First, a little about myself, I was born in 1950 and grew up playing games on the streets of Putney, London. This included many a daredevil game on a bombsite, and many of these sites remained into the late 50's and 60's before being cleared and built upon. These were bombsites where houses, people's homes, stood for in some cases many decades before the Luftwaffe, the Nazi air force planes, dropped thousands of bombs on London, and many other cities and areas of the UK; hitting and destroying homes in which many people lost their lives.

Prior to my birth, during 1939-45, my Father had spent six years in the army helping to overcome the fascism of Nazi Germany under Adolf Hitler, Italy under Benito Mussolini, and Japan under the Emperor Shōwa or Hirohito.

These days, it seems, most politicians are openly keen to embrace fascism once more. But this time it isn't the fascism of the one, two or three nations, but the fascism supported by the majority of governments worldwide. Are the current politicians, who support globalist corporations, the World Economic Forum (WEF), the World Health Organisation (WHO), the United Nations (UN), the North Atlantic Treaty Organization (NATO) and numerous other organisations evil, insane or perhaps 'just' naïve or gullible, or simply self-serving greedy, morally corrupt, and spiritually ignorant individuals? It could of course be a mix of all the aforementioned.

Despite the countless documentaries and films still doing the rounds that show us how heroic, honourable and self-sacrificing our forefathers were, and how evil the fascist dictators were, the current crop seem to have learned nothing from history.

One thing they should have learned is that in the long-term evil is always overcome; defeated, or it self-destructs. After all, where can it go? Once the poor own nothing and the fascist evil elite own everything, control everything, and eliminate all they feel are worthless or non-productive or simply surplus to requirements, what will they do then?

What if then, one 'overlord' decides this or that group of people must go here, or there, and/or be culled, and these include family or friends of one of their loyal government ministers or billionaire partners, what then? What I'm saying is that the compliant politicians and globalist staff of today are deluding themselves if they think that their compliance and co-operation will guarantee their own and their families and friends safety from their masters, the fascist dictators. And if this is their belief, and they think that financially they will flourish and this is all that they care about, then, it is clear they have absolutely no moral integrity. To behave as they are, also suggests that they have no spiritual awareness or concept of the true nature of reality, or at least how natural law operates in the 'afterlife' and the dark conditions they are likely dooming themselves to inhabit, at least for whatever length of time it takes them to realise the error of their actions and the harm they have done. Then to begin to make recompense.

I doubt that anyone has forgotten the 2020 onwards mantra of, "Follow the science".

Taking this advice, I did so. What I found was that hundreds if not thousands of scientists, doctors, nurses, university professors, virologists, climatologists and many other highly credible individuals disagreed with those quoted by governments worldwide. However, two things most do agree upon are that there never was any reason to fear 'Covid' any more than previous annual cases of flu. And, there is no climate crisis.

It seems to me, quite blatantly, that government politicians worldwide are following what the WEF aided and abetted by the WHO dictate. In other words, the agenda of the globalists, the so called, 'elite', the money men; and it is almost always men, although some women are involved in aspects of the agenda.

Should we be asking those who are 'pulling the strings' of the dark agenda 'What they want'?

The World Economic Forum (WEF) a while ago released a video saying that in the future 'we will own nothing and be happy'. It must be assumed that the globalists will own everything. Whether this involves their buying all the land and property from those who currently own it by fair means, such as an offer that is accepted, or by unfair means, such as a compulsory purchase, who can say?

But one thing is for sure, the 'globalists' want total control of everything; the economy, all essential resources, and health to name a few. They already own or control the banks and banking system in the majority of the world. Add to this they own or are controlling share holders in all of the natural resources, such as oil and gas. Then there is the global health (or ill-health) domain of the pharmaceutical industry, they've controlled this for more than a century.

If one looks 'behind the scenes' it seems that a controlling share interest in all these fields is owned by the globalist, and quite likely the same globalists via a comparative few major investment companies. It seems these few investment companies are the leading shareholders in practically every big-business or conglomerate.

To discover more about this I can recommend viewing a video titled: *"MONOPOLY - Who owns the world?"* This is a documentary by Tim Gielen shared by "Stop World Control". The video description says:

'This incredibly eye opening documentary reveals something astonishing: the majority of our world is owned by the very same people. Because of this they can control the entire world and impose their wicked agenda onto all of humanity. This is the time to expose them and to rise up as one to defend our freedom.

'The name of the two companies who virtually owns the world' are Vanguard and BlackRock. They are at the heart of the Deep State or Cabal. Their plan is the Great Reset where they want to enslave every human on Earth.' (See Links)

Many, many people are attempting to share their understanding of the corruption, those behind the dark agenda, and all the rest that constitutes the globalist agenda.

For example, one book I have read and can recommend is by Dr Joseph *Mercola* with *Ronnie Cummins* titled: *The Truth About Covid-19 - Exposing The Great Reset, Lockdowns, Vaccine Passports, and the New Normal – Why We Must Unite in a Global Movement for Health and Freedom (With Foreword by Robert F. Kennedy Jr.).*

The 2021 book goes through the unfolding of the 'story' based on events in the USA, but most were happening in the UK, and Worldwide, at a similar time. This, in itself, I'd have thought people should have considered suspicious.

Below are some abridged passages from the book that I feel are worth sharing herein, as reminders at the very least, of what unfolded. Starting with some of what Robert F. Kennedy Jr. said:

'The medical profession has not proven itself an energetic defender of democratic institutions or civil rights. Virtually every doctor in Germany took lead roles in the Third Reich's project to eliminate mental defectives, homosexuals, handicapped citizens, and Jews. So many hundreds of German physicians participated in Hitler's worst atrocities - including managing mass murder and unspeakable experiments at the death camps - that the Allies had to stage separate "Medical Trials" at Nuremberg. Not a single prominent German doctor or medical association raised their voice in opposition to these projects.

'Big Pharma's $9.6 billion annual advertising budget gives these unscrupulous companies control over our news and television outlets. In 2014, a network president, Roger Ailes, told me he would fire any of his news show hosts who allowed me to talk about vaccine safety on air. "Our news division," he explained, "Gets up to 70 percent of ad revenues from pharma in non-election years".'

The following part of a statement from their book is why Dr Joseph Mercola and Ronnie Cummins (Organic consumers association) say they wrote their book. I believe this confirms that the authors are working for the light, in opposition to the dark agenda.

'The reason we are writing this book is because we believe the Covid pandemic can become, not a dystopian dead end, but a portal to a better world. The current crisis is alarming, but it offers us an opportunity to qualitatively improve public health and planetary health and regenerate the global grassroots. We can cross over from what can only be described as the Disease of Nations to true health and democracy.

'We believe it is possible to educate and empower the average person, and defeat the digital dictators, fear-mongers, mad scientists, medical fascists, and indentured, bought-and-paid-for politicians. Individually and, most important, working together, we can head off the looming threat of the digital dictatorship and so-called Great Reset that is already emerging. We can take control of our health, our communities, and our destiny.

'Now is the time for a global awakening. Now is the time for a local-to-global resistance.'

In their book they comment on what is described as "Medical malpractice", as below.

'Let's not forget that after decades of massively funded research, Big Pharma has never been able to develop an effective vaccine for a Coronavirus. A genetically engineered vaccine designed to modify (perhaps permanently) human RNA has never been allowed on the market, in part because a number of these Coronavirus vaccines seem to create dangerous ADE (antibody-dependent-enhancement) side effects in many of those injected, especially the elderly, making them more susceptible to dangerous disease.

'Then we all have to contend with the mass media, Big Pharma, the WHO, and the tech giants that are censoring information about successful treatments carried out by doctors across the world using low-cost but effective drugs and supplements like Quercetin, Hydroxychloroquine, Ivermectin, both for prevention and for treatment for those hospitalized.'

Continuing from the same source, this once again shows us that these dark forces do not care about public health and never have.

'In 1976 a novel swine flu infected 230 soldiers at Fort Dix, New Jersey, causing one death. Fearing a repeat of the 1918 Spanish flu pandemic, a vaccine was fast-tracked and the government propaganda machine cranked into action, telling all Americans to get vaccinated. What had been a contained outbreak resulted in a massive swine flu vaccine campaign in which more than 45 million Americans were vaccinated.

'Over the next few years, nearly four thousand Americans filed vaccine damage claims with the federal government totalling $3.2

billion. Side effects included several hundred cases of Guillain-Barre syndrome (a rare side effect of flu vaccines). Even healthy 20-year-olds ended up as paraplegics. At least 300 deaths were also attributed to the vaccine. Meanwhile, the death tally from this "pandemic virus" itself never rose above one.

'Then came the swine flu scare of 2009. In that year major news outlets warned that the swine flu could kill 90,000 Americans and hospitalize 2 million. It was an echo of the fearmongering that went on during the 2005 bird flu pandemic, which never materialized.

'In response to the 2009 swine flu pandemic, what did the Centres for Disease Control and Prevention suggest? Swine flu shots for all! As the Washington Post reported, the CDC said: "As soon as a vaccine is available, try to get it for everyone in your family." This, even though the severity of the 2009 H1N1 virus was moderate - generally requiring neither hospitalization nor even medical care. In fact, most cases had mild symptoms that cleared up on their own.'

One of the main 'players' in promoting and profiting from vaccines is a name familiar to most people these days, Bill Gates, someone I feel is completely 'disturbed' and disconnected from all spiritual understanding and reality. Although, I could probably say the same for many people who are attempting to force the dark agenda on us all.

The following is reported in the same book.

'Gates's answers to the problems of the world are consistently focused on building corporate profits through highly toxic methods, be they chemical agriculture and GMOs, or pharmaceutical drugs and vaccines. Vaccines and various surveillance technologies have been his go-to answers throughout, and these are the very industries he has vested interests in.

'From the beginning, Gates was out in front saying that nothing will go back to normal until or unless the entire global population gets vaccinated and countries implement tracking and tracing technologies and "vaccine passports." At the same time, he's pouring money into digital ID projects and cashless society plans. Ultimately, all of these things will be connected, forming a "digital prison" in which the technocratic elite will have complete control over the global population.

'In an August 21, 2020, article in Columbia Journalism Review, Tim Schwab highlights the connections between the Bill and Melinda Gates Foundation and a number of newsrooms, including NPR. These outlets routinely publish news favourable to Gates and the projects he funds and supports. Not surprisingly, experts quoted in such stories are almost always connected to the Gates Foundation as well.

'Upon scrutiny, it becomes abundantly obvious that when Gates hands out grants to journalism, it's not an unconditional handout with which these companies can do whatever they see fit. It comes with significant strings, and really amounts to little more than the purchasing of stealth self-promotions that are essentially undisclosed ads.'

'There's a lot of evidence pointing to COVID-19 being a planned event that is now being milked for all it's worth, even though it didn't turn out to be nearly as lethal as initially predicted. In October 2019, just 10 weeks before the COVID-19 outbreak first began in Wuhan, China, the Bill and Melinda Gates Foundation co-hosted a pandemic preparedness simulation of a "novel Coronavirus," known as Event 201, along with the Johns Hopkins Centre for Health Security and the World Economic Forum.'

A well known phrase is "Follow the money" (rather than the bought and paid for science). How about this from page 69 of the same book, surely this ought to wake a few people up?

'In December 2020 the total wealth of US billionaires reached $4 trillion, more than $1 trillion of which was gained since March 2020 when the pandemic began, according to a study by the Institute for Policy Studies.

'While 45.5 million Americans filed for unemployment, 29 new billionaires were created, the Institute for Policy Studies reported in June 2020, and five of the richest men in the US – Jeff Bezos, Bill Gates, Mark Zucherberg, Warren Buffett, and Larry Ellison – grew their wealth by a total of $101.7 billion (26 percent) between March 18 and June 17, 2020, alone.'

As previously mentioned PCR tests serve no purpose other than propagating fear and promoting the illusion that more people are ill than is the reality; and, let us not forget, making certain people lots and lots of money. In the Mercola-Cummins book it also speaks of these tests, as follows.

'At present, the polymerase chain reaction test is the primary method used to test people for COVID-19. The problem with that is twofold. First of all, the PCR test cannot distinguish between inactive viruses and "live" or reproductive ones. This is a crucial point, since inactive and reproductive viruses are not interchangeable in terms of infectivity. If you have a non-reproductive virus in your body, you will not get sick and you cannot spread it to others. For this reason, the PCR test is grossly unreliable as a diagnostic tool.'

An article from https://off-guardian.org/ was also featured in The Light, January 2021 (page 13) concerning the PCR tests being pointless; having been ruled "unreliable" in a court hearing in Portugal back in November 2020. Below is just a snippet from the article titled:

Portuguese Appeal Court Rules PCR Test 'Unreliable'

'The court's summary of the case reads as follows: "Given how much scientific doubt exists — as voiced by experts, i.e., those who matter — about the reliability of the PCR tests, given the lack of information concerning the tests' analytical parameters, and in the absence of a physician's diagnosis supporting the existence of infection or risk, there is no way this court would ever be able to determine whether C was indeed a carrier of the SARSCoV-2 virus, or whether A, B and D had been at a high risk of exposure to it."'

What about treatments other than an experimental so-called vaccine, and why not a vaccine manufactured in the tried and tested way?

The traditional way, in my layman terms of understanding and explanation is that, usually, a dead cell of a virus or whatever one wants immunity from is added to a concoction that when injected into a person's body, that person's own body (their own immune system) responds by attacking the intruding cell. Then, at the same time as eliminating the cell its genetic make-up is 'mapped' and stored so that if the live version ever enters their body, it is easily overpowered and destroyed, and therefore carries no threat to the person's health.

However, when it came to the so-called Covid virus, it is well known that existing drugs could easily have helped with this, and it seems, can more or less help with any flu like symptoms. So it beggars the question of why this information is not made public knowledge, and for reminders of this issued each flu season?

Below is something on this from the Mercola-Cummins 'Truth about Covid' book.

'The efforts to prevent medical professionals from using Hydroxychloroquine is further evidence that the Covid pandemic has an ulterior motive. If the medical establishment really wanted to save as many people as possible from this infection, wouldn't they embrace any and all things that work? The fact that they went out of their way to vilify a decades-old drug with an excellent safety profile shows we aren't dealing with a real medical establishment; we're dealing with medical technocracy. The censoring and manipulation of medical information are part and parcel of the social engineering part of this system.

'Now, in addition to treating COVID-19 patients and minimizing deaths, the related drug chloroquine has been shown to inhibit influenza A, and this may be yet another reason for the suppression of Hydroxychloroquine. If an inexpensive generic drug can prevent influenza, then what would we need seasonal influenza vaccines for?

'In short, the drug poses a significant threat to the drug industry in more ways than one. It could also eliminate one of the most powerful leverages for geopolitical power that the technocrats have, namely biological terrorism. If we know how to treat and protect ourselves against designer viruses, their ability to keep us in line by keeping us in fear vanishes.

'All of this helps explain the outright fraudulent studies published on Hydroxychloroquine, which were then used as media fodder to frighten the public, all while positive studies were censored and suppressed. In one instance the authors pulled the data set out of thin air. They made it up. That study was ultimately retracted, but the bad publicity had already done its job. In other instances, they used doses known to be toxic.

'While doctors reporting success with the drug are using standard doses around 200 mg per day for either a few days or maybe a couple of weeks, studies such as the Bill and Melinda Gates-funded RECOVERY Trial used 2,400 mg of Hydroxychloroquine during the first 24 hours - three to six times higher than the daily dosage recommended - followed by 400 mg every 12 hours for 9 more days for a cumulative dose of 9,200 mg over 10 days.

'Similarly, the Solidarity Trial, led by the World Health Organization, used 2,000 mg on the first day, and a cumulative dose of 8,800 mg over 10 days. These doses are simply too high. More is not necessarily better. Too much, and guess what? You might kill the patient.'

As I have said before; those following the dark agenda do not care if they kill people. We are of course meant to believe, as everyone queues for the next round of never ending jabs, that the fact they get richer and richer in financial terms is just a coincidence.

An article by Darren Smith was featured in The Light of January 2021 (page 14) about how the already financially wealthy were 'raking it in' while so many, many people lost their jobs and got poorer. Below is a snippet from the article, titled:

Rich Got an Incredible $1.9 Trillion Richer in 2020
While Everyone Else Lost Out

'The roughly 2,200 billionaires are now 20% richer, bringing their combined total value to $11,400,000,000,000, despite the suicidal economic policies of governments across the world to shut down and thus decimate their own populations and tax bases, leading to the estimated permanent closure of more than 50% of businesses.'

What else could those of the dark agenda get up to? Well, it turns out that The WHO, as the Mercola-Cummins book comments, are attempting to rewrite the definition of Herd Immunity.

The following couple of extracts from the book shows the nonsense the WHO put on their website and would like us to believe and accept as factual.

'According to WHO (October 2020) "Herd immunity", also known as "population immunity", is a concept used for vaccination, in which a population can be protected from a certain virus if a threshold of vaccination is reached.'

'Achieving herd immunity with safe and effective vaccines makes diseases rarer and saves lives.'

"Safe and effective" the WHO said and perhaps still say; one could say they are having a laugh. But the joke is on us. Especially it is on those who have had severe adverse reactions (or 'died') from a jab. I bet the victims and their families don't find it remotely funny. The WHO and every government worldwide were spouting off, "Get jabbed and be protected", and, "It will not be transmissible to others". What liars they have proven themselves to be; and in multiple ways still are. In 2023 even the likes of Bill Gates has said these statements haven't proved accurate. Saying this after it is reported he sold 86% of the shares he held in one jab corporation; and I don't doubt, assuming the figure to be accurate, that he made a huge profit on them. But of course, to repeat, they do not care about people, only profits.

One final extract from the same Mercola-Cummins book comments on what those with a dark agenda want to unfold.

'Ask yourself, does concern for public health really justify censoring and eliminating financial transaction capabilities of those who raise questions about vaccine safety and mandatory vaccination policies? The fact that they're trying to shut down all conversations about vaccines - using warfare tactics and economic blackmail, no less - suggests that the planned mass vaccination campaign has little if anything to do with keeping the public healthy and safe. It's about controlling the public and ensuring compliance.'

'The question is: Why?'

'The problem we face now is that censorship fortifies power and is very difficult to end once it has taken hold. This in turn does not bode well for individual freedom or democracy as a whole. Censorship is a direct threat to both. With that in mind, the fact that U.S. and U.K. intelligence agencies are getting involved in censoring tells us something important.'

'It tells us it's not really about protecting public health. It's about strengthening government control over the population. The fact that intelligence agencies view vaccine safety advocates as a national security threat also tells us that government is now in the business of protecting private companies, essentially blurring the line between the two.

'If you criticize one you criticize the other. In short, if you impede or endanger the profitability of private companies, you are now viewed as a national security threat, and this falls squarely within the parameters of technocracy, in which government is dissolved and replaced with the unelected leaders of private enterprise.

'Don't listen to nonsense about asymptomatic transmission, the PCR pandemic, and all the false stats used to scare you. Seek out the truth, take control of your health, and have frank and open discussions with family and friends to help show them the way out of fear, too.'

A truth teller in the USA, Caroline Chang, runs *"Awake 2 Oneness Radio"* and I would describe her as a spiritual teacher. She also writes articles (or Blogs) sharing with us the truths she finds that help to expose such as the following.

Dr. Paul Thomas MD Independent Study

'Dr. Paul Thomas is one the few paediatricians that actually gave all of his patient's parents INFORMED CONSENT about vaccines. He informs each parent about ALL the possible side effects with each vaccine.

'The CDC absolutely refuses to do a study of fully vaccinated children compared to completely unvaccinated children. "I wonder why?" I would think if the CDC wanted to prove that vaccinating children is the best thing for our children's health, they would surely want to do this study and share the results with everyone.

'Because Dr. Paul has some patients that are completely unvaccinated, some partially vaccinated and some fully vaccinated; he was in the perfect position to do his own independent study comparing unvaccinated children with fully vaccinated children. He did not include the partially vaccinated children in his study.

'His independent study proves that unvaccinated children are FAR HEALTHIER than fully vaccinated children.

'He is not the only doctor who has done this study, and they have had the SAME results.

'Because Dr. Paul is an honest doctor and speaks TRUTH; he has been heavily censored by the medical establishment. They took away his medical license for telling the TRUTH! His research is extremely valid, and he is an extremely credible medical doctor.

'Why does the medical establishment NOT want everyone to know about the dangers of vaccines? Why are they injecting newborn babies with Aluminium, which can cause brain damage? Why is ALL TRUE information about the possible harm of vaccines being CENSORED?

'A newborn baby is injected with 250 micrograms of Aluminium regardless of the baby's weight. By the time a baby is 18 months old they will have had 3000 to 5000 micrograms of Aluminium infected into them.

'These injections continue until children are 18 years old on the CDC childhood vaccine schedule. In 1986 the CDC childhood vaccines schedule was 24 doses from birth to 18 years old. Now the CDC childhood vaccine schedule starts before a child is born, by injecting pregnant mothers. Before birth to 18 years old is now over 76 doses.

'With the National Childhood Vaccine Injury Act of 1986 the pharmaceutical Industry is shielded from all liability. It is "We" the Taxpayer that pays for vaccine injuries in Vaccine Court. And only about 10% of claims actually receive compensation.

'Dr. Paul Thomas is an award-winning Dartmouth-trained paediatrician with nearly 30 years of experience in paediatrics. He is an expert on addiction and in Addiction Medicine. He is the co-author of the book, The Vaccine-Friendly Plan: Dr. Paul's Safe and Effective Approach to Immunity and Health - from Pregnancy through Your Child's Teen Years.'

In the fifteen different conditions mentioned in Dr Thomas' study all indicate that the unvaccinated children were healthier. This does not surprise me at all. I have watched films such as Vaxxed and Vaxxed 2 and in these can be seen the terrible harm done to many children, and parents confirming that their unvaccinated children are generally

245

healthier than their vaccinated children. "The Truth about Vaccines" is also a website with half a million subscribers and a free e-book. (See Links)

There are countless people I could quote, top people in their fields of expertise, who have spoken out about one or more aspects of the dark agenda or those people implementing or advocating for one ridiculous or unnecessary thing or another. Many genuine, honest scientists do not support what the general public are told are facts. Many genuine, honest medical professionals do not support what the general public are told to believe. Countless people have spoken out in opposition to what we are told via the mainstream media (MSM); I am only mentioning a few in this book. Be under no illusion, and do not feel that what is included can be dismissed because it is just a comparatively few people.

Where possible, if in doubt, please do some open-minded research. Do not blindly accept and believe what the politicians and those supporting the dark agenda say, "That it is all a conspiracy theory", because it is not, it is a conspiracy fact.

Continuing, next, I include a little from an October 2022 article about the 'great reset' by F. William Engdahl, an award-winning geopolitical analyst, strategic risk consultant, author, professor and lecturer. In this he shares some of the plans of the globalists. (See Links).

Davos, in Switzerland, is where many of the globalists often meet to discuss their plans. It is run by the WEF and the most recent event, the 53rd annual meeting, took place in January 2023.

The Dark Origins of the Davos Great Reset

'Important to understand is that there is not one single new or original idea in Klaus Schwab's so-called Great Reset agenda for the world. Nor is his Fourth Industrial Revolution agenda his or his claim to having invented the notion of Stakeholder Capitalism a product of Schwab. Klaus Schwab is little more than a slick PR agent for a global technocratic agenda, a corporatist unity of corporate power with government, including the UN, an agenda whose origins go back to the beginning of the 1970s, and even earlier.

'The Davos Great reset is merely an updated blueprint for a global dystopian dictatorship under UN control that has been decades in development. The key actors were David Rockefeller and his protégé, Maurice Strong.

'This is the dark origin of Schwab's Great Reset agenda where we should eat worms and have no private property in order to "save the planet." The agenda is dark, dystopian and meant to eliminate billions of us "ordinary humans".'

Dr Vernon Coleman
Proof that Masks Do More Harm than Good

One more doctor who has helped to 'open the eyes' of many people, is Dr Vernon Coleman. He is a Sunday Times bestselling author who has written over 100 books, selling over two million copies in the UK alone. They have been translated into 25 languages and sell in over 50 countries.

His medical bestsellers include, "How to Stop Your Doctor Killing You"; "Anyone who tells you vaccines are safe and effective is lying"; and "Why and How Doctors Kill More People than Cancer"; and still another, "Covid-19: The Greatest Hoax in History: The startling truth behind the planned world takeover".

Some of his books have been serialised in newspapers and magazines all over the world, and many have been turned into television and radio series. He was the Television Doctor on British television and the first agony uncle on the BBC.

Dr Coleman is a general practitioner principal and a former Professor of Holistic Medical Sciences at the International Open University in Sri Lanka. He has an honorary DSc. He has given evidence to the House of Commons and the House of Lords in the UK. (In past times when, perhaps, there was a little less corruption plaguing the world).

Like all qualified medical doctors who have told the truth about covid-19, he has been repeatedly lied about and libelled on the internet and in the mainstream media.

In March 2020, after studying the Covid death figures and comparing the death statistics in the UK to that of previous years, Dr Coleman said that the threat of Covid-19 had been wildly exaggerated and that there was no pandemic. In that first video, he warned that the pandemic fraud, or hoax, as he called it, would result in the deaths of many old people, which it did, and the introduction of mandatory vaccinations, which has happened in certain professions and countries, and the disappearance of cash, now a serious threat.

As a result of his video, his Wikipedia page was deliberately and dramatically changed "by government employees" he believes, and used to discredit him. All his many lifetime achievements were removed. Without any evidence or justification he was, among other things, labelled a "conspiracy theorist". (It is well known to many people that scientists who researched and proved as fact the 'afterlife', and others, have been effectively slandered on Wikipedia).

Dr Coleman shares many videos and articles on his two websites. One subject he covered was "Face Masks", at one point he had a downloadable version of a book he had produced titled, *"Proof that Masks Do More Harm than Good"*.

He still has a shorter version of this at his (.org) website. In his conclusion regarding masks he said:

'Having studied the evidence I believe that mask wearing is likely to do no good but a great deal of harm. The available evidence shows clearly that masks do not work but do have the potential to cause a variety of health problems.'

A couple of the points he makes on his website, are these (numbers 24 and 40):

'There were no mask requirements in Sweden, and the mortality rate there remained below a bad flu season. The average age of Swedish citizens who died of covid-19 was well over 80 years.'

And:

'Mask wearers are more likely to develop infection than non-mask wearers. This may be due to the fact that masks reduce blood oxygen levels and adversely affect natural immunity. It is likely that anyone who wears a face mask for long periods will have a damaged immune system – and be more susceptible to infection. Studies have shown that hypoxia can inhibit immune cells used to fight viral infections. Wearing

a mask may make the wearer more likely to develop an infection – and if an infection develops it is likely to be worse.'

In the earlier version of the book that I previously downloaded from his website, I think the following two points (38 & 99) are still well worth reading. Because these really do highlight the folly of trusting corrupt politicians and their equally corrupt scientists and advisors.

'Dr Margarite Griesz-Brisson MD PhD is a leading European neurologist and neurophysiologist. In October 2020, she warned that re-breathing our exhaled air, because of wearing masks, will create oxygen deficiency and an excess of carbon dioxide in the body. 'We know,' she said, 'that the human brain is very sensitive to oxygen deprivation. There are nerve cells in the hippocampus that cannot last longer than three minutes without oxygen.' Dr Griesz-Brisson pointed out that the acute warning symptoms of oxygen deprivation are headaches, drowsiness, dizziness, difficulty in concentration and slowing down of reaction times. The real danger is, however, that when the oxygen deprivation becomes chronic, the symptoms disappear because the body gets used to them. However, efficiency remains impaired and the damage to the brain continues. 'We know that neurodegenerative disease takes years to decades to develop. If today you forget your phone number, the breakdown in your brain would have already started two or three decades ago.'

'Dr Griesz-Brisson explains that while the mask wearer thinks that they are becoming accustomed to re-breathing exhaled air, the problems within the brain are growing as the oxygen deprivation continues.

'She also points out that brain cells which die, because of a shortage of oxygen, will never be replaced. They are gone forever. She goes on to argue that everyone is entitled to claim exemption from mask wearing because oxygen deprivation is so dangerous – and masks don't work.

'Finally, Dr Griesz-Brisson points out that children and teenagers must never wear masks, partly because they have extremely active and adaptive immune systems but also because their brains are especially active and vulnerable. The more active an organ is the more oxygen it needs. And so the damage to children's brains is huge and irreversible.

'She warns that dementia is going to increase in ten years, and the younger generation will not be able to reach their potential because of the mask wearing.

'*Oxygen deprivation adversely affects the heart and the lungs but it also damages the brain.*

'*And the damage will be permanent.* "*My conclusion has to be that no one has the right to force us to deprive our bodies of oxygen for absolutely no good reason. Depriving individuals of oxygen is a crime perpetrated by those demanding that we wear masks. Those who let it happen and those who collaborate are also guilty. And those who wear masks in situations where they are not legally required are cooperating in a criminal activity.*"

'Inevitably, Dr Griesz-Brisson's interview was removed from YouTube as part of the global suppression of medical information.'

And.

'A report by Boris Borovoy, Colleen Huber and Maris Crisler reported: "Masks have been shown through overwhelming clinical evidence to have no effect against transmission of viral pathogens. Penetration of cloth masks by viral particles was almost 97% and of surgical masks was 44%. Even bacteria, approximately ten times the volume of corona-viruses, have been poorly impeded by both cloth masks and disposable surgical masks. *After 150 minutes of use, more bacteria were emitted through the disposable mask than from the same subject unmasked.*

'A paper by these authors entitled, Masks, false safety and real dangers, Part 2: Microbial challenges from masks is available on the internet and contains a list of 62 scientific journal references showing that masks have no significant preventative impact against any known pathogenic microbes. These authors conclude. "Specifically, regarding covid-19, we have shown that mask use is not correlated with lower death rates nor with lower positive PCR tests." The authors add that, "*Masks have also been demonstrated historically to contribute to increased infections within the respiratory tract*", and they conclude that "*the use of face masks will contribute to far more morbidity and mortality than has occurred due to covid-19.*"'

An article by Arthur Firstenberg was featured in the Light, September 2020 (page 14) also showed that even during surgery masks were more harmful than beneficial; below are just a few snippets from the article, titled:

Scientific Studies on Masks show Inefficacy

'As a person who went to medical school, I was shocked when I read Neil Orr's study, published in 1981 in the Annals of the Royal College of Surgeons of England.'

'... they discovered, to their amazement, that when nobody wore masks during surgeries, the rate of wound infections was less than half what it was than when everyone wore masks.'

'... to my surprise the medical literature for the past forty-five years has been consistent: masks are useless in preventing the spread of disease and, if anything, are unsanitary objects that themselves spread bacteria and viruses.'

The same Neurologist that Dr Coleman mentioned, Dr Margarite Griesz-Brisson, is also featured in The Light of November 2020 (page 5), and is worth reading if pursuing this subject.

It may seem that I am saying more on this issue than is necessary for some readers; but I do want to remind everyone that during the worst of the scare-mongering government led propaganda times people were being coerced into believing that the wearing of a mask helped to protect other people, not necessarily themselves. People who trusted them were, in some instances, quite hostile to those who entered a shop without one. Yet, when one looks at all the evidence, it was those wearing a mask, mostly endangering their own health by doing so, but also potentially putting others at risk by what they might develop and then pass on to those they come into contact with.

Another honest doctor, **Sam Bailey**, lives in New Zealand, like Australia, they have faced the onslaught of 'establishment' dictates that have zero to do with health and helping people and everything to do with control and denying people their God given human rights.

Dr Bailey was a television presenter for "The CheckUp", a nationwide New Zealand health show that debunks common health misconceptions. This inspired Sam to start her own YouTube channel in late 2019, questioning the scientific evidence of mainstream health narratives and answering questions from her viewers.

In early 2020, with the arrival of Covid-19, Sam began researching the scientific evidence behind lockdowns, social distancing and PCR tests. After releasing a YouTube video in September 2020, where she stated she would not take a Coronavirus vaccine, she was sacked halfway through filming a second series of "The CheckUp". Subsequently, she lost some of her employment as a medical doctor and has had ongoing legal battles with the New Zealand medical authorities who are attempting to silence her views on Covid-19.

What was her crime? Like Dr Coleman, it was speaking the truth as she saw it as a medical doctor. Like many, many other doctors worldwide who spoke out and challenged what they were sometimes told to say or told not to say. Having expertise accounted for nothing, as far as those following the orders of their 'dark overlords' were, and are, concerned.

She is the co-author of a book titled, *Virus Mania,* and below is from the book description on Amazon.

'The population is terrified by reports of so-called COVID-19, measles, swine flu, SARS, BSE, AIDS or polio. However, the authors of "Virus Mania," investigative journalist Torsten Engelbrecht, Dr. Claus Köhnlein, MD, Dr. Samantha Bailey, MD, and Dr. Stefano Scoglio, BSc PhD, show that this fearmongering is unfounded and that virus mayhem ignores basic scientific facts: The existence, the pathogenicity and the deadly effects of these agents have never been proven.

'The book "Virus Mania" will also outline how modern medicine uses dubious indirect lab tools claiming to prove the existence of viruses such as antibody tests and the polymerase chain reaction (PCR). The alleged viruses may be, in fact, also be seen as particles produced by the cells themselves as a consequence of certain stress factors such as drugs. These particles are then "picked up" by antibody and PCR tests and mistakenly interpreted as epidemic-causing viruses.

'The authors analyze all real causes of the illnesses named COVID-19, avian flu, AIDS or Spanish flu, among them pharmaceuticals, lifestyle drugs, pesticides, heavy metals, pollution, malnutrition and stress. To substantiate it, the authors cite dozens of highly renowned scientists, among them the Nobel laureates Kary Mullis, Barbara McClintock, Walter Gilbert and Sir Frank Macfarlane Burnet as well as

microbiologist and Pulitzer Prize winner René Dubos, and it presents more than 1,400 solid scientific references.

'The topic of "Virus Mania" is of pivotal significance. Drug makers and top scientists rake in enormous sums of money and the media boosts its audience ratings and circulations with sensationalized reporting (the coverage of the "New York Times" and "Der Spiegel" are specifically analyzed). The enlightenment about the real causes and true necessities for prevention and cure of illnesses is falling by the wayside.'

To emphasis my point about the numbers of doctors amongst others who never supported the actions undertaken by politicians worldwide, is *"The Great Barrington Declaration"*.

This declaration, authored 4th October 2020 initially by Dr. Martin Kulldorff, Dr. Sunetra Gupta, and Dr. Jay Bhattacharya, and subsequently by many more doctors (43 of them, co-signers listed as "Medical and Public Health Scientists and Medical Practitioners", are named), and when I looked January 2023, a total of over 936,000 people had signed the declaration, as below.

The Great Barrington Declaration

'As infectious disease epidemiologists and public health scientists we have grave concerns about the damaging physical and mental health impacts of the prevailing COVID-19 policies, and recommend an approach we call Focused Protection.

'Coming from both the left and right, and around the world, we have devoted our careers to protecting people. Current lockdown policies are producing devastating effects on short and long-term public health. The results (to name a few) include lower childhood vaccination rates, worsening cardiovascular disease outcomes, fewer cancer screenings and deteriorating mental health – leading to greater excess mortality in years to come, with the working class and younger members of society carrying the heaviest burden. Keeping students out of school is a grave injustice.

'Keeping these measures in place until a vaccine is available will cause irreparable damage, with the underprivileged disproportionately harmed.

'Fortunately, our understanding of the virus is growing. We know that vulnerability to death from COVID-19 is more than a thousand-fold higher in the old and infirm than the young. Indeed, for children, COVID-19 is less dangerous than many other harms, including influenza.

'As immunity builds in the population, the risk of infection to all – including the vulnerable – falls. We know that all populations will eventually reach herd immunity – i.e. the point at which the rate of new infections is stable – and that this can be assisted by (but is not dependent upon) a vaccine. Our goal should therefore be to minimize mortality and social harm until we reach herd immunity.

'The most compassionate approach that balances the risks and benefits of reaching herd immunity, is to allow those who are at minimal risk of death to live their lives normally to build up immunity to the virus through natural infection, while better protecting those who are at highest risk. We call this Focused Protection.

'Adopting measures to protect the vulnerable should be the central aim of public health responses to COVID-19. By way of example, nursing homes should use staff with acquired immunity and perform frequent testing of other staff and all visitors. Staff rotation should be minimized. Retired people living at home should have groceries and other essentials delivered to their home. When possible, they should meet family members outside rather than inside. A comprehensive and detailed list of measures, including approaches to multi-generational households, can be implemented, and is well within the scope and capability of public health professionals.

'Those who are not vulnerable should immediately be allowed to resume life as normal. Simple hygiene measures, such as hand washing and staying home when sick should be practiced by everyone to reduce the herd immunity threshold. Schools and universities should be open for in-person teaching. Extracurricular activities, such as sports, should be resumed. Young low-risk adults should work normally, rather than from home. Restaurants and other businesses should open. Arts, music, sport and other cultural activities should resume. People who are more at risk may participate if they wish, while society as a whole enjoys the protection conferred upon the vulnerable by those who have built up herd immunity.'

I do not agree with everything said in the above declaration, however, one must ask: *"Why did the governments ignore such professionals?"*

I say again, they ignored them because they were following the orders given to them by those with a dark agenda that has zero to do with protecting public health and everything to do with power, money and control.

If their policies cause some (or many) to 'die' earlier than nature might have dictated, they do not care. In fact, many believe that a "Eugenics" (the selection of desired heritable characteristics in order to improve future generations) and depopulation policy is 'in play' that connects with much of what has and is happening.

I may have mentioned this before, so take this as a reminder, but people should not forget about all the 'vaccine passport' imposition that governments worldwide attempted to force upon their citizens, and is still being discussed, and is most certainly desired, by those who wish to control us. Those people who are still pushing for this are, without any shadow of doubt, working for the dark side.

It may or may not surprise people to learn that some people, including a 'Pharma boss' knowing the dangers of Covid jabs, obtained false certificates to indicate that they had been vaccinated, when they had not. An article by Paul Bennett about this featured in The Light, August 2022 (page 19), below is from the article, titled:

Pharma boss caught falsifying jab status
Investigation uncovers fake vaccine certificates scam

'A police investigation in Spain, code-named 'Operation Jenner', has discovered that at least 2,200 prominent people paid a nurse for fake vaccine passports - people seeking to have their names added to a covid vaccine database despite not getting the trial jab.

'According to the Spanish newspaper El Mundo: 'A vast network of celebrities and elites paid money to have their names fraudulently entered on the National Immunisation Register, despite refusing to be vaccinated.'

'Euro Weekly News reported:

'The leader of the network was a nursing assistant at the La Paz University Hospital, where he is accused of charging more than 200,000 euros for fraudulently registering 2,200 people as vaccinated in

the Spanish National Registry against covid-19. He has been arrested and is currently in custody.'

'Prominent people from the world of music, film, business, sport, and medicine were caught fabricating their jab status. One of the most interesting and high-profile names listed was Jose Maria Fernandez Sousa-Faro, the Spanish boss and founder of the large pharmaceutical company PharmaMar.

'PharmaMar is one of the largest pharmaceutical companies in Spain, and specialises in researching drug treatment for Alzheimer's, cancer and ironically covid.

'According to ABC News in Spain, the 76-year-old businessman and pharma boss used the illegal scheme to make it appear that he had had the third dose in the official Spanish database, while other relatives also used the same service, according to police sources.

'ABC News reported that the Pharma boss paid an organisation a 'VIP fee' of between 1,000 and 2,000 euros to be added to the Spanish vaccine register. It is alleged that Sousa-Faro was injected with a saline solution, instead of the covid jab.

'Acclaimed Dr. Sousa-Faro has worked in the pharmaceutical industry for over 35 years, and has more than 90 scientific publications and patents in the fields of biochemistry, antibiotics, and molecular biology to his name.

'When a powerful and wealthy CEO of a large Pharma company goes to such extreme lengths not to take the experimental jab, one really needs to take serious note.'

The fact that the above reported that, *'Prominent people from the world of music, film, business, sport, and medicine were caught fabricating their jab status'* does not shock or surprise me one bit. While it seems absolutely understandable why someone from big Pharma would avoid a jab; such a person would know for certain that it would be a foolhardy and dangerous thing to do.

It does, I feel, confirm my suspicions in regard to those so-called celebrities who were featured on TV saying, "Get your jab"; my suspicion being that, perhaps unknown to them, they, or at least some of them, were given harmless placebo jabs (if any at all). A 'reward' one might say, for their co-operation. Although, unlike the Pharma boss, I doubt they understood the dangers of the real thing. Although, as we have been informed by the spirit guides, not all jabs are the same and some are harmless placebos.

Thinking about 'celebrities', during my research for this book I have come across a number of well known names, individuals who are awake to the dark agenda and have written or spoken out concerning it. Matt Le Tissier, former Southampton and England footballer being one. I remember him saying he questioned things early on in 2020 when he heard that three psychologists where on the government team. No doubt they have the expertise of how to convince people to do as the dark agenda prescribed. Even the term, "get your jab" is part of this, no jab is "your" jab; all jabs are "their" jabs. The psychology made it sound as though it were like a gift, or a raffle prize won by jab receivers. What lucky people we are, all getting it for free! (They have used this same psychology for what I consider dodgy flu vaccines for years).

While getting close to publishing this book I came across a question and answer interview by Darren Smith with Matt Le Tissier published in The Light, January 2023 (page 7). I found it of interest and I feel worth sharing herein, as follows.

Footballers are no longer being asked to have vaccines

Darren: Are you getting private support from others in football who agree but don't want to speak out?

Matt: *Yes absolutely. I got a letter together to get a meeting with the FA and PFA regarding vaccines for footballers and the amount of players that were collapsing on the field last year. When I rang around my contacts, I spoke to about 90 ex-players, and I think only two didn't want to put their names to a letter calling for an investigation. So people are aware of it, they will sign letters, but whether they are prepared to speak out in public is a different thing.*

Darren: It seems to have calmed down – we've just had the World Cup and there were no collapses?

Matt: *I sent stuff to the FA doctor whenever people collapsed on the pitch, investigations were taking place, or scientific papers regarding Myocarditis in young men were released – and the last time I sent one, I was told that the footballers are no longer being asked to have vaccines.*

That may be one of the reasons why it's calmed down a bit – they've stopped taking them. Although I had lunch with a former team-mate of mine, who confided in me that he'd had the booster and has since been suffering with heart problems. So it's hard because there are still people taking them and they obviously don't realise the risks involved, and it's sad.

Darren: But there was no big announcement from the Premier League clubs, because that would end it, wouldn't it?

Matt: *Yes, it was all done very quietly. I didn't know until the FA doctor told me about it two weeks ago; it came as a surprise to me. I don't know how long that's been in place for. I played golf with a couple of Premier League players last summer, and they said it was probably about 50/50 in their squad who were vaccinated or not. You could see when the clubs went on preseason tours, the ones that had 'niggling injuries' were the ones who couldn't get into the country because they hadn't had it, so they had to stay at home.*

Darren: Couldn't people say you're in a position to speak out because you've retired, you've got your life set, not relying on pundit income etc...?

Matt: *To be honest, I'm not set for life – I have to work. I still have a mortgage and a lot of outgoings every month, so I still have to have work.*

But I knew the risks of speaking out, and I lost my job at Sky. That was a scary time, because I didn't know where the money was going to come from. I wasn't in a position where I could say 'I'm rich enough and I can say what I want'. I still had sacrifices to make, and I knew what could happen by speaking out, and I still chose to anyway because I believe it's right, and things have worked out.

I have picked up other work, and managed to keep going and pay all my bills, and I believe that's a bit of karma. I did the right thing, and got rewarded for good actions and good deeds – that's something I'm quite at peace with.

Darren: Was it the covid scam that woke you up?

Matt: *I've always tried to have my own thoughts on things, and not be manipulated into thinking in a certain way. The first thing I can think of is probably 9/11, where nothing made sense. Just little things that happened that made you go 'hang on a minute!' One of the things was the conveniently found passport of one of the terrorists. I went 'that* *whole building's collapsed and they found a passport in the debris that just happens to be from the bloke on the plane!' Then you have architects and engineers' testimonies who say 'that can't happen', and all of it is being suppressed.*

Then covid came along and I started looking into it, and saw some credible people who said 'this has been planned for a long time, and this is what's coming next – we're going to have mandatory vaccinations and digital passports'. You watch it all play out and that should make you very suspicious.

Darren: Terrain theory or germ theory?

Matt: *Something I hadn't heard of until about a year ago, but I've asked that question to a couple of doctors who I've had on the podcast. There are more and more doctors now who are questioning the germ theory, and thinking what they've been taught isn't quite right. Dr Tess Lawrie was very open, and said she was going to look into this more because of what's gone on in the last two years.*

You have to question everything you've been taught, and re-evaluate it with a different set of eyes.

Darren: Are any vaccines safe or effective?

Matt: *Last time I had a flu vaccine was about 25 years ago. It made me quite ill for a couple of weeks and so I haven't had another one, or the flu, ever since.*

I've seen some interesting graphs which pointed out that a lot of the diseases that vaccines are claimed to have successfully cured were actually reducing anyway, because of clean water and better sanitation etc., and the vaccines were only brought in late on and didn't change any trajectory.

I'm not qualified to say whether any are safe or effective, but I would need more evidence now to believe they were. Then you start looking into scientific research and who funds it – the pharmaceutical industries who are some of the most corrupt organisations in the world.

If you look at how many times they've been fined criminally, and the amount they've been fined for the unethical things they've done - I no longer trust the pharma industry and scientists who are funded by them.

Darren: I'm completely confident that they won't get their chip implants, and I don't think they're even going to get to cashless, because we're going to fight so hard against it.

Matt: *I think they'll definitely try to implement a cashless society, hoping people won't see what that is and what that leads to.*

It's not difficult to imagine what goes on after you don't have any cash. When you have CBDC, they can turn your money off. So it's far more dangerous, and when they take away cash as an option, that's when you're in serious trouble.

I've learned that everything that happens, they need your consent to do it, so they're very sneaky about it. That's why mass noncompliance is the way forward, because if you don't comply, they then have to resort to illegal measures, and that's when we win, because that wakes everyone up.

Darren: What do you think our best hope is?

Matt: *Keep pounding away and keep making people aware of what governments are trying to do to us – when people realise just how bad these things are they're trying to implement, and how much control they will have over us, then I think it only stops when enough people realise. I don't think there's anything legally that can happen, they seem to have got all that stitched up.*

But if enough people just don't comply, mass peaceful noncompliance, that would make the biggest difference. Once you don't allow these people to implement their laws on you, you take their power away from them.

Matt mentioned 9/11, and yes, this was another event orchestrated by those of the dark agenda; and a way to 'justify' a war.

Another 'celebrity' truth teller is **Neil Oliver**, well known by many of us in the UK for presenting such BBC TV programmes as "Coast" and "A History of Scotland". He has an excellent YouTube channel and a Patreon website.

Below is a snippet from one of Neil's video presentations. He is talking about another of the dark agenda plans, as mentioned by White Feather, to micro-chip everyone, and no doubt one day turn us (future generations) into 'Borg like beings' (a scary race seeking to enslave all others in Star Trek), who are infused with all sorts of technology. As for us, it will of course be presented as 'for our own good and convenience'. If those of the dark agenda have their way, which they won't, it would eventually become inescapable, being artificially infused into all from birth. Honestly, I kid no one. These ideas, and 'test tube designer babies' are all 'out there' as genuine proposals and objectives supported if not directed by the WEF. Just take a discerning look at their website and see.

Neil Oliver – 9th December 2022

Transhumanism

'It's anti-human, anti-human is the agenda, it goes all the way up to transhumanism, this objective that floats about without enough people paying attention to it. This idea of blending the natural human with technology; and it's sold as something that's going to help the quadriplegics to walk again, or it's going to cure blindness, and all the rest of it, and I'm sure that's hypothetically the case.

'But ultimately, I promise you this, it's about putting something into the human organism that will facilitate external control of the human organism at some point in the future, and that objective, this idea that we need to be upgraded, updated, is based fundamentally on the fact that the a narrow Elite believes that human beings aren't good enough.

'World Economic Forum 'preacher' Yuval Noah Harari is on record saying that the mass of the population are just useless eaters. Now who, gets to decide which eaters are useless? I mean objectively speaking, what makes Yuval Noah Harari a useful eater, what makes Klaus Schwab a useful eater, and who gets to sit in judgment on who of the rest of 8 billion people are useless?

'So it's predicated this transhumanism, this idea that we need to be augmented, that we need to be fused with technology in order to come up to scratch, is an expression of a manifestation of the new reality which is the 'elites' don't think we are good enough as we are.

'It's not enough to be human and alive, you've got to have some better kit, some silicon chip, shoved into the back of your head, to elevate you to the point where you become a useful eater, or at least not a useless eater.'

What Neil Oliver said reminds me of what White Feather said in chapter 2, No. 59 "Q&A - On the planned end game".

'.. it is planned, that you will be connected to a computer, a super intelligent computer, that will not involve any emotional decisions, any empathy, any compassion, but merely to work as a slave to serve the system of the chosen few.'

Another aspect of the dark agenda I will briefly touch upon is to say that the war in Ukraine is not simply the good guys versus the bad guys. I'm not for one second suggesting that Vladimir Putin is some misunderstood good (or bad) guy. Although earlier in his career he was a KGB (Russian security agency) operative at one time based in East Germany.

But nothing is as simple as it should be in this physical reality when the media can demonise one person or group of people and praise another as trustworthy and honest. When looking at the bigger issues in this world one should bear in mind that vested material interests might be involved, so what is presented to us may not be the full or in some cases even part of the true facts. Those of the dark agenda have no qualms about starting a war causing many 'deaths' and inflicting suffering on millions of innocent people.

Below is an article on Ukraine by Brett Redmayne-Titley featured in The Light, June 2022 (page 16). Brett is reported to have spent the last decade travelling and documenting the 'Sorrows of Empire'. An archive of his many articles can be found at the website: https://watchingromeburn.uk/

Ukraine's Nazi connections and the British cover-up

'The origin of the war in Ukraine and its propagation of neo-Nazism can be traced back to the 2014 Ukrainian revolution, which saw America help overthrow the legitimately elected president, Viktor Yanukovych, and create the terror of Maidan Square.

'Months before, Assistant U.S. Secretary of State, Victoria Nuland, had publicly stated that the U.S. had spent $5 billion to support democracy in Ukraine. When that 'democracy' spiralled into predictable national violence, much to the dismay of European leaders, Nuland famously stated, "Fuck the EU." A three-word synopsis for U.S. democratic diplomacy then and now.

'Regionally and culturally Ukraine is divided East to West, on either side of the Dnieper River with the capital, Kyiv at the north end. Eastern Ukraine is primarily culturally Russian and has been for centuries. The 1939 Molotov/ Ribbentrop Pact divided Poland and Ukraine along new borders and today western Ukraine is far more aligned culturally and politically with Western Europe and the U.S. For these reasons, western Ukraine has great animosity towards the East, hence the 2014 election was very close and violent.

'Yanukovych was from the Donbas of far eastern Ukraine and until the 2014 election, the people of the city regions of Luhansk (LPR), Donetsk (DPR), and the Donbas had little to fear from the Ukrainian government. These regions are the important industrial, manufacturing and mining centres of Ukraine while the western half is far more agrarian. Regardless, east and west lived in relative harmony post-1939 until 2014. On February 20 that year, pro-democracy snipers murdered in cold blood forty-nine innocent Ukrainians and four policemen in one night, during the U.S.-backed post-election protests against Yanukovych at Maidan Square.

'The murders - falsely blamed on Russia - had the intended effect of sending Ukraine into a tailspin of East vs. West anti-Russian ultra-violence. Yanukovych abandoned the presidency and went to Russia; Parliament installed Arseniy Yatsenyuk as temporary president until new elections brought to power Petro Poroshenko, who was aligned with U.S. interests and did nothing to restrict the growing influence of the neo-Nazi Right Sector or Azov Battalion.

'Thus began the Ukraine war.

'Before 2014, the Armed Forces of Ukraine (AFU) had been rife with anti-Russian/Jewish sentiment for decades but were held in check by Yanukovych and other Russia-aligned leaders. During WWII, Ukrainian Nazi collaborator, Stepan Bandera, achieved hero status in western Ukraine for his genocide against Ukrainian Russians and Jews, and statues were erected in his honour after he was assassinated in 1959. Bandera was unabashedly a neo-Nazi and created his legion of the like-minded. However, his death only galvanised his underground supporters, many of whom remained within, not only the Ukrainian Army, but the political structure itself.

'This is evidenced by a Ukrainian politician, Andriy Parubiy. He has served as Deputy Speaker and Speaker of the Ukrainian parliament from 2014 to 2019, and Secretary of National Security and the Defence Council of Ukraine. Andriy Parubiy is a Nazi. He has proudly proclaimed this many times before his parliament, before the Ukrainian military and the public on TV.

'When Poroshenko was elected, Washington used this opportunity to open the floodgates into Ukraine for U.S. weaponry and military training, in preparation for its eventual de facto assault on the East and Russian influence there. As such, Ukraine incrementally became the largest military in Europe. It was also at this time, that the previously suppressed "Banderists" dominated the AFU and Ukrainian politics, much to the pleasure of the U.S. and NATO.

'The Right Sector are admittedly disciples of Stepan Bandera, and exert neo-Nazi influence as they act as a political watchdog, propagating their philosophy across Ukraine. The AFU is not exclusively Banderist but the massive Azov battalion stationed in the east is predominately so. Like Bandera, they hate Ukrainian Russians and Jews.

'The United Nations Human Rights Commission reported that over 14,000 Eastern Ukrainians have been killed since 2014, as they repeatedly begged Russia for military assistance to help their regional militias fight back.

'To stop this slaughter in 2014, Russia brokered a truce called the Minsk Protocols which the AFU ignored. This was followed in 2015 by Minsk II which also had no practical effect on the AFU genocide. For seven years, this terror continued unchecked, as Washington salivated in the wings for more dead Russians.

'**In 2019, Volodymyr Zelensky, a comedian and actor famous for his role in the TV series, Servant of the People, defeated Poroshenko in a landslide by promising peace through honouring the Minsk accords and controlling corruption and the rising violence of the Right Sector. But it took mere months for the Ukrainians to become the brunt of this comedian's dark joke that saw him become, not a leader for peace, but a U.S. and Banderist puppet.**

'With the collapse of the Soviet Union and the divestiture of its many satellite countries in 1990, NATO had promised not to expand into these countries. However, almost without exception NATO expanded and began to ring Russia with U.S. weapons and NATO influence. With Ukraine being the launching point for past wars against Russia, the

Kremlin had made it clear to the U.S. that Ukraine joining NATO was a red line.

'For the UK media to suggest that Russia was not incrementally provoked into defending both Eastern Ukraine and its own national interests is to turn the truth on its head. With spring being historically the best time to begin a war, during February Zelensky ordered the Azov Battalion and the AFU to begin amassing 100,000 troops and munitions towards the east in preparation for a massive attack designed to take back the autonomous eastern regions.

'The DPR, LPR and Donbas militias again begged Russia for intervention but Putin still refused. Instead, the Russians tried diplomacy and repeatedly contacted Washington and Kyiv in an effort not to militarily intervene. The demands were simple and rational: Abide by Minsk I & II; not attack the East; de-Nazify the AFU and not join NATO.

'The U.S. and Kyiv did not respond. In an effort to get a negotiated response, and with the AFU continuing to amass forces eastward, Russia began to prepare its army on the Russia/Ukraine border. Instead of negotiating with Russia for peace, Ukraine and the Western media falsely screamed 'Russian aggression'.

'Then, in the last week of February, Zelensky did the unthinkable. He informed the U.S. that he was now willing to allow U.S. nuclear weapons into Ukraine.

'The next day, the Russian army crossed into Eastern Ukraine. Thus began the Russian/Ukrainian war and the incredible barbarity of the AFU.

'For the Western media to cover up the neo-Nazi connection in Ukraine is the biggest lie of this war. I have recently returned from two months' reporting in and around Ukraine. Certainly, both sides are guilty of atrocity, but I have seen a different kind of barbarity by the AFU that is beyond the pale of war because the AFU and the Avovs consider and treat all Ukrainian Russians, Jews and even peace advocates as vermin. They have given up all morality. I can bear witness to the killings of the innocent, the torture and killings of prisoners, the firing on civilian targets, the mining of the humanitarian corridors to prevent escape, and the execution of anyone who suggests peace, much less negotiation,

and I have seen the Swastikas and pro-Nazi tattoos scrawled on the hands, arms, necks and chests of the AFU killers.

'Many facts are being ignored, such as the network of U.S. bio-weapons labs discovered across Ukraine and that the Ukrainian army is not winning this war, it is being decimated. Air Force, Navy, fuel refineries, supply and railway lines destroyed. 50,000 men dead with so many surrendering that the Russians are building larger POW camps. All men 16-60 being - by law - conscripted as replacements. NATO munitions supplies destroyed as soon as they cross the Polish border, and command and control communications centres are in ruins.

'This day Boris Johnson's favourite democratic champion, President Zelensky, signed a new law banning all opposition parties from existence, after already arresting five generals and the main opposition leader, Viktor Medvedchuk as 'anti-heroes' for the treasonous crime of suggesting peace.'

The facts are that the 'elites' want a World Government run by them; and Russia, as far as I can see, want to retain their independence. The fact that Russia also has vast natural resources may also be desired by those seeking domination over everyone and everything? While at this time those in the USA, UK and so forth who, via our corrupt politicians, are happy to surrender our own sovereignty to what would probably be presented as a WEF world government (with those 'pulling the strings' remaining hidden in the dark shadows).

Shifting back to the injection agenda, I could go on and on adding more and more revelations about how 'dodgy' (to say the least) the Covid jabs, in some cases at least, are, and the harm caused to many and the 'deaths' of others. This is happening worldwide, for instance, as the following abridged article by Paul Bennett featured in The Light, November 2022 (page 16) shows.

Vaccine damage cover-up in Israel

'In a monumental and game changing development, a leaked video of a meeting has revealed the Israeli health authorities knew the vaccines were harming people, and intentionally failed to disclose their findings to the public.

'The videoed meeting showed that a research team commissioned by the Ministry of Health in Israel found evidence of serious, long-lasting side-effects from the covid jabs.

'They found that the covid vaccines were much more dangerous to people than the world authorities admitted. They found serious adverse events that were never disclosed by Pfizer or any world government. These adverse events were also not found to be short-term as the public was told.

'In his detailed report, Kirsch said: "In short, the panel determined that the government was misleading the people of Israel.

'"We still don't know the whole extent of how dangerous the vaccines are, because the outside team only looked at the top 5 most frequently cited events.

'"Both the Israeli authorities and scientists analysing the Ministry of Health data acted to cover up the harms by releasing a fabricated report to the public, to make the vaccine look perfectly safe and claim that there was nothing wrong."

'In the secret video recording, the research team warned the Israeli health officials: "You have to think very, very carefully about how you communicate this to the public, because you may open yourself to legal lawsuits and liability issues, because what you promoted is, in fact, not the reality in what we see in the reports."

'Regarding collecting relevant data about serious side-effects, Kirsch said: "They only started collecting safety data in December 2021, one year after rolling out the vaccines to the public. Few people knew this."

'Kirsch commented on the silence across the world about the stark disclosure by saying: "Leaders of our 'trusted institutions' all over the world said absolutely nothing after the news broke on August 20, 2022. This suggests that there is widespread corruption in the medical community, government agencies, among public health officials, the mainstream media, and social media companies worldwide; they will not acknowledge any event that goes against the mainstream narrative. This is a level of corruption that is unprecedented. The atrocities here are clear-cut. Everyone should be speaking out and calling for a full investigation and fully evaluating the safety data collected by the Israel government.

'"This is a gross example of the perversion of medicine from its moral mission as a healing profession. We are bearing witness AGAIN to the *mass weaponisation of medicine. Not since the Nazi medical crimes against humanity has medicine been perverted on such a mass scale. Why didn't they release the original presentation made by the safety team?*

'Kirsch concluded by saying: "They should be prosecuting all these people as criminals, because that's what they did: they conspired to bury the safety information which could have saved lives.'

There are, as I have said, many things that I could have added in this chapter. Undertakers (or 'Funeral Directors'), being one, who have spoken out about finding blood clots never before seen in the dead bodies of many people they embalm. (It seems they drain the blood from a body as part of the embalming procedure). Also the number of babies and aborted remains they are encountering. But for now the following may give some indication of just how many are 'dying' (and far more haven't died but have had severe adverse reactions – to jabs).

An article by Richard House featured in The Light, October 2022 (page 5) highlights just how many people, following the jab, have 'gone home' to spirit life, the article is titled:

Covid jab: 48,000 Harold Shipmans - and counting

As 'vaccine' genocide toll reaches 12 million, we have still seen nothing in the mainstream media

'Most will know something of the history of the late medical doctor and mass murderer, Harold Shipman.

'Over a period of many years, general practitioner Shipman is estimated to have murdered around 250 of his patients - with that paragon of unbiased information, Wikipedia, describing him as "The most prolific serial killer in modern history". Nicknamed 'Dr Death' and 'The Angel of Death' by the media, many will remember the prurient coverage of his crimes by the mainstream media at the time (Shipman was convicted on January 31, 2000.)

'Contrast such media coverage with their deafening non-coverage of the deaths attributed to the covid experimental jab. U.S. entrepreneur Steve Kirsch will likely be well known to readers. A previously strong supporter of the political left in the USA pre-2019 (having donated some $20 million to the Democrat Party), Kirsch woke up around the start of

the plandemic - and since then he has used his fortune to amass a huge database, based on which he periodically releases telling newsletters that give readers the real statistics about what's going on with covid and the jab (see https://stevekirsch.substack.com/). Notably, Kirsch has also offered U.S. $1 million to anyone who can refute any of his analyses - and as yet (and predictably), no one has cashed in.

'In a recent newsletter (August 2022), Kirsch estimates - conservatively - that the covid jab has killed 12 million people worldwide. Needless to say, there has been a deafening silence about this global genocide in the mainstream media. Just let that sink in. Over TWELVE MILLION people have died (to date) worldwide from an imposed experimental medical treatment, and not a peep from the captured mainstream media. Incredible.

'There is a well known saying about death, attributed to Joseph Stalin: 'One death is a tragedy; one million is a statistic.'

'So, to date as I write, the covid-jab genocidal outrage amounts to 48,000 Harold Shipmans. Precisely because of the truth of Stalin's quotation, and the numbing effect that mass death has on the psyche, it's extremely difficult to let in the full reality of this. In effect, 48,000 Harold Shipmans, each criminally killing 250 medical patients, and this unspeakable crime has unfolded before our eyes over the last two years. Some sage commentators are saying that 'we ain't seen nothing yet'.

'With outrageously biased non-reporting such as this, no wonder the number of viewers and readers of the mainstream media platforms are in freefall. Ex-chief executive of ITV, Mark Sharman, said in a recent UK Column interview that his BBC licence renewal had recently arrived - and he wasn't paying it because, he said, "The BBC has broken its public service contract with me."

'It's clear from the BBC's recent accounts that Mark Sharman is far from alone, with erstwhile faithful licence-payers deserting the BBC in droves. This is a direct outcome of the BBC relinquishing any reputation it ever had (however chimerical) for unbiased public service broadcasting, and becoming a demonstrably captured mouthpiece for government, the security services and corporate interests - for anyone sufficiently free-thinking and unduped to see.

'If current trends continue (and everything suggests they will, if anything, accelerate), at some point the curves will cross, and more

people will be seeking their news from truth-telling independent media sources like The Light, UK Column News, Off-Guardian, Windows on the World and the rest, rather than from mainstream sources. When that day comes, no longer will the globalists have majority control over the way people think and the views they hold. And for huge numbers of free-thinking truth-seekers, that day can't come soon enough.'

The list of people who have spoken out about one or more aspect of this whole cruel agenda is absolutely vast and I mention just a comparative few that I have 'stumbled across' in my research. For example, in an article courtesy of https://freewestmedia.com/ that was featured in The Light, September 2021 (page 14) from which I include a couple of short quotes below, it was titled:

German chief pathologist sounds alarm on vaccine fatalities

'Peter Schirmacher, director of the Pathological Institute of the University of Heidelberg, expresses his concerns after conducting more than 40 autopsies on people who died within two weeks of a covid shot'.

'Even if his results are only a snapshot, it is a dramatic one: 30 to 40 percent died from the vaccination itself. The pathologist cited "rare, severe side effects of the vaccination – such as cerebral vein thrombosis or autoimmune diseases".'

I mentioned Undertakers in the UK a couple of pages back, and there is an article by Paul Bennett (https://www.thegatewaypundit.com/) concerning autopsies in The Light, February 2023 (page 17), and below is just a little from the article titled:

Japanese team finds alarming abnormalities during autopsies

'Japanese doctors conducting autopsies have discovered disturbing results regarding the experimental covid jabs. In a detailed report, Professor Masataka Nagao, a medical specialist in forensic medicine from the Hiroshima University School of Medicine, reported how the bodies of vaccinated individuals he autopsied were unusually warm, with body temperatures over 100 degrees Fahrenheit (about 40 Centigrade).

'He said: "We believe the vax is related to serious immune abnormalities. The first concern was that the body temperatures of the corpses were very high when the police performed the autopsy."

'Nagao's research team also observed significant changes to the genetic make-up of vaccinated autopsied patients' immune systems. The thorough investigation has led Nagao to conclude that the vaccine causes immune system abnormalities that prompt inflammation throughout the body, which is likely the cause of the high body temperatures at the time of autopsy.'

Also:

'Sano added, "I don't know if I should say this, but it has been found that vaccinated people are more likely to get coronavirus than unvaccinated people. Sometimes, things that are not good are introduced into the human body. Vaccination may cause our overall immune system to fail to fight against such bad things."'

The 'dark agenda' is worldwide and far worst in some countries; for example, it has been rife in Canada, as the following article by Dr Francis Christian featured in The Light, September 2021 (page 15); informs us, and below is just a little from this article titled:

Persecution of Canada's outspoken physicians and scientists mirrors totalitarian Iron Curtain

'There is a medical and societal tyranny now afoot in Canada.

'It is based on a single-minded, totalitarian and anti-science opposition to anything other than what constitutes the 'official narrative' with regard to the covid-19 pandemic and its solution.

'It has evolved into a well-coordinated campaign to smear, de-platform, persecute and silence anyone who questions the official propaganda constantly emanating from government-sanctioned sources.

'This Orwellian tyranny has extended to include the persecution of Canadian scientists and physicians.

'If their scientific utterance or statement is perceived by the authorities to stray from the official narrative, there are concerted, coordinated moves by health authorities, government public health agencies and licensing bodies, with a compliant media in tow, to persecute and *'discipline' the offender for simply expressing an opinion or pointing out ethical obligations for physicians, such as informed consent.'*

In the same September 2021 edition of The Light (page 19), if we remember the evidence Undertakers were finding while embalming, supporting this, another Canadian doctor is quoted having made an alarming find; and below is just a little from the article by https://www.worldtribune.com/ titled:

Doctor finds 62% of vaccinated have blood clots

'A Canadian doctor who has given the covid vaccine to more than 900 patients has reported that 62 percent of them tested positive for blood clots.

'Dr Charles Hoffe, who has been practicing medicine for 28 years in British Columbia, said he has given about 900 doses of the Moderna experimental mRNA vaccine and the core problem he has seen are microscopic clots in his patients' tiniest capillaries.

'Hoffe said the blood clots are "Occurring at a capillary level. This has never before been seen. This is not a rare disease. This is an absolutely new phenomenon."

'Hoffe continued: "Blood vessels in the lungs are now blocked up. In turn, this causes the heart to need to work harder to try to keep up against a much greater resistance trying to get the blood through your lungs. This is called pulmonary artery hypertension – high blood pressure in the lungs because the blood simply cannot get through effectively. People with this condition usually die of heart failure within a few short years."

'In an April letter to the provincial Ministry of Health, Hoffe cited a high rate of serious side-effects from the vaccine he was administering: "It must be emphasized, that these people were not sick, being treated for some devastating disease. These were previously healthy people, who were offered an experimental therapy, with unknown long-term side-effects, to protect them against an illness that has the same mortality rate as the flu. Sadly, their lives have now been ruined."'

Those behind or carrying out the wishes of the overlords of the dark agenda try to undermine honest researchers, calling them, "Conspiracy theorists", or saying that they are "Racist", or whatever else they think will deter members of the general public from paying attention to them. Yet, today, we find that much of what they have said is now clearly upon us, and is true or coming true, and can no longer be considered nonsense or theory, but factual. So it *is* time for people to 'wake up' and pay attention, if they do not wish to become enslaved by, or at least under the control of, those with a dark agenda; and allow this fate to befall their children or grandchildren, or future generations in general.

As I have said, I could have added more in this chapter; but perhaps I have said enough for most people to realise, if they did not before, that many corrupt people are currently trying to take away personal liberty and freedom of speech and choice.

One of the things I could have commented on is the number of freedom rallies, or protests marches, that have taken place worldwide since the beginning of the dark agenda pre-planned so called pandemic. From London (UK) to Melbourne (Australia) and many cities in between I have seen footage showing hundreds of thousands of people standing up for their rights. One in Berlin (Germany) it is estimated had between one and two million people taking to the streets. In London a friend went on at least one occasion, and the spirit guide Monty said that 625,000 people on that occasion took part.

In March 2021 many rallies were taking place worldwide, and an article by Darren Smith and Jess Peters featured in The Light, April 2021 (page 3) mentioned this, below are a few snippets, it was titled:

Worldwide Rallies For Freedom

'Hundreds of thousands of people across the world demonstrated against the extreme, draconian year-long overreach of their governments on Saturday 20th March 2021, as they peacefully rallied in major cities across Argentina, Australia, Austria, Belgium, Brazil, Britain, Bulgaria, Canada, Croatia, Denmark, Finland, Germany, Ireland, Italy, Japan, Netherlands, Poland, Portugal, Romania, Serbia, Sweden, Switzerland and the U.S.'

'In London, despite the lame attempts by the bought media to portray the crowds as "a few hundred", more than 70,000 rallied and marched through the capital, people from all walks of life coming together in solidarity against the insanity and tyranny of our times.'

When I showed video footage of some of these rallies to a friend without access to the Internet he was amazed; since he had never seen any of this on the mainstream TV news. I would wonder why not if I didn't already know that it was because of corrupt media censorship.

Our UK government, in majority, do not have any respect for the general population and are even willing to vote in such a way to deny us our human rights, which were supposedly guaranteed by the Nuremberg code. How so? Because the majority of them voted to deny certain people, certain workers in fact, the right to refuse an experimental medical procedure for those working in care homes. Below is a little about this from an article by Darren Smith and Jessica Peters featured in The Light, August 2021 (page 2), it was titled:

MPs vote for forced vaccines

'On July 13, after a 90 minute debate in a vote the public hardly knew about, MPs voted 319-246 in favour of forcing care workers and all those working in care homes to receive experimental injections, which are part of the mass mRNA drug trials being carried out until 2023.

'Perhaps they are still under the impression there really is a deadly, contagious disease out there, but after 18 months with no evidence of one whatsoever, one must now really start to question the sanity of these so-called representatives. This is exactly how repressive dictatorships are formed: legislation is passed while most of the country is distracted by rather less meaningful events than the total removal of their personal freedom for ever.'

'Just over 75 years after Britain's brave men and women fought off a totalitarian menace to keep our country free, it seems we have surrendered our individual sovereignty and the right to choose for ourselves and prosper, falling for the age-old tyrant's ruse of 'wanting to protect its citizens' and constantly telling us 'it's for your own good' as we are herded and restricted.

'Not only is this parliament quickly shaping up to be similar to that of the Reichstag's in 1933-45, it seems it is determined to far surpass all other lapdogs to tyranny in history.'

Then there are the number of young people, athletes, footballers, and others simply trying to keep fit, having heart attacks. All the evidence

274

suggests that these individuals were those who allowed themselves to be jabbed. At least this should be investigated, but is ignored by the MSM as an article by John Brindley featured in The Light, January 2022 (page 3) pointed out. Below is a little from the article; firstly from former professional football player Trevor Sinclair.

Time to blow the whistle on sudden sporting deaths

'I've now seen reports of another FIVE players who've collapsed/died in past two days. One of them, did so in a CHAMPIONS LEAGUE game v Real Madrid watched all around the world by millions & apparently there have been 108 FIFA registered pro footballers who've died in last 6 months & nearly 200 of them have collapsed… what the f**k is going on?

'In my 19 years as a pro footballer & then my 20+ years watching & commentating, I've never seen ANY players collapse, pass out, etc either live or during any of the thousands of training sessions & matches I've taken part in.

'Something isn't right…. In fact something is happening that is very VERY wrong. Ignore it & keep your head buried in the sand if you wish, but it's not going away.'

'… former England badminton star Gail Emms, aged 44, "I remember 2hrs after vaccine, my HR going through the roof. Then my blood pressure soared. I don't remember the next few hours as I was rushed to hospital with suspected stroke. And I've been told that this has happened lots with very fit people and the vaccine".'

Another article by Louize Small, and I include a couple of paragraphs from this, was featured in The Light, December 2021 (page 4); and this also concerns heart issues, it was titled:

New study shows mRNA vaccines
DOUBLE chances of heart attack

'A new study published in the American Heart Association's online medical journal, Circulation, shows that patients who have received their second shot of the Moderna or Pfizer covid 'vaccines' have more than doubled their chances of having a heart attack.

'A group led by renowned cardiologist Dr Steven Gundry used the PULS cardiac test - a blood test - to accurately detect risk of heart attack in the coming five years.'

Obviously I hope the risks reduce over time and that new Earth treatments will benefit all in need. The best advice, I think, is clearly to never comply in the first place, but all is never lost even for those who have suffered adverse reactions after complying. One must, also, never forget that life is eternal; and that if one does depart the Earth as a consequence of taking a jab I believe it is a choice accepted, to some degree at least, by one's higher self. Although, that said, we do at the same time have personal responsibility over how we treat our physical bodies, and if we compromise them too much, then perhaps the intended life-plan becomes compromised in some way and the higher self feels the lifetime can end. Obviously, the same applies for any family or friends departing because of the agenda. Some, I believe, may be departing to help raise awareness of the dark agenda. They are, of course, going home to a far superior world and state of being; as sad as it may be for those who miss them.

It is easy to say do not comply; what would happen one might ask? Well, let us see, if we use the following as a guideline. In an article by Bushiri featured in The Light, March 2022 (page 18) is an inspiring account that I include in full. The original president, Magufuli, the writer says was murdered, and I have no doubt that this was the case. I remember seeing a video of him saying that, for one thing, the PCR test was nonsense. He had all sorts tested; fruit and animal included, gave them false identities as though the swabs were from people, and got results that in a number of cases said the 'people' had tested positive. Effectively proving that the tests where meaningless.

He embarrassed the 'Covid establishment', defied them. Consequently, as White Feather confirms happens, they got rid of him and installed a puppet made in their false image. The article was titled:

It took just one week for 50 million
Tanzanians to stop complying

Subtitle: **An entire nation engaging in peaceful, silent, civil disobedience is one of the most moving phenomena you can experience.**

'It is almost a year since the assassination of the world's one and only sovereign leader who waged open warfare against the covid-19 cabal.

'This is a first-hand account of the situation on the ground in Tanzania since the hit squad was sent in to eliminate the only leader who fought the cabal and their 'vaccines' head-on, out in the open, from day one.

'Within a few weeks of President Magufuli's murder, his replacement, Samia Suluhu Hassan, a World Economic Forum attendee, set about installing the cabal's covid agenda. It was a thoroughly depressing experience. I know. I was there to see it.

'Gone forever were Magufuli's maskless smile and palpable warmth, replaced now by daily images of a cold, insentient president and her entire entourage all muzzled, as per the cabal's orders.

'In rapid succession, in came the following: a campaign of fear launched by the media with images of 'covid patients' in hospitals, tight covid controls at the country's airports and borders, directives to force the public to wear face masks face, masks in all government buildings, a masked police force, masks in hospitals, anti-social distancing, masks in schools, masks in the streets, no handshakes, public transport forced to operate at half capacity, messages from government on our mobile phones, warning us about covid and promoting the 'vaccine', palpable fear between old friends and families, import of covid 'vaccines' banned under Magufuli, "She is poison," were words often heard in the street when Tanzanians compared the new WEF-appointed president with Magufuli.

'But then, after just one week, something happened. Something truly remarkable...

'After just one week of all the fear and insanity, the people of Tanzania had had enough.

'Call it the legacy of Magufuli, call it divine intervention, or perhaps just **plain old common sense**, but it is a fact that within just seven days, great cracks began to appear in the covid narrative in Tanzania.

'First it was the police. Working in the tropical heat, they quickly realised that they were suffocating behind their masks, so they threw them where they belonged - in the bin.

'So, when you see that the police themselves are questioning the narrative and distancing themselves from the nonsense, what happens?

277

'Everyone else follows.

'And so, while the new president and her acolytes appeared on TV daily, all masked up, pumping out fear and promoting covid 'vaccines', **out in the streets the people of Tanzania were having none of it and, believe me, the mass non-compliance was a sight to behold.**

'I do not know how many of you reading this have borne witness to an entire nation engaged in peaceful, silent, civil disobedience, but I can testify first-hand that it is one of the most moving phenomena you can possibly experience: like a warm, silent, gentle current passing from one person to the next, leaving everyone with a smile.

'Quietly, the whole of Tanzania stopped complying.

'That is 50 million people in a land almost five times the size of Britain.

'And so today, with the exception of the country's airports (which 90% of Tanzanians will never enter), life goes on as it always has.

'Children go to school without masks, people work freely unmasked, the police do not enforce any covid rules, public buses are packed to the hilt.

The fishermen sail the ocean, farmers till the land, tourists come from Europe to taste the freedom they once had. The markets are bursting with millions of smiling people buying and selling, hugging and hand-shaking, and the clubs and bars pound out the tunes while men and women are allowed to do what men and women have always done - meet, dance and romance, no passes required, no poison required, exactly as God intended.

'It is a blessing from God to be here.

'I write off with a final anecdote to put a smile on your face.

'In a recent conversation with hospital staff in Tanzania, they informed me that the government had ordered them to launch 'outreach programmes' to inform the public about the danger of covid. I quote from that conversation: "...So we packed the hospital vehicles with equipment and staff and took off to the rural villages deep in the bush to inform them. When we arrived there, we found the people working in the fields and we called them together.

'"We asked them if they had heard of coronavirus, or covid. They all just frowned and looked at each other. 'What?' they asked. They had no *idea what we were talking about. So we tried again. And again they just shook their heads.*

'They were completely bemused. So we stopped what we were doing and thought about it all right there. Then I looked at those villagers. They were fit and healthy. They were born under the hot sun. They worked their fields day after day, and you could see their muscles hewn from physical work, their gleaming skin, their white teeth. They were in perfect health."

'At this point in the conversation the doctor paused and shook his head. He looked embarrassed before concluding, "Then I looked at us people from the hospital. You know what, we were the ones who looked sick compared with those villagers! We were the ones who needed lecturing about health. So I told the staff to get in the vehicles and we drove away. We will not go back. Those villagers should be left as they are. They don't need all this."'

Other honest people, 'rebels' fighting against the dark side, include none other than the Canadian police, also known to many of us as the *"Royal Canadian Mounted Police"* (RMCP). In The Light, December 2021 (page 16) can be found the following article, abridged extracts below, about an 'open letter' they issued. The article is titled:

Canadian police mount massive challenge to covid mandates

Subtitled: Officers defend people's right to bodily autonomy and accuse government of coercion.

'Around 30,000 officers in the Royal Canadian Mounted Police have signed an explosive letter opposing mandatory covid vaccinations and having to enforce them.

'As well as accusing the Canadian Government of coercion and overstepping its authority, the officers have also called on investigators to collect statements from medical professionals and other reliable witnesses who allege they have been silenced – "thereby putting lives at risk".

'In the powerful open letter, sent to RCMP commissioner Brenda Lucki on October 21, they expressed their "sincere concerns and resolute stand against the forced coercive medical intervention of Canadians,

and against the undue discrimination experienced by those exercising their lawful right to bodily autonomy".

"'A complete investigation must include full disclosure of all the facts of the case, even contradictory evidence. Why, then, is there little to no tolerance for free and open debate on this matter? Many credible medical and scientific experts are being censored. "Accordingly, we rightly have concerns about 'the science' we are being coerced to 'follow'.

"'**Police officers are expected to preserve the peace, uphold the law and defend the public interest. We strongly believe that forced and coerced medical treatments undermine all three and, thus, contradict our duties and responsibilities to Canadians. "We believe our federal and provincial governments have failed to uphold the Charter, Bill of Rights and Constitution and we are witnessing the erosion of democracy in Canada.**

"'The choice of whether to receive medical treatment has always been an individual's right in Canada. The Canadian National Report on Immunisation (1996) states 'Immunisation is not mandatory in Canada; it cannot be made mandatory because of the Canadian Constitution'.

"'Though the Nuremberg Code is not a law, it is internationally accepted and falls in line with the spirit of our Charter and Bill of Rights. "A key component of the Nuremberg Code is that participants in a medical experiment need to participate voluntarily without any form of force or coercion. "We have obtained documentation from several Canadian doctors who have explained the current covid-19 treatment options in Canada, being referred to as 'vaccines', were recently authorised as new drugs despite the absence of long-term data. "According to these accredited Canadian doctors, these treatment options did not meet the criteria of true vaccines until very recently when the definition of vaccine was changed. "Without long-term data, these vaccines are still experimental. We believe the act of removing the rights and freedoms of citizens who refuse to participate in specific covid-19 treatment options is a form of coercion.

"'The Criminal Code contains our country's Criminal Offences and explains that a person commits an assault by intentionally applying force to someone else without that person's consent. The Criminal Code further explains that consent is not obtained from a person who submits, or neglects to resist, on the grounds of authority being *exercised over them. "How then can someone give proper consent to a covid-19 treatment injection when doing so under the threat of losing their job, freedoms, or livelihood? Canadian courts have already ruled that medical treatment without proper informed consent is an assault.*

'"As law enforcement officers, we cannot in good conscience willingly participate in enforcing mandates that violate the laws of our country and breach the rights and freedoms of the people we protect".'

Personally I have never accepted even a flu jab despite the fact that here in the UK where I live it has for a long time been offered free to those 'getting on in years'. One article by Richard House featured in The Light, May 2022 (page 9) ought to make a few people think more about vaccines in general. Below is just a little from the article that echoes what Caroline Chang reported in her article (blog), it was titled:

Vaccine harassment is backfiring

'None of the 72 vaccines that are currently mandated for our (U.S.) children has been safety tested against a placebo in pre-clinical trials.'

'An enormous pile of literature exists that comprehensively deconstructs the junk, zombie science underpinning vaccine-centred public health discourse. In a recent interview, one of these writers, Neil Z. Miller, said the following: "(in our research) we discovered that children who'd received vaccines were anywhere from four to over twelve times more likely to develop various negative or adverse health outcomes... **so the unvaccinated children are healthier** *in these respects, in comparison with these children receiving these multiple vaccines."'*

If anyone in the UK thinks that 72 vaccines in the USA for children sounds insane they are right. Nevertheless, it is the true figure. It is a big-big, enormous, profit making scheme. And the fact that these are not even tested against a placebo shows how corrupt, in my opinion, the whole system is. If this shocks anyone reading this, then perhaps they will think twice before they go alone for 'their free jab', and they emphasise "free" to make it sound like they are doing those who accept the offer a favour. Parents might also consider whether jabbing their children truly is advisable.

I am also reminded to say that in one letter I received in the UK from the medical practice that I am registered with it said if I did not get jabbed they would enter it as a "refusal". I did complain about this and said that "refusal" was not right as it wasn't some sort of lawfully ordered procedure I would potentially be receiving. It was an "offer" I was perfectly entitled to decline. The following year I noticed that they had now changed their wording. (So they do sometimes take notice).

In The Light, February 2023 (page 3) a partial glimpse of just how many people have had adverse reactions to the Covid jabs is mentioned.

The Yellow card scheme is the UK adverse reaction (to the jab) reporting procedure. The article is by Professor Richard Ennos, from which I quote just a little, was titled:

Alarming vaccine safety signals revealed by Yellow Card data

Subtitle: No question that the mRNA vaccines should be withdrawn with immediate effect.

'However, an independent analysis of the accumulated Yellow Card data, finally released 18 months after the first Freedom of Information (FOI) request, shows unequivocal safety signals linking the mRNA vaccines to serious damage to the lymph system, the heart and female reproduction.'

'Nearly half a million Yellow Card reports have now been filed, documenting suspected adverse events to the covid-19 vaccines (about one per hundred recipients).

'However, its response to the high number of reports of Myocarditis and pericarditis following mRNA vaccination has not been to withdraw the offending products, but merely to alter the safety information associated with these products, and alert health professionals to look out for these very serious adverse events after the relevant vaccines have been administered.'

Meanwhile, in the USA they have the "Vaccine Adverse Event Reporting System" abbreviated to: "VAERS". When I checked 6th March 2023 they showed a total of 1,527,370 reports with 34,576 deaths and

193,318 hospitalizations. However, it is known that the vast majority of cases go unreported in both the UK and USA. Many people say that no more than 10% are reported. After all, if many doctors are in denial and do not want to acknowledge that something they or their nurses have administered have resulted in someone's earlier than expected demise, who, particularly if a person lives alone, and has no family, is going to file a report?

Climate

Changing the subject to the Earth climate, many scientists know perfectly well that man-made and so called "Climate change" is a lie, a fraud to push an agenda to suit those of the dark agenda, and those with vested financial interests in pursuing the policies that are intended to be imposed on citizens of all nations. Honest scientists are, like the doctors who speak out about the so-called vaccine - jab them all agenda, are censored so what they say rarely, if ever, gets mainstream media coverage.

Below, is just a little from the Clintel.org website.

World Climate Declaration
There is no climate emergency

'Climate science should be less political, while climate policies should be more scientific. In particular, scientists should emphasize that their modelling output is not the result of magic: computer models are human-made. What comes out is fully dependent on what theoreticians and programmers have put in: hypotheses, assumptions, relationships, parameterizations, stability constraints, etc. Unfortunately, in mainstream climate science most of this input is undeclared.

'To believe the outcome of a climate model is to believe what the model makers have put in. This is precisely the problem of today's climate discussion to which climate models are central. Climate science has degenerated into a discussion based on beliefs, not on sound self-critical science. We should free ourselves from the naïve belief in immature climate models. In future, climate research must give significantly more emphasis to empirical science.'

During my last glance during January 2023 at the above website I noticed that 1499 Scientists and professionals have signed the declaration that, *"There is no climate emergency"*. Those of the dark agenda who, via the MSM, and for many years, have pushed the narrative that 'most scientists agree that climate change is man-made' have no such list of scientists to support their bogus claim.

Meanwhile The Light, September 2022 (page 3) published an article that one can read, headlined: **"1,100 eminent Scientists declare: There is No climate emergency"**.

The Ambassadors of Clintel who say, *"There is no climate emergency"* include the following, and I list these to show that this is not some 'run-of-the-mill' easily misled 'conspiracy theorists' but highly credible and qualified individuals:

Nobel Laureate Professor Ivar Giaever – Norway/USA

Professor Guus Berkhout - The Netherlands

Dr Cornelis Le Pair - The Netherlands

Professor Reynald Du Berger - French Speaking Canada

Dr Patrick Moore - English Speaking Canada

Professor Laszio Szarka - Hungary

Professor Seok Soon Park - South Korea

Professor Jan-Erik Solheim - Norway

Professor Richard Lindzen - USA

Professor Ingemar Nordin - Sweden

Professor Ian Plimer - Australia

Dr Blanca Parga Landa - Spain

Professor Alberto Prestininzi - Italy

Professor Benoit Rittaud - France

Dr Thiago Maia - Brazil

Professor Fritz Vahrenholt - Germany

The Viscount Monckton of Brenchley - United Kingdom

The last name on the list I have included, *The Viscount Monckton of Brenchley,* in an article I found on the Clintel website, answered a number of questions put to him. These may help confirm for readers that the whole subject is built on a lie.

He was asked:

After decades of research, what has been the most plausible conclusion regarding the "climate emergency"

Answer: *'There is no "climate emergency". The notion of large and dangerous (rather than small and net-beneficial) global warming arose from an elementary error of physics. At the temperature equilibrium in 1850 the direct warming by the preindustrial greenhouse gases was 8 K, but the total natural greenhouse effect that year was 32 K, of which 24 K was feedback response. It was, therefore, incorrectly assumed that, thanks to feedback response, a 1 K direct warming by doubled CO_2 in the air would cause about 4 K final warming. In reality, the multiple of direct warming to allow for feedback response was not 32/8 = 4. Climate scientists had forgotten the Sun was shining, and that, without any greenhouse gases in the air, the average temperature would be 260 K. That crucial feedback-driven multiple of direct temperature was (260 + 32) / (260 + 8), or less than 1.1. After correcting this climatologists' error, there will not be 4 K warming this century, as currently imagined, but little more than 1 K, which will be globally beneficial. Warming is already proving beneficial.'*

He was also asked:

How did the "97% consensus" about global warming turn out to be a 0.3% consensus?

Answer: *'Cook et al. (2013) reported that 97.1% of 11,944 scientific papers on climate and related topics published in the 21 years 1991-2011 had stated that global warming was chiefly manmade. That result was – and still is – widely publicized in the far-Left Western news media. In response to that paper, Mr. Obama tweeted that "global warming is real, manmade and dangerous". However, Legates et al. (2015) showed that Cook et al., in their own list of all 11,944 papers, had marked only 64, or 0.5%, as stating that recent warming was chiefly manmade. Legates et al. read all 64 papers and found that only 41 of them, or 0.3% of the entire sample, had actually stated that recent warming was chiefly manmade. At the request of a citizen of Queensland, the site of Cook's university, the police investigated and concluded that a deception had been perpetrated. A private intranet used by Cook and his conspirators was penetrated. It revealed that they were self-declared Communists.'*

The above confirms why so many people wrongly believe that man-made climate change is real, when it is a lie. In fact, as the first quote finishes, *Warming is already proving beneficial.* In other words the current situation of a slight natural warming is a good thing for us. This full article is available online for anyone to read. (See Links)

David Bellamy

Millions of people in the UK will remember David Bellamy, an enthusiastic and popular TV presenter. But how many of those millions know that the former botanist and broadcaster for the BBC (who returned to spirit life in 2019) spoke publicly about how he was effectively sacked from the BBC because he refused to 'play along' with telling the public that man-made climate change was real. This, he said, is why he 'suddenly' vanished from our TV screens. Like honest doctors, sacked, honest journalists, sacked, honest scientists, ignored and censored if they cannot be sacked. I thought he is worth remembering and mentioning, a good, honest man. Although I'm not suggesting that all presenters on TV realise that they are going along with lies. Many, if not the majority of the public, having been bombarded with the lie for decades now, truly believe that carbon dioxide is a threat to the climate.

During 2022 I purchased a book titled: ***"There Is No Climate Crisis"*** by David Craig. It contains near to 350 pages that also go to expose the current fictional climate crisis as nonsense. He shows that weather scares were around as far back as 1871; and that 'global warming' scares were aired in the 1920's and 1930's and during other decades. That 20-30 years back certain islands we were told would by now be under water and, guess what, they are currently under no more water than they were then.

There is a vast amount more in this book that I could mention that exposes so-called man-made climate change as a lie, but it might be 'overkill' and repetitive to say too much when readers can do some research and purchase such books themselves if they so wish.

"The Great Global Warming Swindle" was also a programme made for UK TV by Channel 4 in 2007 - when they were permitted to present genuine facts rather than 'obeying censorship orders' like the obedient puppets that the entire main stream media now are. This documentary can be viewed at my Bitchute channel. (See Links)

People should be aware that air and waste pollution that is rife on this planet, as we all know, has such a tiny affect on climate to be totally and absolutely insignificant. It is horrible and a disgrace, of course. It is another insult to humanity that can be placed firmly at the door of those with the dark agenda; the globalists and their corporations. One simple example is plastic bags; these could very easily have been removed from production and circulation a number of years back. I remember seeing something I think was on Facebook that showed alternative bags made from Hemp, and Mushroom or Fungi packaging is also an alternative that it is reported will decompose in a garden in weeks. With Hemp (and perhaps both) we were told are harmless to both land and sea, since they composted down easily; and in the sea they can, as they breakdown, be safely eaten by fish. Our worldwide governments are quick to attempt to impose legislation on limiting our God given freedoms, but slow to do anything as simple as stopping the use of slow or non-biodegradable plastic bags that are not land or sea friendly.

The corporations or supermarkets blame the public and say it is them who like their fruit and vegetables, for instance, in plastic bags 'for convenience'. But what choice do they always have? Buy in plastic or buy nothing, sometimes. NO, the public are not to blame; certainly not at the root cause. If no such packaging was used, the public would soon adjust to buying such produce loose. And, of course, hemp or paper bags could be used.

People need to be aware that blaming the general population for all the troubles in this world is a mind game to those of the dark agenda. It is a way of eliciting co-operation with our own enslavement. They tell us we are to blame and must therefore expect to suffer the consequences. And all too often people largely believe what they are effectively told to believe. It is the abuser telling the abused that they brought it on themselves. It is the rapist blaming the victim, saying they 'asked for it'. The psychopath, who lacks empathy and is incapable of showing any remorse for their actions.

If anyone still doubts that a dark agenda is in play in the UK and worldwide, they probably have not paid sufficient attention to what the 'baddies' have planned for us and the world. One tip; if the MSM go out of their way to say something is a 'conspiracy theory' then in all likelihood it contains some and perhaps plenty of truth.

If anyone believes that 'those at the top' are perhaps simply misunderstanding the true state of the climate they should think again. They know it is a lie. The 'second-string' foot soldiers may not, but those at the top know perfectly well. The lie is one they are using to help implement their own plans; and, of course, some of them are making fortunes out of the ruse.

One of the ways in which they plan to control people is through "Climate Lockdowns". Again, this is no joke or theory, this is fact, and it is one that anyone can discover more about online.

These Climate Lockdowns are planned, starting in different cities around the globe. One 'trial' of this, due to be implemented in 2024 is in Oxford (UK). One report of this featured in a 30th November 2022 article in "Vision News" edited by Darren Birks. Below is part of the article.

Climate Lockdowns

'At the end of November 2022 Oxfordshire County Council approved plans to lock residents into one of six zones to 'save the planet' from global warming.

'Residents will be confined to their local neighbourhood and have to ask permission to leave it all to 'save the planet'.

'The latest stage in the '15 minute city' agenda is to place electronic gates on key roads in and out of the city, confining residents to their own neighbourhoods.

'Under the new scheme if residents want to leave their zone they will need permission from the Council who gets to decide who is worthy of freedom and who isn't.

'Under the new scheme residents will be allowed to leave their zone a maximum of 100 days per year, but in order to even gain this every resident will have to register their car details with the council who will then track their movements via smart cameras round the city.

'Every resident will be required to register their car with the County Council who will then monitor how many times they leave their district

via number plate recognition cameras. And don't think you can beat the system if you're a two car household. Those two cars will be counted as one.

'Under the new rules, your social life becomes irrelevant. By de facto Councils get to dictate how many times per year you can see friends and family. You will be stopped from fraternising with anyone outside your district, and if you want a long distance relationship in the future, forget it, you are confined to dating only those within a 15 minute walk of your house.

'A single person's life will be at the mercy of Communists in central office, dictating the same type of draconian rules we had to avert the last crisis, a mild flu virus so deadly 80% of people didn't even know they had it.

'An entirely new social structure is being imposed on Oxford's residents (and more cities are to follow) under the lie of saving the planet; but what it really is, is a plan for Command and Control. There will be permits, penalties and even more ubiquitous surveillance. Council officials will determine where you can go and how often, and will log every time you do. 15 minute cities, or 15 minute prisons?'

How long could it be before the 15 minute city (or town) becomes our ghetto, if we, collectively, allow such acts of blatant control and infringement upon our natural and common law rights?

If we do allow this, we could next be told that we are never allowed outside of our zone without a permit. If anyone thinks I'm joking, then think again. It is the plan of the dark agenda to utterly dominate and control every action of our lives. These things have happened in the past, just watch documentaries about Germany under the Nazi regime and you will see this. Not everything then unfolded overnight, Hitler was appointed as the chancellor of Germany on 30th January 1933. It was then a gradual process to 'persuade' the people towards evermore fascist extremes with worse and worse acts of evil spread over a number of years; one step at a time, until millions of men, women and children could be murdered by men who once, in some cases, were their friendly neighbours.

Those who practice any spiritual 'gifts' or abilities should also be forewarned, and have good reason to ensure that they do not 'go along' with any aspect of the dark agenda. They need to consider that in some countries, dictatorships effectively, it has been and still is in some, illegal to practice healing other than perhaps through the established medical profession, which is overwhelmingly drug based medicine. Also, how long before mediums who 'speak to those in spirit life' are considered mentally ill? Before they are locked away for 'corrective treatment', "To help them with their mental health", people will be told. Those of the dark agenda have no qualms about taking such action. They are largely atheists anyway, so to them it seems all who accept spiritual healing and communication are self-deluded or gullible people; it is a small step from this position to declaring such people as insane and locking them away. And this reminds me of what Rudolf Steiner said, included in chapter 2, No. 2.

'The time will come, and it may not be far off, when people will say: It is pathological for people to even think in terms of spirit and soul. 'Sound' people will speak of nothing but the body. It will be considered a sign of illness for anyone to arrive at the idea of any such thing as a spirit or a soul.'

I do not believe it will not come to such extremes in the UK or the USA, but, if we collectively succumb to an agenda we intuitively and spiritually know lacks integrity, then we leave ourselves open to the one step at a time rollout of whatever controlling and restricting and medical dictates those of the dark agenda wish to enforce upon us. Referring back again to the Nazi regime, their agenda didn't just stop at a certain point, it got worse year after year. It was only their defeat in war that ended their agenda; and it can also be questioned whether it did really end; or whether it simply transferred, as many of its scientists did, to the USA to work on projects and experiments there. These truths are not secret; those who have investigated so much of the dark agenda for decades, such as James Corbett (Corbett Report), and Polly St George (Amazing Polly), and David Icke, have commented on these facts in videos. (See Links)

As for 'going green', personally, I don't have a car. I do not like car fumes. I will be glad to see the back of them. But, even more than I dislike carbon dioxide emissions in with the air I breathe I dislike being told lies. I'm absolutely convinced that there exist alternative more air-friendly fuel sources and even better (more or less free) power sources.

Some, I'm sure have been suppressed, why let us have something free, when they can sell the current energy services to us for never-ending profits? But this is another story.

In the meantime, until all the cover-ups and corruption is exposed and dealt with (and this could take a number of years, even though it is inevitable and is already underway), whenever we see or feel that we are being told lies about anything, then it is our duty as custodians of Earth to challenge what we are told. In this way we help to empower the construction of new Earth.

There are these days an enormous number of people awake to the corruption and to some aspects, and in many cases much, of the dark agenda. Several of them I have mentioned in this book. Although there are some investigative researchers who have been attempting to enlighten the rest of us for a number of years. And although it might be an overstatement to suggest that in everything they say they are one-hundred per cent correct, like all of us, they can only 'say it as they find it' at a particular point in time. And I'm quite sure that much of what they say is reliable, or at least worthy of our serious consideration. (In my opinion, what a number of investigative researchers say is without doubt far more reliable and honest than what many politicians say!).

One more thing about 'climate' that people should be aware of is called: *"Geo-engineering or Climate engineering"*, and this involves the spraying of our skies on a regular basis.

Personally, I have been aware of this agenda for some years now. As have some of my friends, including those who have written to their MP's (in the UK) to ask them to investigate and hopefully end this atrocity. The replies all turn a blind eye to the truth and say these are normal airplane vapour trails. Clearly they are not, and with even an elementary online effort hundreds of reports of Geo-engineering will be found. One can even find videos with panels of people discussing these, including the likes of botanists and environmentalists discussing the spray impacts on the soil.

Below is just one paragraph from an article by J. Marvin Hendon featured in The Light, May 2022 (page 4), which can be read in full online at the paper's website.

It highlights how 'insane' those with a dark agenda truly are, and the fact they have zero regard for public, animal, or any life form.

The headline for the article was:

Climate engineering: We're being sprayed

'For at least fifteen years covert weather/climate modification activities have been taking place with ever-increasing scale and frequency that involve spraying pollutant particles into the troposphere. The scientific community has been grossly remiss in ignoring the now near-daily, near-universal spraying of particulate-pollution matter into the troposphere, which evidence indicates is coal fly ash, a substance containing toxins injurious to virtually all biota, including us.'

There are a number of music videos that effectively incorporate messages. On my *'Find Truth'* webpage I include links to a number of these. I particularly enjoyed, *"I Bought Myself A Politician"* by the Mona-Lisa twins and, *"I will not comply"* by Blind Joe. The latter was removed by YouTube for, they say, 'violating their terms of service'. This being just one more example of censorship, be it speech, or song. Obviously the writers of the lyrics of these songs are awake to world events. Watching the videos is recommended. (See Links)

Summary and Final Thoughts

This book can be considered an historic record of 'what the spirit guides had to say' before and during this time on Earth.

'The Great Awakening', spoken of by our spirit friends and guides, in some cases for a very long time, is in the process of unfolding and no 'dark agenda', globalist, corporation, mega-financially wealthy family, or all their combined forces of darkness and bought and paid for media, politicians, scientists and medical practitioners and others will stop this.

The world will change, year by year, but not the way the globalists' desire. It will change for the better; with ever-greater spirit and spiritual principles coming 'online', as it were, and a new world, a new Earth, will take shape. It may not be 'overnight', there may still be challenging times, but it will happen.

At this time, in fact always but more so now, it is important to remain calm and try to avoid becoming fearful or angry about anything. I say this because these emotions are negative and help no one, least of all any individual that feels this way. They also have a negative effect on the collective whole.

If certain 'baddies', I'll call them, start to annoy anyone then it may help to think of them as mischievous children, three year-olds, let's say. Not yet old enough to fully realise how 'naughty' they are being. No one sensible would scream and shout at such a young child; they would simple say, "No", to them, and hopefully explain why. It can also be considered that these 'baddies' are younger souls, or souls that have yet to learn to live and express themselves in a way that the inner or higher soul might desire. So we do not give in to their whims, just as no one ought to over-spoil a child by giving in to their whims and tantrums. So it is up to each person to say "No" and refuse to allow our would-be rulers to get away with nonsense; however, just as with a child, we must also wish them no harm. They will, one day, learn by their mistakes. As the child will grow, such souls must come to understand themselves and to live with integrity; whether this is fulfilled in the current or a future lifetime.

As may be gathered, there is much more that I could have said in this book; particularly in regard to the dark agenda, and I have emphasised this fact to make sure everyone realises that it is not any conspiracy theory or fantasy or illusion or misjudgement by those in positions of power on Earth, nor them simply making bad choices.

Readers can be assured that the dark agenda is being revealed by vast numbers of people these days; while other people have and are starting projects to help humanity and the planet. While still others are taking legal actions to 'fight' and prosecute those who have abused their positions or attempted to impose or coerce some dark agenda that benefits the few and harms or tramples over the rights of the people.

I think for now I have said enough, and I hope it is enough to help those who were unaware of just what was and is happening on this planet to awaken to at least some of the reality and, most importantly, to begin to question everything that those who claim authority over us tell us to believe, and try to impose upon us. And, repeating myself, to say "No" when they tell us that 'this or that' is true, and that doing as they say is for our own good, when, if we follow our hearts, and our inner knowing, or intuition, it tells us that what they are saying is a lie, or certainly not the whole truth and nothing but the truth.

Whether they try to make a law, or coerce our co-operation with their dark plans, whatever they may be, just say, "No", and do not accept or obey them. **Never fear saying, "No".** Life is eternal; remember this at all times. And, although I do not believe it will come to it, it would be one-hundred percent better to 'die' being true and honest to our own integrity and soul awareness than to submit to the dictates of tyranny.

The people supporting and trying to implement the dark agenda have no right whatsoever to seek domination over any sovereign human being. We must remain true to ourselves. **Indeed, doing so might be one of the 'tests' that we are currently on Earth to 'pass'. We must not fail our higher self.**

As mentioned early in this book, at present, it is my likely intention to write another book; one that will share any further spirit revelations that may be received during 2023. If I do write another book I will also try to feature a number of other 'truth tellers on Earth' who I never managed to include within this edition. It is also possible that I may have more dark agenda info to share. These (dark agenda) people can be rather sneaky in trying to get their own way. So trust nothing from those who have any links to the dark agenda organisations; and to repeat, feel, feel with the heart and inner knowing or inner voice, 'the gut', some say, whether something has integrity behind it, or whether it is driven by some ulterior motive, power, control, money, and so forth.

Until next time, dear readers, goodbye, and be happy in the certain knowledge that life is eternal and that we are all immortal souls.

Note: If any other trance mediums are themselves channelling communications they feel might be appropriate to include in a future book, and they are happy to share these, I will be delighted to hear from them.

Likewise, if anyone finds any inspiring new Earth projects that they feel more people could benefit hearing about, then I will be delighted to learn about these.

I can be contacted via Facebook or by the email address shown at my "Find Truth" webpage. (See Links)

Reference List of What the Spirit Guides Say in Chapter Two

Below is a list of the spirit guides quotes in chapter two.

1. Rudolf Steiner – October 1917 - The Fall of the Spirits of Darkness – Part One

2. Rudolf Steiner – October 1917 - The Fall of the Spirits of Darkness – Part Two

3. Magnus - Q. Can you tell us a little bit about the Earth Changes? – circa 1990's-2000's

4. White Feather - A Glimpse of the Future – circa 2008

5. White Feather - From: The Collected Wisdom 2010

6. White Feather - Speaking in 2011 - Cancer Cure Deliberately Covered-Up for Financial Gain

7. White Feather - Speaking of the NWO in 2011

8. White Cloud – 2nd December 2016 - The World Needs Your Prayers

9. Dr Peebles - May 2018

10. White Cloud – 1st June 2019 - You Must Stand Up and Speak the Truth

11. Copernicus – 2nd December 2019

         - The Measure of Time on Earth is Very Different than in the Celestial Heavens

12. Augustine – 3rd December 2019 - So Goes the World, So Goes the Catholic Church

         - A Variety of Souls, Some Light and Some Dark

13. White Cloud – 16th February 2020 - It is Time to Come Together as One

14. Sanaya - March 2020 - Coronavirus Perspective from the Spirit Realms

15. Dr Peebles - March 2020

16. Keea Atta Kem – 15th March 2020 - Changing Earth Conditions

17. Jonathan - April 2020 - Reasons for Spiritual Awakening

18. Josephus – 27th April 2020 - Free Will and Its Impact on Earth

19. Dr Peebles - 8th July 2020

20. Dr. Peebles - 3rd August 2020

21. Monty - August 2020 - Concerning Emotions

22. Dr Peebles - 12th August 2020

23. Jonathan - October 2020 - The Great Spiritual Awakening

24. Dr Peebles - 22nd October 2020

25. Zac - October 2020 - Truth Revelations

26. Zac - October 2020 - Time Travellers

27. Monty - November 2020 - Forthcoming Jabs

28. Jonathan - November 2020 - Knowing Yourself & The Awakening

29. Abraham Lincoln – 28th December 2020

         - Lincolns Speaks of the Condition of America And Implores Us to Reach for the Light

30. Zac - January 2021 - Cycles of Change

31. Jesus – 11th March 2021 - Earth Changes

32. Zac - May 2021 - We Have the Ability to Overcome Anything

33. Jesus – 19th May 2021 - Life on Other Planets Poised to Help Us on Earth

34. Monty - June 2021 - With a Warning

35. Jesus – 2nd June 2021 - Humanity Will Awaken with Coming Earth Changes

36. Jonathan – 16th July 2021 - Awakening and Earth Changes

37. Dr Peebles - 11th August 2021

38. Dr Peebles - 7th September 2021

39. Dr Peebles - 29th September 2021

40. Dr Peebles - 13th October 2021

41. Simeon - 14th October 2021 - Equilibrium

42. Dr Peebles - 27th October 2021 - Trust in God

43. Dr Peebles - 3rd November 2021

44. The Philosopher - 12th November 2021 - Truth and Trust

45. Dr Peebles - 17th November 2021

46. Jonathan - November 2021 - Earth Changes

47. Dr Peebles - 2nd December 2021

48. Monty – 14th December 2021 - The Great Awakening

49. Archangel Michael – 17th December 2021
                    - Declaration of the Beginning of the Transformation of Our World

50. Orion – 12th February 2022 - Escalating Earth Changes are Coming

51. Zac - February 2022 - Schumann Resonance & Harmonising with the Cosmos

52. Nikola Tesla - 15th May 2022 - Discourse on Spirit and Power of Love

53. Zac - May 2022 - This Cuboid of the Universe

54. Zac - May 2022 - Truth and Empathy

55. Zac - May 2022 - DNA Optimisation

56. White Feather- 7th June 2022 - Stand in Your Light - Introduction Talk

57. White Feather – 7th June 2022 - Q&A on Jabs

58. White Feather – 7th June 2022 - Q&A on Cash Banking

59. White Feather – 7th June 2022 - Q&A - On the Planned End Game

60. Monty - June 2022 - They Want Your Homes, They Want It All

61. Dr Peebles - 29th July 2022

62. Sanaya - June 2022 - Major Shift in Evolution

63. Jonathan - July 2022 - The Light and the Awakening

64. Zac - July 2022 - Universal Integrity

65. Zac - July 2022 - DNA Change Makers

66. Zac – August 2022 - Rocket Fuelled Inspiration

67. White Feather – 1st September 2022 - Seeds in the Wind

68. White Feather – 30th September 2022 - The Love Revolution

69. Chief Joseph – October 2022 - Mother Earth

70. Zac - October 2022 - In conversation with Pam Gregory - Astrologer

71. Sanaya – 13th October 2022 - Growing

72. Sanaya – 31st October 2022 - The Tools

73. White Feather – 6th November 2022 - It is Always Darkest Just Before the Dawn

74. Dr Peebles - 5th December 2022

75. Dr Peebles ~ 30th December 2022 - Surrender to God

76. Dr Peebles ~ 30th December 2022 - Time to Live Our Truth

Chapter 2 - Quote Numbers for each Medium

Al Fike
Quotes 8, 10-13, 16, 18, 29, 31, 33, 35, 49, 50, 52

Catherine Stegner Cowan
Quote 69

Colin Fry
Quote 3

Elaine Thorpe
Quotes 17, 23, 28, 36, 46, 63

Janet Treloar
Quotes 25, 26, 30, 32, 51, 53-55, 64-66, 70

Jacqui Rogers
Quote 41

Ray Edwards
Quote 44

Robert Goodwin
Quotes 4-7, 56-59, 67, 68, 73

Rudolph Steiner
Quotes 1, 2

Summer Bacon
Quotes 9, 15, 19, 20, 22, 24, 37-40, 42, 43, 45, 47, 61, 74-76

Suzanne Giesemann
Quotes 14, 62, 71, 72

Warren James
Quotes 21, 27, 34, 48, 60

Links

Al Fike
https://divinelovesanctuary.com/
Podcasts: https://divinelovesanctuary.podbean.com/

Brandon J. Kim
Facebook: https://www.facebook.com/brandontek.it

Catherine Stegner Cowan
Facebook: https://www.facebook.com/kate.cowan.33

Elaine Thorpe
https://www.elainethorpe.com/
YouTube: https://www.youtube.com/c/ElaineThorpe
Spotify Podcasts: https://open.spotify.com/show/1q7TjRdGdyVgiow2kPOro8

Estelle Roberts
https://estelleroberts.co.uk/

Grace Cook
https://www.white-eagle.org.uk/

Janet Treloar
https://www.planet-therapies.com/
YouTube: https://www.youtube.com/user/Hazel2609/playlists

Jacqui Rogers
http://simplyspiritual.org.uk/

Ray Edwards
Facebook: https://www.facebook.com/ray.edwards.3910

Robert Goodwin
https://www.whitefeatherspirit.com/
YouTube: https://www.youtube.com/user/joyouscar33132/featured

Rudolph Steiner & Steiner Online Library
https://www.rudolfsteiner.org/
https://rsarchive.org/

Summer Bacon
https://www.summerbacon.com/

Suzanne Giesemann - spirit communicator - Sanaya
https://suzannegiesemann.com/
YouTube: https://www.youtube.com/c/SuzanneGiesemann

The Lucas Trust (Alice Bailey books):
https://www.lucistrust.org/

Warren James
https://trancemedium.org/
YouTube: https://www.youtube.com/channel/UCrnq-yrcYX1X7vKKBtijKdA/featured

Truth Tellers on Earth

Bracha Goldsmith – Astrologer
https://yourastrologysigns.com/
YouTube: https://www.youtube.com/@BrachaGoldsmith

Bruce H. Lipton PhD
https://www.brucelipton.com/
YouTube: https://www.youtube.com/@BruceHLiptonPhD

Caroline Chang - Awake 2 Oneness Radio
https://www.awake2onenessradio.org/
https://www.awake2onenessradio.org/post/dr-paul-thomas-md-independent-study?cid=b37db337-9167-4638-a66c-0fb3b2a2cd6e

Climatecite
https://climatecite.com/

Clintel – There is no climate emergency
https://clintel.org/
The Viscount Monckton of Brenchley: https://clintel.org/interview-with-lord-monckton-in-italian-newspaper/

David Icke
https://davidicke.com/
Bitchute: https://www.bitchute.com/channel/weBLW8e6mglB/

Dr Joseph Mercola
https://www.mercola.com/
Podcast: https://www.mercola.com/downloads/podcast.htm

Dr Sam Bailey
https://drsambailey.com/
Odysee: https://odysee.com/@drsambailey:c
YouTube: https://www.youtube.com/c/DrSamBailey

Dr Vernon Coleman
https://vernoncoleman.org/
https://www.vernoncoleman.com/index.htm
Face Masks: https://vernoncoleman.org/articles/proof-masks-do-more-harm-good
https://childrenshealthdefense.org/wp-content/uploads/Masks-false-safety-and-real-dangers-Part-1-Friable-mask-particulate-and-lung-vulnerability.pdf
https://mask-covid.info/wp-content/uploads/2020/11/Mask_Risks_Part2.pdf

300

Find Truth (James McQuitty webpage)
https://findtruth.mystrikingly.com/

F. William Engdahl
http://williamengdahl.com/gr22October2022.php

James Corbett – The Corbett Report
https://www.corbettreport.com/
Bitchute: https://www.bitchute.com/channel/GwPziiQZrVT3/

James McQuitty
Bitchute: https://www.bitchute.com/channel/vY0gWZKmZauR/
The Great Global Warming Swindle: https://www.bitchute.com/video/QXy1musBtvL4/
Blind Joe: https://www.bitchute.com/video/LROfTl2WjVI7/

Joni Patry – Astrologer
https://www.galacticcenter.org/
YouTube: https://www.youtube.com/c/JoniPatryVedicAstrologer

Mona-Lisa Twins
https://www.youtube.com/watch?v=_QAKz_cxTIQ

Neil Oliver
https://www.patreon.com/neiloliver
https://www.youtube.com/watch?v=CFuMk9Bahes

Not on the Beeb
https://www.notonthebeeb.co.uk/

Pam Gregory – Astrologer
https://www.thenextstep.uk.com/
YouTube: https://www.youtube.com/c/PamGregoryOfficial

Polly St George – Amazing Polly
https://www.amazingpolly.net/
Bitchute: https://www.bitchute.com/channel/ZofFQQoDoqYT/

Rachel Elnaugh
https://rachelelnaugh.com/
Odysee: https://odysee.com/@RachelElnaugh:7

Richard Vobes
YouTube: https://www.youtube.com/@RichardVobes/videos

Russell Brand
https://www.russellbrand.com/
Rumble: https://rumble.com/c/russellbrand

Stand in the Park - We 'Stand in the Park' to celebrate freedom, diversity, and fairness for all.
https://www.astandinthepark.org/

Stop World Control
https://www.stopworldcontrol.com/
MONOPOLY - Who owns the world? Documentary by Tim Gielen
https://rumble.com/vmyx1n-monopoly-who-owns-the-world-documentary-by-tim-gielen.html

The Expose – Our aim is to bring you, honest, trustworthy and reliable journalism.
https://expose-news.com/

The Freedom Network - We're bringing individuals and communities together to retain their freedom.
https://www.thefreedomnetwork.co.uk/

The Great Barrington Declaration
https://gbdeclaration.org/

The Light Paper
https://thelightpaper.co.uk/archive

The People's Health Alliance
https://the-pha.org/

The Truth about Cancer
https://thetruthaboutcancer.com/

The Truth about Vaccines
https://thetruthaboutvaccines.com/

UK Column - independent news organisation.
https://www.ukcolumn.org/

UK Medical Freedom Alliance - Professionals supporting medical choice and informed consent.
https://www.ukmedfreedom.org/

Vaccine Impact - Mislabelling Vaccination Deaths for 50 Years.
https://vaccineimpact.com/

VAERS Statistics of Covid Vaccine Adverse Event Reports (USA)
https://www.openvaers.com/covid-data

Vision News - Independent journalism at its best.
https://www.visionnews.online/
https://www.visionnews.online/post/oxfordshire-county-council-pass-climate-lockdown-trial-to-begin-in-2024

Watching Rome Burn
https://watchingromeburn.uk/

World Doctors Alliance - An independent non-profit alliance of doctors, nurses, healthcare professionals.
https://worlddoctorsalliance.com/

James McQuitty - Books

All are available on Amazon worldwide in

Paperback and Kindle formats

Every book is moderately priced since the author's primary motivation is a desire to share spiritual knowledge.

Amazon reviewers have said:

GOLDEN ENLIGHTENMENT

Twenty Year Anniversary Edition

Now Featuring:

60 Q's & A's for Seekers of Spiritual Knowledge, Truth and Wisdom

'Anyone starting out on the spiritual pathway, and requiring a guide in the form of a book, will find that Golden Enlightenment will be that book. Easy to read and understand, this book stands out among the hundreds available as one that is reliable, honest, informative and very, very interesting. What more could a seeker want? It really is a case of what is written on the label / outside can be found on the inside!'

Myra Bowman

Spiritual teacher and Registered Approved Medium

The Institute of Spiritualist Mediums

www.ism.org.uk

GOLDEN ENLIGHTENMENT

TWENTY YEAR ANNIVERSARY EDITION

JAMES MCQUITTY

Escape from Hell

Hell of our own making! (T.R.)

'Escape from Hell is an apt title. This book describes in detail a number of the lower planes in the spirit world and the horrible beings that inhabit these dark, vile and dismal realms. It is a wake up call for all of us to put 'right' any wrongs before we pass on from this life on earth. Well worth reading!'

A recommended read for all! (Salsaroo)

'This book is in many ways the opposite of books such as 'The Secret': the account of 'Antonio' after he died indicates the hellish experiences you can manifest for yourself if you give in to your baser nature and live a cruel, corrupt life.

'More scary than a William Peter Blatty novel, it may be easy to dismiss Antonio's grisly account as fiction, although the author offers supporting evidence in the form of accounts of the baser realms from other sources.

'Furthermore, the basic message is in alignment with the message that we have been given loud and clear from various sources for millennia; live life according to your own conscience as much as you can, and make love, care, kindness, and service your central aim.'

Wonderfully full of spiritual knowledge (Sam McD.)

'Absolutely beautiful book. Read it twice, loved it. I would love to see this book made into a movie. Strongly recommend, especially if you have unanswered spiritual questions.'

The Reason Why You Were Born

Straightforward, honest and informative (GMax)

'This book gives one of the most straightforward and clear explanations of spiritual matters that I have ever read and the truth shines out through the words. I have often wanted a book I could recommend to those who are awakening spiritually and who need some good grounding information that's down to earth and without any religious connotations. His style is concise and emanates a loving warmth that is almost tangible. Highly recommended.'

I have to say I thoroughly enjoyed this book (Geoff Langford)

'I have to say I thoroughly enjoyed this book. It was well written. No matter whether you are new to Spirit or like me had an interest for the last 10 years or so, there is something of interest for you in this book. It has served to remind me of some of the Spiritualist things I had forgotten and it has also taught me many new things about Spiritualism. It is a book I will be dipping into in the future and on top of that it is a good read. Enjoy.'

Excellent book! This book is short and to the point (Dave B.)

'Excellent book! This book is short and to the point (just how I like them). 'It covers the topic in sufficient detail to enable the reader to get a clear understanding of why we are here, where we are going, and to help us follow a path that will help our understanding of spirituality during this lifetime.'

Adventures in Time and Space

Very, very, interesting (Mr L J Simpkins)

'Very calming, and informative, try it.'

Everyone should read this book (James Aylward)

'Many who do may not believe it.

'Those who do will increase their trust in life, accept personal responsibility, be less critical of others and help make this world a better place.'

I recommend it to all seeking proof of life after death (Robert Goodwin)

'James McQuitty is one of a rare breed - an author possessing real spiritual insight, able to convey his wisdom in ways accessible to everyone through the written word. This book combines challenging (to some) information with sound common sense and age old truth. I recommend it to all seeking proof of life after death and the knowledge that life is a wonderful journey, leading ultimately to the realisation that we are all one.'

Immortality: A reminder of life's eternal nature

An interesting read for beginners (Lord P.)

'As a reader already familiar with the evidence for survival after death, I needed no persuading of this book's main message - that death is not an 'end' involving fearful total annihilation; that instead there is such a thing as 'spirit' and a 'next life'. The book is essentially 'spiritist', with the author assuring us we need to learn lessons about goodness and mutual consideration; the golden rule, you might say. Also, he points out that bad behaviour on Earth can have negative consequences for our personal development in the afterlife.

'One of its novel features is that the author has collected and used for illustrative purposes the lyrics of over 30 modern songs that reflect the ideas he is talking about in each chapter. The twelve chapters cover such things as the spiritual implications of war, accidents, suicide, getting old and the consequences of negative actions, and more.

'James McQuitty has endeavoured to make this book positive and uplifting, and I'd say he has achieved that. Personally, I would have liked more emphasis on 'evidence' at the expense of 'lyrics', but then it would have been a different creature and probably not what he intended.

'This book on immortality will appeal to those considering the philosophy for life that virtually all spiritualists and spiritists already accept. At the end, a suggested reading list covers the work of over 20 authors.'

Very Positive and Enlightening Book! (Jeff Altaffer – Amazon.com)

'I thought this was a very positive and enlightening book! I liked how each chapter began with song lyrics related to the subject of each chapter. I knew a lot of the things talked about, but I liked how the author kept reminding the readers that we're immortal spirit beings having a physical experience. I would recommend!'

The Evolvement of the Soul: The Origins and Development of Life

In this book the author asks: How does spirit justice relate to the animal kingdom? Is a cat, for instance, destined to always remain a cat? Can our feline friends only ever become smarter and brighter and evermore loving and "highly evolved" cats?

The author continues: As a cat lover, and in fact loving all our animal friends, it seemed rather unfair to me if this was the case. These were my thoughts as I "meditated" on the subject. I was thrilled when a sudden understanding or "revelation" came to me. Afterwards, I wondered why I hadn't previously realised what then seemed so blindingly obvious to me. I have since advanced my understanding by adding to what I received. This I am presenting to readers in the chapters of this book.

This explains how the human soul evolves. Furthermore, it explains that evolution and progression of spirit is not limited to human life alone; rather it encompasses all life; and this includes the life of my furry feline friends.

Very Informative Book! (Jeff Altaffer - Amazon.com)

'I liked how this book was very informative in talking about the origins and development of life! Also it's not that long of a read. It's also very thought provoking. I'd recommend!'

BEHOLD THE TRUTH (Clive A. Siegner)

'If you want to know the truth about who you really are and what your purpose as a Human Being is, then I suggest you read this book. This book is not long but the Author really knows what he is talking about.'

Spiritual Astro-Numerology: The Complete Guide

Spiritual Astro-Numerology combines a mixture of Astrology and Numerology to analyse a subject's spiritual pathway.

The book includes an analysis for each of the Chinese Animal Years, along with Traditional Astrological Birth Signs and Ruling Planets. Also a Numerological analysis of the Inner and Outer Personality, Soul and Life Lesson Pathways, and Current and Future Years influence of the numbers. Readers will even discover their Colour Ray.

This guide is easy to use, enlightening, and fun.

Fantastic! (assirekaevas – Amazon.com)

'This is the best book on numerology that I've read yet! It's comprehensive, provides ample instruction on how to find your numbers and tells you everything from horoscope to soul number!'

Great (Dena Shores – Amazon.com)

'A very thorough and complete book to do your analysis or start doing someone else's.

'Great read. Will be on my bookshelf for future reference.'

Know Thyself, Be Thyself

If we do not know ourselves how can we be true to ourselves? This book shows us who we truly are and shares a number of observations to highlight how we can more authentically express our true identity. Inspiring and empowering us to consider where we may benefit from making some positive changes in how we approach life and interact with our families, friends, colleagues, and everyone else we meet in life. Can we live and act with soul awareness? The alternative may well be to follow the flock or to adhere to the expectations of other people; and this may not be in harmony with one's own soul.

The Wisdom Oracle: An Aid to Accessing Your Inner or Higher Self Wisdom

Please note: It is recommended that dice are used to aid selection with this oracle, preferably two different coloured dice, alternatively, one dice used twice will suffice. (Not supplied).

The objective of this oracle is to help users to access their own inner or higher self wisdom.

Within, the author uses proverbs and totem animals as tools to help users to open their minds to greater self-awareness or self-reflective guidance.

Readers will find this oracle, which contains 36 different readings, informative and fun to use.

How Psychics and Mediums Work, The Spirit and the Aura

This book will help readers to understand how psychics and mediums work; and about the human spirit and the energies which surround each person - often referred to as the "aura."

The wealth of information James shares in his books he gathered over a number of decades. One can start reading them as a novice to the subjects covered and finish highly informed and greatly inspired.

Christianity: The Sad and Shameful Truth

The author says: I am not in any sense an 'academic religious scholar' who has devoted decades of his life to the subject. So those readers who want every "i" dotted and every "t" crossed and to find material written in a way that suggests 'academia', or for that matter some new 'revelation' derived from some ancient manuscript, should look elsewhere.

What I am, is a sensible individual who even as a child had the commonsense to never for one second fall for the 'crazy' zealous and guilt ridden teachings of the Christian Church.

In this book readers will find is plenty of simple and easy to read explanations of the origins of Christianity and the sad and shameful truth of how over its history it has directly or indirectly abused billions of people. Read this book if you dare.

Worldwide Rallies For Freedom

Here are some images from The Light…

These show some of the articles mentioned within this book.

It took just one week for 50 million Tanzanians to stop complying

'Footballers are no longer being asked to have vaccines'

Time to blow the whistle on sudden sporting deaths

1,100 eminent Scientists declare: 'There is NO climate emergency'

Ukraine's Nazi connections and the British cover-up

Printed in Great Britain
by Amazon

44186940R00175